New England Nature

Centuries of Writing on the Wonder and Beauty of the Land

David K. Leff and Eric D. Lehman

Globe
Pequot

Essex, Connecticut

Globe
Pequot

An imprint of The Globe Pequot Publishing Group, Inc.
64 South Main Street
Essex, CT 06426
www.globepequot.com

Distributed by NATIONAL BOOK NETWORK

British Library Cataloguing in Publication Information available

Library of Congress Control Number: 2020944833

ISBN 9781493052189 (cloth : alk. paper) | ISBN 9781493052196 (ebook) | ISBN 9781493084241 (paper)

∞™ The paper used in this publication meets the minimum requirements of American National Standard for Information Sciences—Permanence of Paper for Printed Library Materials, ANSI/NISO Z39.48-1992.

Nature is what we see—
The Hill—the Afternoon—
Squirrel—Eclipse—the Bumble bee—
Nay—Nature is Heaven—
Nature is what we hear—
The Bobolink—the Sea—
Thunder—the Cricket—
Nay—Nature is Harmony—
Nature is what we know—
Yet have no art to say—
So impotent Our Wisdom is
To her Simplicity.

—Emily Dickinson, Poem 668

Contents

CONTENTS

CONTENTS

Acknowledgments

We would like to thank Laura Caserta, Taleesa Scott, and David and Trena Lehman for their editing advice, as well as the University of Bridgeport's Magnus Wahlstrom Library and the Eli Whitney Library at the New Haven Museum. Special thanks to Becky Fullerton, Archivist, Appalachian Mountain Club, for assistance finding documents in the club's early journals and library collection; Elizabeth Van Ness, Reference and Adult Services Librarian at Canton Public Library, for tracking down books, articles, and obscure biographical facts; and our wives, Mary C. Fletcher and Amy Nawrocki, for their encouragement and ideas.

New England:
Gateway to American Nature Writing

Spend even a little time in the natural world, and it's hard not to encounter moments of awe and wonder. Such instants may steal upon us along a wilderness path alive with birdsong, or beneath a colonnade of trees in an urban park. We might find them while afloat on a lake, or atop a rocky summit. Often, we struggle to express the power and elation we experience. So we turn to nature writers whose work gives us a grammar and syntax, even an entire language, to articulate the blend of amazement and reverence we experience in these encounters. Nature writers connect the physical world to the imagination. They enable us to see more clearly, by guiding us how to look. They help us understand our relationship to the plants and animals around us, and link us to the substance and cycles of natural phenomena. Nature writing cultivates our sense of beauty, inflaming curiosity and the passion to explore. It opens us to deep, primal experiences that enrich life.

To fully understand American nature writing, we must look at its origins in New England. Why should the six-state region of Connecticut, Maine, Massachusetts, New Hampshire, Rhode Island, and Vermont, tucked into the nation's northeast corner and less than 2 percent of its land, punch so far above its weight when it comes to nature writing? The early settlement and exploration of the region may be partially responsible, but the best answer probably lies in the countryside itself. In this place people develop an intimate relationship with their landscape, where nature and culture are inextricably entwined and most everything is close at hand. What it lacks in grandeur and scale it makes up for in diversity and proximity. It is a landscape of fine detail and astonishing beauty that is easily accessible.

Here you can find seacoast and mountains, valleys and forests, rivers and beaches. You can explore bogs, marshes, swamps, and other wetlands; paddle across myriad lakes and ponds; and hike across bare traprock ridges or red-leafed hills. Underlying it all is a complex geology with a wide range of rocks and minerals supporting many different habitats sustaining diverse plant and animal communities. Above is our famously fickle weather, generated by our four distinct and nearly perfect seasons, in which our temperate climate gets small tastes of both the Arctic and the tropics.

This natural world has had an uneasy relationship with human beings since the last ice age at least. Our encounters leave traces on the land—from the rock shelters and middens, to the stone walls of old farms, to the sluiceways and dams of early factories. Suburban developments rise next to ruins disappearing into the woods. Here in New England, humankind and nature have long struggled in partnership, and the successive cycles of exploitation and healing remain all around us.

With so much, so close, it is no wonder that people have been writing about these islands and highlands since they had the means to do so. This sort of writing has gone under different names over the centuries, but today we call it "nature writing" or "environmental writing"—an established and important genre that continues to grow in popularity. "An argument can be made," Bill McKibben has written in his Library of America anthology *American Earth*, "that environmental writing is America's single most distinctive contribution to the world's literature." In addition to its allure to readers, nature writing has played a significant role in getting millions of people outdoors; in the development of public parks, forests, and preserves; and in the passage of legislation and adoption of regulations protecting the environment.

Nature writing today is most familiar in the first-person essay that takes deep notice of natural features and phenomena through a lens of personal meaning. These essays often reflect consequences for the world at large, increasingly arguing for a sustainable human relationship with nature. Although this trajectory owes a lot to the pen of Henry David

Thoreau, it flows from a number of styles and sources, much as a network of creeks and streams in a watershed contribute to the main-stem river.

This anthology covers material from the seventeenth century to the 1920s, the roots of contemporary literature. Included are landscape descriptions by the early pioneers; scientific investigations by Enlightenment thinkers; tales of outdoor adventure; works of advocacy and nature education; romantic celebrations of beauty; and contemplative, philosophical essays. There are excerpts from works of fiction where the natural world exerts a powerful influence on the story or is practically a character itself. Beyond the scope of this anthology are poetical works which, it should be acknowledged, are among the earliest pieces of nature writing and continue to exert a strong influence on our views of the natural world.

There are other missing voices, to be sure. There has historically been a lack of representation by women and people of color, particularly Native American voices. Those early voices that could have told us much about living close to the earth were often oral traditions that were tragically silenced, and we learn about them secondhand, or not at all. But hopefully their philosophy worked its way into the spirits of some who did leave their words in print. Within these pages you will find famous names known to every student of history, and names forgotten by that history. This collection digs deep to find voices rarely heard.

We begin with the explorers and settlers of the 1600s, who find both a land of abundant resources and a frightening wilderness to overcome. Writing about both this richness and the struggle to conquer it continues through the 1800s, with hunters, loggers, and whalers all adding their stories. By then, though, concern for decreasing abundance has already begun. In 1817, on what is now Earth Day, Noah Webster published an essay called "Domestic Consumption" on the front page of the *Connecticut Courant*, calling for stewardship of natural resources. "We are not to waste and destroy for the sake of present enjoyment," he wrote, "we must not strip the inheritance of wood and its fences and its timber, and leave it barren and impoverished to the next generation." His concerns are echoed with increasing fervor throughout the nineteenth century by figures as diverse as Celia Thaxter and P. T. Barnum. As the twentieth century dawns, writers like Gifford Pinchot and Frederic Walcott begin the process of conserving what is left of our ecological home.

But there is more. Between these covers Lydia Sigourney finds pleasures in winter, Elizabeth Agassiz finds scientific intricacies in sea urchins, and Henry Ward Ranger finds artistic inspiration in the rural landscape. Jonathan Edwards and Helen Keller both find miracles, while Samuel Peters and Mark Twain find humor. Author Nathaniel Hawthorne discovered a place to hide his metaphors, while the enslaved James Mars discovered an actual hiding place. Through it all is the apprehension of a profound and lasting splendor. "Beauty breaks in everywhere," writes philosopher Ralph Waldo Emerson in 1850. Seventy years later, W. E. B. Du Bois said much the same: "the glory of physical nature; this, though the last of beauties, is divine!"

Our relationship with the natural world has existed long before our consciousness, and will continue long after we are gone. It is more than a temporary bond—it is our connection to the continuum of life that binds us to the earth. Both spirit and science agree on that. And so, it seems worthy of a few scribblings, a few pages, to study the bark of a beech tree or learn the patterns of the waves. In reading nature, we discover nothing less than ourselves.

"Penobscot to Cape Cod"
by John Smith

From A Description of New England *(1616)*

English explorer, soldier of fortune, and adventurer John Smith (1580–1631) left home at age 16 and became a mercenary in Europe and the Middle East. In 1605 he returned to England, and at age 27 he signed on with the Virginia Company and sailed with the Jamestown colonists. Assuming a leadership role, he proved able at dealing with the Native Americans, exceedingly resourceful and audacious. While in Virginia, he explored the Chesapeake Bay area and was involved in a variety of political intrigues, some of them life-threatening. He returned to England in 1609 amidst political controversy.

Hired by London merchants in 1614 in the hope he would find gold and harvest whales for oil and other products, he set out to explore the coast from Massachusetts to Maine. His return with furs and fish disappointed investors. After two more unsuccessful attempts, he spent the rest of his life in the British Isles, where he wrote several books about his experiences. He coined the name "New England" by publishing a map with that title in 1616. That same year he published A Description of New England, *which is excerpted here.*

"PENOBSCOT TO CAPE COD"

The most Northern part I was at, was the Bay of *Pennobscot*, which is East and West, North and South, more than ten leagues: but such were my occasions, I was constrained to be satisfied of them I found in the

Bay, that the River ran far up into the Land, and was well inhabited with many people, but they were from their habitations, either fishing among the Iles, or hunting the Lakes and Woods, for Deer and Bears. The Bay is full of great Islands, of one, two, six, eight, or ten miles in length, which divides it into many faire and excellent good harbors. On the East of it, are the *Tarrantines*, their mortal enemies, where inhabit the *French*, as they report that live with those people, as one nation or family. And Northwest of *Pennobscot* is *Mecaddacut*, at the foot of a high mountain, a kind of fortress against the *Tarrantines*, adjoining to the high mountains of Pennobscot, against whose feet doth beat the Sea: But overall the Land, Iles, or other impediments, you may well see them sixteen or eighteen leagues from their situation. *Segocket* is the next; then *Nusconsus*, *Pemmaquid*, and *Sagadahock*. Up this River where was the Western plantation are *Aumuckcawgen*, *Kinnebeck*, and diverse others, where there is planted some corn fields. Along this River 40 or 50 miles, I saw nothing but great high cliffs of barren Rocks, overgrown with wood: but where the Savages dwelt there the ground is exceeding fat and fertile. Westward of this River, is the Country of *Aucocisco*, in the bottom of a large deep Bay, full of many great Iles, which divides it into many good harbors. *Sowocotuck* is the next, in the edge of a large sandy Bay, which hath many Rocks and Iles, but few good harbors, but for Barks, I yet know. But all this Coast to Pennobscot, and as far I could see Eastward of it is nothing but such high craggy Cliffy Rocks and stony Iles, that I wondered such great trees could grow upon so hard foundations. It is a Country rather to affright, then delight one. And how to describe a more plain spectacle of defoliation or more barren I know not. Yet the Sea there is the strangest fish-pond I ever saw; and those barren Iles so furnished with good woods, springs, fruits, fish, and fowl, that it makes mee think though the Coast be rocky, and thus affrightable; the Valleys, Plaines, and interior parts, may well (notwithstanding) be very fertile. But there is no kingdom so fertile hath not some part barren: and *New England* is great enough, to make many Kingdoms and Countries, were it all inhabited. As you pass the Coast still Westward, *Accominticus* and *Passataquack* are two convenient harbors for small barks; and a good Country, within their craggy cliffs. *Angoam* is the next; This place might content a right curious judgement: but there are many sands at the entrance of the harbor: and the worst is, it is inbayed too far from the deep Sea. Here are many rising hills, and on their tops and descents many corn fields, and delightful groves. On the East, is an Ile of two or three leagues in length; the one half, plain moorish grass fit for pasture, with many faire high groves of mulberry trees gardens: and there is also Oaks, Pines, and other woods to make this place an excellent habitation, being a good and safe harbor.

Naimkeck though it be more rocky ground (for *Angoam* is sandy) not much inferior; neither for the harbor, nor any thing I could perceive, but the multitude of people. From hence doth stretch into the Sea the faire headland *Tragabigzanda,* fronted with three Iles called the three *Turks heads*: to the North of this, doth enter a great Bay, where we found some habitations and corn fields: they report a great River, and at least thirty habitations, do possess this Country. But because the *French* had got their Trade, I had no leisure to discover it. The Iles of *Mattahunts* are on the West side of this Bay, where are many Iles, and questionless good harbors: and then the Country of the *Massachusets*, which is the Paradise of all those parts: for, here are many Iles all planted with corn; groves, mulberries, savage gardens, and good harbors: the Coast is for the most part, high clay sandy cliffs. The Sea Coast: as you pass, shows you all along large corn fields, and great troupes of well-proportioned people: but the *French* having remained here near six weeks, left nothing for us to take occasion to examine the inhabitants relations, *viz.* if there be near three thousand people upon these Iles; and that the River doth pierce many days journeys the entrails of that Country. We found the people in those parts very kind; but in their fury no less valiant. For, upon a quarrel we had with one of them, he only with three others crossed the harbor of Quonahassit to certain rocks whereby we must pass; and there let fly their arrows for our shot, till we were out of danger.

Then come you to *Accomack*, an excellent good harbor, good land; and no want of any thing, but industrious people. After much kindness, upon a small occasion, we fought also with forty or fifty of those: though some were hurt, and some slain; yet within an hour after they became friends. *Cape Cod* is the next presents it self: which is only a headland of high hills of sand, overgrown with shrubby pines, hurts, and such trash; but an excellent harbor for all weathers. This *Cape* is made by the main Sea on the one side, and a great Bay on the other in form of a sickle: on it doth inhabit the people of *Pawmet*: and in the bottom of the Bay, the people of *Capawack*. Towards the South and South west of this *Cape*, is found a long and dangerous shoal of sands and rocks. But so far as I encircled it, I found thirty fathom water aboard the shore and a strong current: which makes mee think there is a Channel about this shoal; where is the best and greatest fish to be had, Winter and Summer, in all that Country. But, the Savages say there is no Channel, but that the shoals begin from the main at *Pawmet*, to the Ile of *Nausit*; and so extends beyond their knowledge into the Sea. The next to this is *Capawack*, and those abounding Countries of copper, corn, people, and minerals; which I went to discover this last year; but because I miscarried by the way, I will leave them, till God please I have better acquaintance with them.

"Hurricane and Earthquake"
by William Bradford

From Of Plimoth Plantation *(1651)*

Born in England, William Bradford (1590–1657) lost his parents at an early age and was raised by relatives. As a boy he joined a radical branch of Puritanism known as Separatists and eventually left for the Netherlands with other church members to escape persecution. More than ten years later, in 1620, he sailed for America on the Mayflower. *The following spring he was elected governor of the Plymouth Colony and served in that capacity, with some breaks, for most of the remainder of his life.*

Bradford was intimately involved in all phases of the colony including economic, judicial, and religious matters. He kept meticulous notes on the founding and ongoing life of the Plymouth Colony. About 1630 he began his History of Plimoth Plantation, *which he completed in 1651. In it he records the origins of the Separatist movement, the flight from England to Holland, the voyage of the* Mayflower, *the founding of the colony, and every aspect of life in the new settlement from crops to storms, commercial transactions to crimes, relations with the natives to colonial political intrigue. After Bradford's death the manuscript passed through several hands and was not printed in its entirety until 1856.*

This excerpt from his journal, edited into a more readable form, describes two successive disasters, a hurricane in 1635 and an earthquake three years later.

"HURRICANE AND EARTHQUAKE"

1635

This year, the 14 or 15 of August (being Saturday) was such a mighty storm of wind and rain, as none living in these parts, either English or Indians, ever saw. Being like (for the time it continued) to those Hurricanes and Typhoons that writers make mention of in the Indies. It began in the morning, a little before day, and grew not by degrees, but came with violence in the beginning, to the great amazement of many. It blew down sundry houses, and uncovered others; diverse vessels were lost at sea, and many more in extreme danger. It caused the sea to swell (to the southward of this place) above 20 foot, right up and down, and made many of the Indians to climb into trees for their safety; it took off the boarded roof of a house which belonged to the plantation at Manamet, and floated it to another place, the posts still standing in the ground; and if it had continued long without the shifting of the wind, it is like it would have drowned some part of the country. It blew down many hundred thousands of trees, turning up the stronger by the roots, and breaking the higher pine trees off in the middle, and the tall young oaks and walnut trees of good bigness were wound like a wreath, very Strange and fearful to behold. It began in the southeast, and parted toward the south and east, and veered sundry ways; but the greatest force of it here was from the former quarters. It continued not (in the extremity) above 5 or 6 hours, but the violence began to abate. The signs and marks of it will remain this 100 years in these parts where it was sorest. The moon suffered a great eclipse the 2nd night after it.

1638

This year, about the 1st or 2nd of June, was a great and fearful earthquake; it was in this place heard before it was felt. It came with a rumbling noise, or low murmur, like unto remote thunder; it came from the northward, and passed southward. As the noise approached nearer, the earth began to shake, and came at length with that violence as caused platters, dishes, and such like things as stood upon shelves, to clatter and fall down; yea, persons were afraid of the houses themselves. It so fell out that at the same time diverse of the chiefs of this town were met together at one house, conferring with some of their friends that were upon their removal from the place, (as if the Lord would hereby show the signs of his displeasure, in their shaking a pieces and removals one from another). However it was very terrible for the time, and as the men were set talking in the house, some women and others were without the doors, and the earth shook with that violence as they could not stand without catching hold of the posts and pails that stood next them; but the violence lasted not long. And about half an hour, or less, came another noise and shaking, but neither so loud nor strong as the former, but quickly passed over; and so it ceased. It was not only on the sea coast, but the Indians felt it within land; and some ships that were upon the coast were shaken by it. So powerful is the mighty hand of the Lord, as to make both the earth and sea to shake, and the mountains to tremble before him, when he pleases; and who can stay his hand? It was observed that the summers, for diverse years together after this earthquake, were not so hot and seasonable for the ripening of corn and other fruits as formerly; but more cold and moist, and subject to early and untimely frosts, by which, many times, much Indian corn came not to maturity; but whether this was any cause, I leave it to naturalists to judge.

"Secondly, of Beasts" by John Josselyn

From New England's Rarities, Discovered in Birds, Beasts, Fishes, Serpents, and Plants of that Country *(1672)*

Born in Kent, England, John Josselyn (?–1675) was a mysterious traveler about whom not much is known. He visited New England in 1638, meeting with John Cotton and John Winthrop and staying over a year. He made the difficult Atlantic crossing again in 1663, after which he published New England's Rarities, Discovered in Birds, Beasts, Fishes, Serpents, and Plants of that Country *(1672) and* An Account of Two Voyages to New England *(1674). He has been criticized for his extreme "credulity"—believing everything told to him about the New World—but also praised by writers like Henry David Thoreau for his attention to natural history. The slightly modernized excerpt below might be very funny to twenty-first-century readers, but also contains some priceless details.*

"SECONDLY, OF BEASTS"

The Bear, which are generally Black

The bear. They live four months in caves; that is, all winter. In the spring, they bring forth their young ones. They seldom have above three cubs in a litter; are very fat in the fall of the leaf, with feeding upon acorns; at which time they are excellent venison. Their brains are venomous. They feed much upon water-plantain in the spring and summer, and berries, and also upon a shell-fish called a *horse-foot*; and are never mankind—i.e., fierce—but in rutting-time; and then they walk the country,—twenty, thirty, forty, in a company,—making a hideous noise with roaring, which you may hear a mile or two before they come so near as to endanger the traveler. About four years since, acorns being very scarce up in the country, some numbers of them came down amongst the English plantations, which generally are by the sea-side. At one town called Gorgiana, in the Province of Meyn (called also New Sommersetshire), they kill'd fourscore.

For Aches and Cold Swellings

Their grease is very good for aches and cold swellings. The Indians anoint themselves therewith from top to toe; which hardens them against the cold weather. A black bear's skin heretofore was worth forty shillings; now you may have one for ten: much used by the English for beds and coverlets, and by the Indians for coats.

For Pain and Lameness upon Cold

One Edw. Andrews, being foxt [drunk], and falling backward cross a thwart in a shallop or fisher-boat, and taking cold upon it, grew crooked, lame, and full of pain; was cured, lying one winter upon bears' skins newly flayed off, with some upon him, so that he sweat every night.

The Wolf

The wolf, of which there are two kinds,—one with a round-ball'd foot, and are in shape like mongrel mastiffs; the other with a flat foot. These are liker greyhounds; and are called deer-wolfs, because they are accustomed to prey upon deer. A wolf will eat a wolf new-dead: and so do bears, as I suppose; for their dead carcasses are never found, neither by the Indian nor English. They go a-clicketing twelve days, and have as many whelps at a litter as a bitch. The Indian dog is a creature begotten 'twixt a wolf and a fox; which the Indians, lighting upon, bring up to hunt the deer with.

The wolf is very numerous, and go in companies,—sometimes ten, twenty, more or fewer; and so cunning, that seldom any are kill'd with guns or traps: but, of late, they have invented a way to destroy them, by binding four maycril-hooks a cross with a brown thread; and then, wrapping some wool about them, they dip them in melted tallow till it be as round and as big as an egg. These (when any beast hath been kill'd by the wolves) they scatter by the dead carcass, after they have beaten off the wolves. About midnight, the wolves are sure to return again to the place where they left the slaughtered beast; and the first thing they venture upon will be these balls of fat.

For Old Aches

A black wolf's skin is worth a beaver-skin among the Indians; being highly esteemed for helping old aches in old people worn as a coat. They are not mankind, as in Ireland and other countries; but do much harm by destroying of our English cattle.

The Raccoon

The raccoon liveth in hollow trees, and is about the size of a gib-cat. They feed upon mass, and do infest our Indian-corn very much. They will be exceeding fat in autumn. Their flesh is somewhat dark, but good food roasted.

For Bruises and Aches

Their fat is excellent for bruises and aches. Their skins are esteemed a good, deep fur; but yet, as the wild-cats, somewhat coarse.

The Porcupine

The porcupine, in some parts of the country eastward towards the French, are as big as an ordinary mongrel cur; a very angry creature, and dangerous,—shooting a whole shower of quills with a rouse at their enemies; which are of that nature, that, wherever they stick in the flesh, they will work through in a short time, if not prevented by pulling of them out. The Indians make use of their quills, which are hardly a handful long, to adorn the edges of their birchen dishes; and weave (dying some of them red, others yellow and blue) curious bags or pouches, in works like Turkie-work.

The Beaver, Canis Ponticus Amphibius

The beaver, whose old ones are as big as an otter, or rather bigger; a creature of a rare instinct, as may apparently be seen in their artificial damheads to raise the water in the ponds where they keep; and their houses having three stories; which would be too large to discourse. They have all of them four cods hanging outwardly between their hinder legs: two of them are soft or oily, and two solid or hard. The Indians say they are hermaphrodites.

For Wind in the Stomach

Their solid cods are much used in physick. Our English women in this country use the powder, grated—as much as will lye upon a shilling—in a draught of Fiol wine, for wind in the stomach and belly; and venture many times, in such cases, to give it to women with child. Their tails are flat, and covered with scales, without hair; which, being flayed off, and the tail boiled, proves exceeding good meat; being all fat, and as sweet as marrow.

"Of the Rainbow"
by Jonathan Edwards

From the Library of American Civilization
(1895, first written 1710s)

Born in East Windsor, Connecticut, by the precocious age of 13, Jonathan Edwards (1703–1758) was ready for Yale College, where he studied both theology and natural history. He became the pastor of the church in Northampton, Massachusetts, where he instigated what was later called the Great Awakening, first through the conversion of hundreds of people, and then by the publication of his account, A Faithful Narrative of the Surprising Work of God, *which took the local revival around the country and across the seas. He became the most important American preacher of the eighteenth century and influenced religious thought far beyond his time.*

Seeing nature as proof of the designs of God, Edwards often took long walks and rides through the New England forests to be close to this divine beauty. His earlier writings shed light on the scientific part of his questing mind, as he studied optics and the behavior of spiders. The following essay, "Of the Rainbow," does not discuss the biblical symbol, but rather Sir Isaac Newton's theory of light and color.

"OF THE RAINBOW"

We shall endeavor to give a full account of the rainbow and such an one as we think if well understood, will be satisfactory to anybody, if they are fully satisfied of Sir Isaac Newton's Different Reflexibility and Refrangibility of the Rays of Light; and if he be not, we refer him to [what] he has said about it, and we are assured if he be a person of an ordinary logacity and anything versed in such matters, by that time he has thoroughly considered it, he'll be satisfied; and after that let him peruse what we are about to say.

The first question then shall be what is that reflection which we call a rainbow from. I answer from the falling drops of rain, for we never see any rainbow, except it be so that the sun can shine full upon the drops of rain, except the heavens be so clear on one side as to let the uninterrupted rays of the sun come directly upon the rain that falls on the other side. Thus, we say it is a sign of fair weather when there is a rainbow in the east, because when there is a rainbow in the east, it is always already fair in the west. For if it be cloudy, there the rays of the sun will be hindered from coming thence to the opposite of drops of rain. It cannot be the cloud from whence this reflection is made, as was once thought, for we almost always see the ends of rainbows come down even in amongst the trees below the hills and to the very ground, where we know there is no part of the cloud there, but what descends in drops of rain; and [I] can convince any man by ocular demonstration in two minutes on a fair day that the reflection is from drops, by only taking a little water in my mouth and standing between the sun and something that looks a little darkish, and spurting of it into the air so as to disperse all into fine drops; and there will appear as complete and plain a rainbow with all the colors as ever was seen in the heavens, and there will appear the same if the sun is near enough to the horizon upon fine drops of water dashed up by a stick from a puddle. The reason why the drops must be fine is because they won't be thick enough, but here and there a drop, if they are large, and I have frequently heard my countrymen that are used to sawmills say that they have seen a rainbow upon the drops that are dispersed in the air by the violent concussion of the waters in the mill, and what is equivalent to a rainbow. If one take a drop of water upon the end of a stick and hold it up on the side that is opposite to the sun and moving it along towards one side or t'other, you will perceive where the drop is held just as such a distance from the point opposite to the sun that the rays of the sun are much more vividly reflected by it to your eye, than at any other place nearer or further of, and that in the colors of the rainbow too; so that if there had been enough of these drops, there would have appeared a perfect rainbow; and if you have a mind to see more distinctly, you may fill a globular glass bottle with water, the glass of it must be very thin and clear, and it will serve your turn as well as so big a drop of water, and by that means you may also distinctly see that the reflection is from the concave and not from the convex surface.

The next thing that wants a solution is what should cause the reflection to be circular, or which is the same thing what should cause the reflection to be just at such a distance everywhere from the point that is opposite to the sun, and no reflection at all from the drops that are within or without that circle. Why should not all the drops that are within the circle reflect as many rays as those that are in the circle or where the circle is? To resolve this we must consider this one law of reflection and refraction to wit. If the reflecting body be perfectly reflexive, the angle of reflection will be the same as the angle of incidence, but if the body be not perfectly, so the angle will be less than the angle of incidence. By a body perfectly reflexive, I mean one that is so solid as perfectly to resist the stroke of the incident body and not to give way, and does not obstinately resist the stroke of the incident body. So I say that if body a. b. be perfectly reflexive and does not give way at all to the stroke of the incident ray c. d., it will reflect by an angle that shall equal to that by which it fell upon the body a. b. from d. to e. But if the body a. b. is not able to resist the stroke of the ray c. d. but gives way to it, it will neither be able to reflect by so big an angle but will reflect it. It may be by the line d. f. or d. g., according as the reflexive force of a. b. be greater or lesser. And the bare consideration of this will be enough to convince any man, for we know that there is need of greater force by a great angle than by a little one. If we throw a ball against the floor or wall, it will much easier rebound sideways than right back again, and [if] we throw it sideways against a body that gives way to the stroke of (it may be tried at any time), it will not rebound in so big an angle as if the body were quite hard. So, it is the same thing in the body a. b. It might give way so much as to let the ray proceed right on with very little deviation from its old path, and if so, the deviation will be greater and greater in proportion to the resisting power of the body; and if it gives way at all, it will not deviate so much as if it did not at all. Now these drops of water is one of these imperfectly reflexive bodies. If they were perfectly reflexive, we should see those drops that are right opposite to reflect as many rays as those that are just so much on one side, had the liquor but resistance enough to reflect the rays so directly back again. But those rays that fall perpendicularly, or near perpendicularly, upon the concave surface of the drop as from a. to b., falling with much greater force than the ray, which falls sideways upon it from e. to b. after the refraction at e., which is made in all pellucid globes. The concave surface has not force enough to stop it and reflect it (what the reflexive force of the concave surface is we are not now disputing), but let's go through and pass right on uninterruptedly. Now the ray h. e. b. and the rays which fall about so obliquely coming with a far lighter stroke the concave surface, has force enough to resist it, and what falls obliquely being far more easily reflexible, reflects it along in the line b. g.; and so in the same manner, the ray c. i. b. will be reflected to k., so that an eye so much sideways as g. or k. will take the rays thus reflected from the drops and nowhere else; and it being only those ray[s] whose obliquity is adjusted [to] the refractive power that are reflected by it, and they being all reflected out again with such a degree of obliquity, we hence see why the rays be not reflected all ways equally. We hence also see why the rays are only reflected out at the sides of the drop and not directly back again, by that why the eye does not take the rays from any drops but those that are so much sideways of, or on one side of the point that is right opposite to the sun, and so why the parts that are so opposite look dark, and why the parts that are just so much on one side at such a distance all round from the opposite point alone are bright, or which is the same thing why there is such a bright circle.

The next grand question is what is it causes the colors of the rainbow, and this question indeed is almost answered already, for it is very evident.

"Frogs and Caterpillars"
by Samuel Peters

From A General History of Connecticut, from
Its First Settlement Under George Fenwick to its
Latest Period of Amity with Great Britain *(1781)*

*Born in Hebron, Connecticut, Samuel Peters (1735–1826) attended Yale Col-
lege and served as rector of St. Peter's Church in Hebron. In 1763 he climbed
Killington Peak, and afterwards claimed he was the first to name the area "Verd
Mont." A firm Tory supporter of the king, Peters fled the colony in 1774 after
several confrontations with local Sons of Liberty, including Benedict Arnold.
During the Revolution he wrote* A General History of Connecticut, *which
painted an insulting and inaccurate picture of the colony and its people. However, it is also filled with amusing anecdotes, including the one below featuring
the famous Windham "frog fight."*

*Unlike many of the other tales in his book, though, this one is apparently
true, with an early version memorialized in a 1754 ballad by Ebenezer Til-
den. It was repeated in newspapers like the Providence* Gazette *and the Putnam* Patriot, *and in 1788 even turned into an operetta called* The Frogs of
Old Windham, *produced in Willimantic and then performed in a number of
other towns throughout the region. Peters pairs the fight with another similar
"plague" of caterpillars on the Connecticut River, and his tongue-in-cheek attitude toward these natural phenomena and the reactions of human beings must
have been refreshing, even to the most ardent patriot.*

"Frogs and Caterpillars"

Windham, the second county in the ancient kingdom of Sassacus, or colony of Saybrook, is hilly; but the soil being rich, has excellent butter, cheese, hemp, Indian-corn, and horses. Its towns are twelve.

Windham resembles Rumford, and stands on Winnomantic River. Its meeting-house is elegant, and has a steeple, bell, and clock. Its court-house is scarcely to be looked upon as an ornament. The township forms four parishes, and is ten miles square.

Strangers are very much terrified at the hideous noise made on summer evenings by the vast number of frogs in the brooks and ponds. There are about thirty different voices among them, some of which resemble the bellowing of a bull. The owls and whippoorwills complete the rough concert, which may be heard several miles. Persons accustomed to such serenades are not disturbed by them at their proper stations; but one night in July, 1758, the frogs of an artificial pond, three miles square, and about five from Windham, finding the water dried up, left the place in a body, and marched, or rather hopped, towards Winnomantic River. They were under the necessity of taking the road and going through the town, which they entered about midnight. The bull-frogs were the leaders, and the pipers followed without number. They filled the road, forty yards wide, for four miles in length, and were for several hours in passing through the town unusually clamorous.

The inhabitants were equally perplexed and frightened: some expected to find an army of French and Indians; others feared an earthquake, and dissolution of Nature. The consternation was universal. Old and young, male and female; fled naked from their beds, with worse shriekings than those of the frogs. The event was fatal to several women. The men, after a flight of half a mile, in which they met with many broken shins, finding no enemies in pursuit of them, made a hault, and summoned resolution enough to venture back to their wives and children, when they distinctly heard from the enemy's camp these words: Wight, Hilderkin, Dier, Tete. This last, they thought, meant treaty, and, plucking up courage, they sent a triumvirate to capitulate with the supposed French and Indians. These the men approached in their shirts, and begged to speak with the general; but, it being dark and no answer given, they were sorely agitated for some time betwixt hope and fear: at length, however, they discovered that the dreaded inimical army was an army of thirsty frogs going to the river for a little water.

Such an incursion was never known before nor since; and yet the people of Windham have been ridiculed for their timidity on this occasion. I verily believe an army under the Duke of Marlborough would, under like circumstances, have acted no better than they did.

In 1768 the inhabitants of Connecticut River were as much alarmed by an army of caterpillars as those of Windham were at the frogs; and no one found reason to jest at their fears. Those worms came in one night and covered the earth, on both sides of the river, to an extent of three miles in front and two in depth. They marched with great speed, and ate up everything green for the space of one hundred miles, in spite of rivers, ditches, fires, and the united efforts of 1,000 men. They were, in general, two inches long, had white bodies covered with thorns, and red throats. When they had finished their work they went down to the river Connecticut, where they died, poisoning the waters, until they were washed into the sea. This calamity was imputed by some to the vast number of logs and trees lying in the creeks, and to cinders, smoke, and fires, made to consume the waste wood for three or four hundred miles up the Connecticut River; while others thought it augurated future evils, similar to those of Egypt. The inhabitants of the Verdmonts would unavoidably have perished with famine, in consequence of the devastation of these worms, had not a remarkable Providence filled the wilderness with wild pigeons, which were killed by sticks as they sat upon the branches of the trees, in such multitudes that 30,000 people lived on them for three weeks. If a natural cause may be assigned for the coming of the frogs and caterpillars, yet the visit of the pigeons to the wilderness in August has been necessarily ascribed to the interposition of infinite Power and Goodness. Happy will it be for America, if the smiling providence of Heaven produces gratitude, repentance, and obedience, amongst her children!

"River Caves"
by Timothy Dwight

From Travels in New England and New York *(1800)*

Born in Northampton, Massachusetts, Timothy Dwight IV (1752–1817) was descended from Jonathan Edwards and graduated Yale College when he was just 17 years old. He served as a chaplain during the Revolutionary War, inspiring the troops with his sermons, before serving in the Massachusetts State Legislature. He then moved to Fairfield, Connecticut, where he served as minister at Greenfield Hill and ran an academy. Due to his religious and political leadership, he was elected president of Yale College, and his guidance led it into the nineteenth century. He and the professors he hired added science to the curriculum, prompting other schools to do the same.

Dwight's public writings began in 1776, when he gave a valedictory address at Yale that described Americans as having a unique national identity. As a member of the "Hartford Wits" in the 1770s and '80s, he helped gather popular support for the federal union of the states, and combined pastoral and religious imagery in Greenfield Hill *and other poems. The work from which the piece below is taken,* Travels in New England and New York, *was considered his most important and long-lasting work, giving a social and economic overview of the Northeast during the early 1800s. However, it also highlighted natural phenomena like the "river caves" described here.*

"River Caves"

Monday, September 25th, we set out for Charlestown, accompanied by Colonel Tyler, of Guilford, Vermont, who politely offered to point out to us whatever was interesting in Bellows Falls, three miles north of the village of Walpole. These are the falls so fancifully described by Peters in that collection of extravagancies which he has been pleased to style "The History of Connecticut." They are certainly an interesting natural curiosity, although we did not find the water beneath them so hard as to be impervious to an iron crow. They are formed by four successive rifts, with that same number of rapids, and extend in a straight line three fourths of a mile; or, if measured on the circular course of the river, seven eighths. In this estimate I include that part of the river which lies between the two ends of the canal to be described hereafter. All these rifts run from the foot of the Fall Mountain, the base of which at this spot terminates about forty rods eastward of the river. The rocks are very hard gray granite. In the northern and middle rifts there is nothing remarkable, but the southern has long been an object of peculiar attention. The waters of the Connecticut, which both above and below the falls are forty rods in breadth, are here contracted to the narrow compass of twenty feet; and, when the stream is very low, it is said, within that of six. The rapidity of the current may be conjectured from this fact.

An inquisitive traveler, while inspecting this ground, will want no argument to convince him that the river anciently had its channel about fifty rods, where the distance is the greatest, westward of the place where it now runs. Here a canal is dug in its former bed to facilitate the transportation of boats around these falls. The bed of rocks, after crossing the present channel, takes a southwestern direction toward the lower end of the canal. Originally, the bed of the river was from fifteen to twenty feet higher than it is at present, as is unanswerably evident from the great number of excavations which it formerly wrought out in the rocks, chiefly on the western bank, which are now from ten to fifteen feet above the highest present watermark. The river now is often fuller than it probably ever was before the country above was cleared of its forests, the snows in open grounds melting much more suddenly and forming much greater freshets than in forested ground. The river cannot, therefore, have risen to the height of these excavations by having a greater supply of water. Besides, excavation so deep, so large, and wrought in rocks so hard show with absolute certainty that the river ran at this level often and for a long period: a fact which no possible sources of its water could have been the means of accomplishing had it customarily flowed at its present level.

These cavities are very numerous, both above and below the bridge. They are also of various forms, from that of a shallow dish to that of an iron pot, that of a barrel, and in one instance that of an inverted pear; and of various sizes, from the capacity of a pint bowl to that of perhaps two hogsheads. Their greatest depths we could not accurately estimate, because those which were deepest, as well as many others, were partially filled with water, gravel, and stones.

From these cavities and others like them, and generally from the depredations made by falls of water upon the rocks over which they fell, that class of infidels who have discernment exactly fitted to perceive, candor enough to love, and industry sufficient to point out petty objections against revelation have with no small triumph around here, in their own opinion, means of disproving the date assigned to the creation by Moses. An argument founded, as this is, on arithmetical computation requires that the means of computing should be within the reach of him by whom the argument is adduced. Had these gentlemen taken the pains to examine the subject on the spot, they would have found that neither here, nor in any other place of the like nature, are there any possible means of such a computation, and that, therefore, the argument is totally destitute of foundation. The rocks are in some places harder than in others; the water some years rises oftener and higher than in others, and is sometimes more replenished with grit. The gravel and stones exist in greater quantities; the stones are larger, have sharper angles, and are of a harder consistency. From these facts it is evident that nothing like regularity can exist in this operation of nature, nothing which can present materials for any calculation.

The manner in which these cavities commenced, and how the stones and gravel by which they are worn are retained in the same spot before the rock is to a considerable degree hollowed out, it seems not very easy to determine. The best solution of the difficulty which I am able to give is the following. The rocks, although generally of a form approaching toward convexity, are in some places flat, and in others in a small degree concave. There are in all rivers, especially where they are most agitated, innumerable little circular eddies or whirlpools. Wherever one of these exists immediately over such a spot having gravel and stones lying on it, they are driven around in exact conformity to the direction of the water, and are retained in their place by its circular force. In this manner, they grind the rock until they have worn a concavity, whose figure will ever afterwards create a similar whirlpool within its limits.

All the stones and gravel which we saw in these cavities had their angles entirely worn off by the attrition.

On one of the rocks lying in the river below the bridge, we saw two rude Indian attempts at sculpture. They were very coarse copies of the human face: a circular figure cut in the rock serving for the outline, two round holes for the eyes, and an elliptical one for the mouth. For what purpose they were made in this place we were unable to divine. They are not visible except when the water is low.

I have observed that the bed of the river is lower than it was formerly. This change has been chiefly accomplished by the washing away of the earth, gravel, and stones which were of such a size as to yield to the force of the current. In consequence of this process, the stones and rocks of a larger size have gradually subsided. Even these, indeed, have been partially worn, but not so as to contribute perceptibly to any alteration in the channel. Where the bed of a river is a stratum of slate or limestone, very great changes often take place from these attritions of the stream and the influence of the atmosphere; but these rocks are of too firm a texture to be greatly affected by the efficacy of either.

"Account of a Meteor"
by Benjamin Silliman

From Memoirs of the Connecticut Academy of Arts and Sciences, 1810 *(1810)*

Benjamin Silliman (1779–1864) was born in a tavern in what is today Trumbull, Connecticut, after his mother fled the British attack on Fairfield. Seventeen years later he graduated from Yale College and continued on to receive his master's and law degrees. Hired by Yale president Timothy Dwight IV, he began to teach chemistry and natural history, giving the first scientific lectures ever presented at the institution. He founded the American Journal of Science, *became one of the first teachers at the new Yale Medical School, and developed the process by which kerosene could be distilled and thus marketed. Along with his many contributions to science, he also supported coeducation and the abolition of slavery.*

Silliman's interest in geology was sparked by a meteorite that crashed into Weston, Connecticut, on December 14, 1807. In the following excerpt from his essay on the topic, he gives details about the event that combine both the anecdotal style of early naturalists and the precision of scientific inquiry.

"ACCOUNT OF A METEOR"

The meteor which has so recently excited alarm in many, and astonishment in all, first made its appearance in Weston, about a quarter or half past 6 o'clock, a.m. on Monday the 14th. The morning was somewhat cloudy; the clouds were dispersed in unequal masses, being in some places thick and opaque, in others light, fleecy, and partially transparent; while spots of unclouded sky appeared here and there among them. Along the northern part of the horizon, a space of 10 or 15 degrees was perfectly clear. The day had merely dawned, and there was little or no light, except from the moon, which was just setting. Judge Wheeler, to whose intelligence and observation, apparently uninfluenced by fear or imagination, we are indebted for the substance of this part of our account, was passing through the enclosure adjoining his house, with his face to the north, and his eyes on the ground, when a sudden flash, occasioned by the transition of a luminous body across the northern margin of clear sky, illuminated every object, and caused him to look up. He immediately discovered a globe of fire, just then passing behind the first cloud, which was very dark, and obscure, although it did not entirely hide the meteor.

The most northerly fall was within the limits of Huntington, on the border of Weston, about 40 or 50 rods east of the great road from Bridgeport to Newtown, in a cross road, and contiguous to the house of Mr. Merwin Burr. Mr. Burr was standing in the road, in front of his house, when the stone fell. The noise produced by its collision with a rock of granite, on which it struck, was very loud. Mr. Burr was within 50 feet, and immediately searched for the body, but, it being still dark, he did not find it till half an hour after. By the fall, some of it was reduced to powder, and the rest of it was broken into very small fragments, which were thrown around to the distance of 20 or 30 feet. The granite rock was stained at the place of contact with a deep lead color. The largest fragment which remained did not exceed the size of a goose egg, and this Mr. Burr found to be still warm to his hand. There was reason to conclude from all the circumstances that this stone must have weighed about twenty or twenty-five pounds.

Mr. Burr had a strong impression that another stone fell in an adjoining field, and it was confidently believed that a large mass, had fallen into a neighboring swamp, but neither of these had been found. It is probable that the stone whose fall has now been described, together with any other masses which may have fallen at the same time, was thrown from the meteor at the first explosion.

The masses projected at the second explosion seem to have fallen principally at and in the vicinity of Mr. William Prince's in Weston, distant about five miles, in a southerly direction, from Mr. Burr's. Mr. Prince and family were still in bed, when they heard a noise like the fall of a very heavy body, immediately after the explosions. They formed various unsatisfactory conjectures concerning the cause—nor did even a fresh hole made through the turf in the door-yard, about twenty-five feet from the house, lead to any conception of the cause, or induce any other enquiry than why a new post hole should have been dug where there was no use for it. So far were this family from conceiving of the possibility of such an event as stones falling from the clouds. They had indeed formed a vague conjecture that the hole might have been made by lightning, but would probably have paid no further attention to the circumstance, had they not heard, in the course of the day, that stones had fallen that morning, in other parts of the town. This induced them, towards evening, to search the hole in the yard, where they found a stone buried in the loose earth which had fallen upon it. It was two feet from the surface—the hole was about twelve inches in diameter, and as the earth was soft and nearly free from stones, the mass had sustained little injury, only a few small fragments having been detached by the shock. The weight of this stone was about thirty-five pounds. From the descriptions which we have heard, it must have been a noble specimen, and men of science will not cease to deplore that so rare a treasure should have been immediately broken in pieces. All that remained unbroken of this noble mass, was a piece of twelve pounds weight, since purchased by Isaac Bronson, Esq. of Greenfield, with, the liberal view of presenting it to some public institution.

Six days after, another mass was discovered, half a mile north-west from Mr. Prince's. The search was directed by the confident persuasion of his neighbors that they heard it fall near the spot, where it was actually found buried in the earth, weighing from seven to ten pounds. It was found by Gideon Hall and Isaac Fairchild. It was in small fragments, having fallen on a globular detached mass of gneiss rock, which it split in two, and by which it was itself shivered to pieces.

The same men informed us that they suspected another stone had fallen in the vicinity, as the report had been distinctly heard and could be referred to a particular region somewhat to the east. Returning to the place after an excursion of a few hours to another part of the town, we were gratified to find the conjecture verified, by the actual discovery of a mass of thirteen pounds weight, which had fallen half a mile to the north east of Mr. Prince's. Having fallen in a ploughed field, without coming into contact with a rock, it was broken only into two principal pieces, one of which, possessing all the characters of the stone in a remarkable degree, we purchased; for it had now become an article of sale.—It was urged that it had pleased heaven to rain down this treasure upon them, and they would bring their thunderbolts to the best market they could. This was, it must be confessed, a wiser mode of managing the business than that which had been adopted by some others, at an earlier period of these discoveries. Strongly impressed with the idea that these stones contained gold and silver, they subjected them to all the tortures of ancient alchemy, and the goldsmith's crucible, the forge, and the blacksmith's anvil, were employed in vain to elicit riches which existed only in the imagination.

Two miles south-east from Mr. Prince's, at the foot of Tashowa hill, a fifth mass fell. Its fall was distinctly heard by Mr. Ephraim Porter and his family who live within 40 rods of the place and in full view. They saw a smoke rise from the spot, as they did also from the hill, where they are positive that another stone struck, as they heard it distinctly. At the time of the fall, having never heard of any such thing, they supposed that lightning had struck the ground, but after three or four days, hearing of the stones which had been found in their vicinity, they were induced to search, and the result was the discovery of a mass of stone in the road, at the place where they supposed the lightning had struck. It penetrated the ground to the depth of two feet in the deepest place; the hole was about twenty inches in diameter, and its margin was colored blue from the powder of the stone, struck off in its fall.

It was broken into fragments of moderate size, and from the best calculations might have weighed 20 or 25 pounds. The hole exhibited marks of much violence, the turf being very much torn, and thrown about to some distance. It is probable that the four stones last described were all projected at the second explosion, and should one be discovered on the neighboring hill, we must without doubt, refer it to the same avulsion.

Last of all, we hasten to what appears to have been the catastrophe of this wonderful phenomenon. A mass of stone far exceeding the united weight of all which we have hither to described, fell in a field belonging to Mr. Elijah Seeley, and within 30 rods of his house.

A circumstance attended the fall of this which seems to have been peculiar. Mr. Elihu Staples, a man of integrity, lives on the hill at the bottom of which this body fell, and witnessed the first appearance, progress and explosion of the meteor. After the last explosion, a rending noise like that of a whirl wind passed along to the east of his house and immediately over his orchard, which is on the declivity of the hill. At the same instant a streak of light passed over the orchard in a large curve and seemed to pierce the ground.—A shock was felt and a report heard like that of a heavy body falling to the earth; but no conception being entertained of the real cause, (for no one in this vicinity with whom we conversed appeared to have ever heard of the fall of stones from the skies) it was supposed that lightning had struck the ground. Three or four hours after the event, Mr. Seeley went into his field to look after his cattle.—He found that some of them had leaped into the adjoining enclosure, and all exhibited strong indications of terror. Passing on, he was struck with surprise at seeing a spot of ground which he knew to have been recently turfed over, all torn up, and the earth looking fresh, as if from recent violence. Coming to the place, he found a great mass of fragments of a strange looking stone, and immediately called for his wife, who was second on the ground.

Here were exhibited the most striking proofs of violent collision.— A ridge of micaceous schistus lying nearly even with the ground, and somewhat inclining like the hill, to the south east, was shivered to pieces, to a certain extent, by the impulse of the stone, which thus received a still more oblique direction and forced itself into the earth to the depth of three feet, tearing a hole of 5 feet in length and 4½ feet in breadth, and throwing large masses, of turf and fragments of stone and earth to the distance of 50 and 100 feet. Had there been no meteor, no explosions and no witnesses of the light and shock, it would have been impossible for any person contemplating the scene to doubt that a large and heavy body had really fallen from the skies with tremendous momentum.

This stone was all in fragments, none of which exceeded the size of a man's fist, and was rapidly dispersed by numerous visitors who carried it away at pleasure. Indeed we found it very difficult to obtain a sufficient supply of specimens of the various stones, an object which was at length accomplished principally by importunity and purchase. From the best information which we could obtain of the quantity of fragments of this last stone, compared with its specific gravity, we concluded that its weight could not have fallen much short of 200 pounds. All the stones, when first found, were friable, being easily broken between the fingers; this was especially the case where they had been buried in the moist earth, but by exposure to the air, they gradually hardened. Such were the circumstances attending the fall of these singular masses. We have named living witnesses; the list of these may be augmented, but we consider the proof as sufficient to satisfy any rational mind. Farther confirmation will be derived from the mineralogical description and chemical examination of these stones.

The specimens obtained from all the different places are perfectly similar. The most careless observer would instantly pronounce them portions of a common mass, and different from any of the stones commonly seen on this globe.

"Domestic Economy"
by Noah Webster

From the Connecticut Courant *(1817)*

Born in Hartford, Connecticut, Noah Webster (1758–1843) had an unpleasant experience in elementary school, which led him to his life's work reforming American education. He attended Yale College during the American Revolution, and went on to teach school and study law. Failing at both these pursuits, he found more success as a writer of political tracts supporting the Revolution and the Constitution. In 1785 he wrote his iconic "Blue Backed Speller" for elementary students, the enormous sales of which eventually gave him a substantial income and which helped popularize spelling bees. Alone in his rooms in New Haven and Northampton, he then wrote his American dictionary, which took twenty-six years to complete and when published standardized American speech.

During those years, Webster continued to write numerous other books and newspaper articles. The article featured below, "Domestic Economy," takes on the subject of conservation a century before it became popular. In his time, the apparently endless wealth of resources made such arguments unpopular to say the least. But as he did in education, Webster saw the problems ahead, and his plea for managing our limited resources resonates strongly today.

"DOMESTIC ECONOMY"

When our ancestors first planted their habitations in this country, the first object was to clear the land for tillage, mowing and pasture; wood was an incumbrance, and it was consumed without regard to quantity. In conformity to this object wide and deep fire places were constructed; for it was less labor to roll in heavy logs than to cut and split them. Almost two centuries have elapsed, since this work of destruction has been carried on without intermission—our habits have been formed upon this practice, and the annual consumption of thirty or forty cords of wood by a family is considered as necessary, and a matter of course. Provident men, however, begin to cast about for the means of saving fuel.

In truth, our country cannot sustain the present consumption of wood for a century to come—We must either reduce the annual consumption within the limits of the annual growth, or that time will arrive when we must search the bowels of the earth for fuel; and if we are not able to find it in the interior of New England, we must import it; or we must abandon the soil. It is of the more importance to attend in season to this object, as at some future time we must depend more on manufactures for our clothing and utensils, than we now do; and how are our manufactories to be supplied with fuel?

The first object that requires attention is to nourish and increase the growth of trees for fuel and timber. Every farm should contain a tract of land, covered with trees, the annual growth of which should be equal to the necessities of one family at least. Experienced farmers will best judge of the best mode of treating wood land for the preservation of the wood and for encouraging the most rapid growth.

The next object is to reduce the amount of consumption. Within a few years past much attention has been paid to this object, and many experiments have been made, some of them with no inconsiderable success. The great point to be gained in the use of fuel, is to confine the heat and prevent its escape in the current of air which it generates, and by which combustion is supported. In our common fire places, a great part of the heat is entirely lost. A large fire can be nourished only by a strong current, or a continued access of a large quantity of fresh air. But in our common fire places set in chimneys on one side of a room, a large fire is necessary to warm a common room in cold weather and in the current of air generated by such a fire, probably nine tenths of the heat ascend the chimney and is wasted.

To remedy this evil, it is necessary that less fire should be used, and a smaller current of air generated; to effect this object, it is absolutely necessary, that our fireplaces should be brought forward into the rooms to be warmed, or that the heat should be conveyed through them by pipes. It is by no means improbable that if heat could be perfectly confined, a cubic foot of dry wood would evolve best enough to warm a room for twelve hours. But this is not practicable.

⸻

The following facts will exhibit its uses saving fuel. In a school house, in that neighborhood, with two chimneys, one each end; the consumption of wood went formerly from 15 to 18 cords of wood during the time of keeping the winter school. In the stoves or new fire places, which were introduced last fall, the consumption has been, the present winter but five cords and a quarter. But the saving is not the only benefit—the room has been much better heated; so that eighty children might be kept upon their seats, without the necessity of resorting to the fire.

But the greatest consumption of fuel is in our kitchens, and most of our chimneys are so constructed that the fire places cannot easily be altered. To remedy this evil, we can however resort to the modern cooking stoves.

⸻

As timber becomes more scarce, our citizens will build more generally with brick or stone. It deserves consideration, whether a mode may not be devised to convey the warm air and smoke of our kitchens or parlors through the whole extent of the apartments in the house, by means of a flue carried round the upper part of the room just below the ceiling. This flue if formed of thin or narrow bricks would be so far warmed, as to temper the air, and render less fuel necessary in the fire place. I see but one objection to this scheme, which is, that the flue might fill and be ultimately obstructed by soot; and perhaps this evil might be obviated.

Another important object in the economy of fuel, is, never to burn green wood. I say burn it, but it can hardly be said that green wood burns. In truth, it does not burn; for before green wood burns in our fire places, it must be, and in fact is, dried by the fire previously made. Before green wood becomes proper fuel, all the sap or watery substances must be expelled. These substances pass off in smoke, and with them a large portion of heat, in a latent or imperceptible state; in other words the hydrogens, or inflammable substance is conveyed off in combination, without inflammation.

—◆—

These remarks, few and scanty indeed, have reference to the permanent welfare and prosperity of this part of America. The people of America, in general have never been compelled to practice a rigid economy. Many of our people are indeed just and avaricious in the use of money; but in other respects, are far from being provident or economical. They have generally such an abundance of provision, that one family in America consumes what supports three in Europe; the shopkeeper here furnishes an entertainment for a friend that vies with a nobleman's table in England or France. Gentlemen of little property cover themselves and their families with the richest clothes and silks, and their floors with carpets; and apprentices are not satisfied without a pair of ten dollar boots upon their legs and a watch in their pockets.

—◆—

The laws of nature cannot be controlled, nor will the all wise Author of them alter the scheme of his moral government in compliance with our inordinate desires. If men will trespass upon his goodness, abuse his bounties, and waste in vice, and in riot, that portion of good things, which he has commanded them to use with temperance, and with a due acknowledgement of his goodness, they must suffer the evils which he has imposed upon such abuses, as their penalty. Our country has been favored beyond example, for many years' past, in agricultural and commercial prosperity. The effect of this has been, not only to furnish the means of improvement, but the means of buying and ambition. We are habitually disposed to spend all we can get, and something more—and under a depressed state of business, these habits become extremely inconvenient. But it is the ordinance of Providence that men should live within their means—we must come to this sooner or later—and adapt our manner of life to our circumstances. With a determination to do this, we shall soon find that we are not forsaken by a bountiful Providence. But we are not merely to seek the means of subsistence for ourselves—we are not to waste and destroy, for the sake of present enjoyment; we must not strip the inheritance of its wood & its fences and its timber, and leave it barren and impoverished to the next generation. We must not be so improvident as to render our country uninhabitable. Cold as the climate is, New-England may, with provident management, forever supply food and fuel to a numerous population.

Men are too apt to form rash opinions & take precipitate steps under the impulse of temporary adversities. And the failure of a crop or two, may impel men to abandon their country.

The climate of America is indeed as cold in the *fortieth*, as the west of Europe is in the *fiftieth* degree of latitude. But Europe supports a vast population north of that degree.

The failure of crops in the northern section of the United States is much less frequent than in the southern. The cotton and the rice of the south are destroyed by drouth, worm or inundation more frequently than the corn of the north, either by drouth or by frost. The loss of the maize the last year, has had but one parallel instance, if I am rightly informed, within a century, viz.—in 1737, eighty years ago; and in this instance Providence has furnished an alleviation by a super abundant crop of other grains. At this moment New-England has probably an ample supply, and perhaps a surplus of provisions for the year, and a competency of fodder for the cattle.

Unfavorable seasons have occasionally occurred in every country and in every age. Numerous instances are recorded of famine in Asia, Africa and Europe. No instance has yet occurred in America. In addition to this, this country has suffered less than others by other calamities. In the year 810, a pestilential disease swept away a great part of the cattle, in some countries of Europe. In Germany it almost destroyed the species. A similar calamity, but not so destructive, prevailed in 1751. In 1711 and 12, a like calamity destroyed almost all the cattle in Italy. About the year 250 or 252 in the reign of the Emperor Decius, a plague commenced in Africa and extended over Europe, which, in a few years, destroyed a large part of its inhabitants. Gibbon estimates that a "moiety of the human species," fell a prey to the pestilence. The plague of 1347-8-9 destroyed one *third*, and some authors allege, one *half* of the inhabitants of England, and some cities on the continent were nearly depopulated.

What calamity have the inhabitants of the United States ever suffered, that class any proportion to these? Surely we have more cause for gratitude than for discontent. We are not to expect perpetual prosperity.— We must bear our portion of the calamities inflicted upon a guilty world for their sins and ingratitude, and it ill becomes men, inhabiting a healthy country and a productive soil; blessed with a greater share of political and religious freedom, than any other people on earth, to murmur, complain, and abandon their country, because they cannot enjoy perpetual sunshine and uninterrupted prosperity.

I have visited *twelve* of the States, and have resided in *five*—and after the best estimate I have been able to make of all the advantages and disadvantages, physical, civil, moral and religious to be enjoyed or encountered in each, I can declare that I should not be willing to exchange a residence in New-England for one in any other part of the States I have seen. The summer heat and diseases of the south, are, in my apprehension, more than a balance for the cold winters of the north, and the state of society, with the civil and religious institutions of the north, gives, to this portion of America, a decided preference. There are indeed great vices that stain the character of the people, in both sections of the Union; and if I could find a small portion of inhabited territory, in either section, untainted with these vices, I would seek that spot, and there spend the remainder of my days. But no such spot is to be found, almost any part of America however may be rendered an eligible residence, to a man who is disposed to be contented with what steady industry will furnish, and with those enjoyments, which reason and religion permit.

"The Whale's Revenge"
by Owen Chase

From Narrative of the Most Extraordinary
and Distressing Shipwreck of the Whale-
Ship Essex, of Nantucket *(1821)*

A lifelong Nantucketer, Owen Chase (1797–1869) was a whale-ship cap-tain most famous for being first mate on the Essex, *a whaler sunk after being rammed by a sperm whale in November 1820. After the* Essex *sank, Chase was among twenty-one men who began a journey in three whaleboats across thousands of miles of open ocean. Only five survived a harrowing experience of oppressive weather, hunger, thirst, and cannibalism. He returned home in June 1821.*

The book he wrote about the experience, which is excerpted below, served as Herman Melville's inspiration for Moby Dick. *With the help of a ghost-writer, Chase completed his narrative in just a few months and returned to sea in December 1821. He later became a captain and owned his own ship. He retired from whaling in 1840, but the memory of the* Essex *haunted him with nightmares and headaches. Forever fearing hunger, he hoarded food in his attic later in life.*

Chase's narrative is direct and factual, but still provides a sense of the sheer amazement and terror he experienced. It's a rare recorded instance of one of nature's creatures, usually dominated by human beings, fighting back with unmitigated success.

"The Whale's Revenge"

I observed a very large spermaceti whale, as well as I could judge about eighty-five feet in length. He broke water about twenty rods off our weather bow and was lying quietly, with his head in a direction for the ship. He spouted two or three times and then disappeared. In less than two or three seconds, he came up again, about the length of the ship off, and made directly for us at the rate of about three knots. The ship was then going with about the same velocity. His appearance and attitude gave us at first no alarm, but while I stood watching his movements and observing him, but a ship's length off, coming down for us with great celerity, I involuntarily ordered the boy at the helm to put it hard up, intending to sheer off and avoid him.

The words were scarcely out of my mouth before he came down upon us with full speed and struck the ship with his head, just forward of the fore-chains. He gave us such an appalling and tremendous jar as nearly threw us all on our faces. The ship brought up as suddenly and violently as if she had struck a rock and trembled for a few seconds like a leaf.

We looked at each other with perfect amazement, deprived almost of the power of speech. Many minutes elapsed before we were able to realize the dreadful accident. During this time the whale passed under the ship, grazing her keel as he went along. He came up alongside of her to leeward and lay on the top of the water, apparently stunned with the violence of the blow, for the space of a minute. He then suddenly started off in a direction to leeward.

After a few moments' reflection and recovering, in some measure, from the sudden consternation that had seized us, I of course concluded that he had stove a hole in the ship and that it would be necessary to set the pumps going. Accordingly, they were rigged but had not been in operation more than one minute before I perceived the head of the ship to be gradually settling down in the water. I then ordered the signal to be set for the other boats, which scarcely had I dispatched before I again discovered the whale, apparently in convulsions, on the top of the water about one hundred rods to leeward. He was enveloped in the foam of the sea that his continual and violent thrashing about in the water had created around him, and I could distinctly see him smite his jaws together, as if distracted with rage and fury. He remained a short time in this situation and then started off with great velocity across the bow of the ship to windward.

By this time the ship had settled down a considerable distance in the water, and I gave her up as lost. I, however, ordered the pumps to be kept constantly going and endeavored to collect my thoughts for the occasion. I turned to the boats, two of which we then had with the ship, with an intention of clearing them away and getting all things ready to embark in them if there should be no other resource left. While my attention was thus engaged for a moment, I was aroused with the cry of a man at the hatchway: "Here he is—he is making for us again."

I turned around and saw him, about one hundred rods directly ahead of us, coming down apparently with twice his ordinary speed and, it appeared to me at that moment, with tenfold fury and vengeance in his aspect. The surf flew in all directions about him, and his course towards us was marked by white foam a rod in width, which he made with the continual violent thrashing of his tail. His head was about half out of water, and in that way he came upon and again struck the ship.

I was in hopes, when I descried him making for us, that, by a dexterous movement of putting the ship away immediately, I should be able to cross the line of his approach before he could get up to us and thus avoid what I knew, if he should strike us again, would prove our inevitable destruction. I bawled out to the helmsman, "Hard up!!" But she had not fallen off more than a point before we took the second shock. I should judge the speed of the ship to have been at this time about three knots and that of the whale about six. He struck her to windward, directly under the cathead, and completely stove in her bow. He passed under the ship again, went off to leeward, and we saw no more of him.

"Excursion from Providence to Bristol"
by Charles T. Jackson

From Report on the Geological and Agricultural Survey of the State of Rhode-Island *(1840)*

A Boston-based physician and geologist, Charles T. Jackson (1805–1880) was born in Plymouth, Massachusetts, and received a medical degree from Harvard in 1829. He then studied medicine and geology in Europe. Upon his return in 1832, he spent a few years in medical practice before starting an analytic chemistry lab where he taught.

Jackson went on to write geological surveys and served as state geologist of Maine, New Hampshire, and Rhode Island. A brilliant polymath, he claimed to have played a role in the invention of the telegraph and anesthesia, assertions which resulted in highly contentious disputes. His sister Lydian married Ralph Waldo Emerson, and the couple defended Jackson. Suffering from mental illness, in 1873 he was admitted to an asylum where he spent the rest of his days.

Although a man of science, Jackson's writing about Rhode Island's geology marries the factual and poetic, evoking a sense of wonder.

"EXCURSION FROM PROVIDENCE TO BRISTOL"

In Apponaug, in the township of Warwick, there is a curious mass of rock delicately balanced upon two points, so as to be moved with great ease by the hand, and as it is said, is even rocked by the wind. When put in motion, it strikes audibly upon its pedestal, and produces a sound similar to the cantering of a horse upon frozen ground. It has received the descriptive appellation of the Drum Rock.

It is situated upon the land of Mr. John Carpenter, three quarters of a mile southwest of the village of Apponaug, just on the edge of a wood lot, and near a spring of good water, said to have been much resorted to by the aboriginal inhabitants. The rock is said to have served the Indians as an alarm or call, for by rocking it a sound is produced audible to a great distance, and I was informed it could be heard during the stillness of night to the distance of six or eight miles.

I measured the dimensions of the rocking stone, and found them to be 7½ feet in length, 5½ in width, and 15 inches in thickness, so it must weigh about 34 tons. It is composed of compact grauwacke, and rests upon the same kind of rock, from which it was doubtless separated by the action of frost and by decomposition effected through the medium of a natural fissure.

Purgatory, and the Hanging Rocks of Paradise, are examples of geological importance, as showing the effects of aqueous action. At Purgatory we see a very hard and finely cemented mass of conglomerated pebbles, varying in size, from an inch to a yard in length, and all oval shaped, with their long axes parallel to each other as if affected by a powerful current, or the surf of a former ocean. These pebbles are of the hardest kind of quartz rock, and yet present polished surfaces, evidently the result of long abrasion, produced by friction upon each other, effected by the action of water. Now we find the pebbles cemented together, by a finer paste, of a similar nature, but presenting all the usual appearances of fusion. I remarked also an infinity of minute crystals of magnetic iron ore on their surfaces, and in many cases that substance served to attach the pebbles to each other. Magnetic oxide of iron could never have been deposited in that state from water, and I regard it as an absolute proof of the agency of fire, which has fused the cement and crystallized the oxide of iron.

By means of a simple lens, or common microscope, any person may discover a great abundance of these Magnetic crystals, and even to the naked eye, when the sun shines upon the rock, they are very apparent. The chasm called Purgatory, is a fissure, in the conglomerate rock, produced by an ancient disruption of the strata, and was once of the rent, to attest its former presence. This rent is in a S. E. and N. W. direction, and by measurement, was found to be of the following dimensions: The width was from 8 to 10 feet, the depth is 36 feet on one side, and 44 feet on the opposite or highest point. The pebbles are arranged in parallel directions, their long axes coinciding and running north and south. They consist of very hard quartz rock and flinty slate, and the pebbles have been cut in two by the power that up-hove the rock.

Purgatory is a place of resort for the curious, and a singular legend is connected with the name which it bears. It is said that a young man being challenged to prove his love for a fair maiden, actually sprang across this ravine, and declared his transit as one from Purgatory to Paradise; hence the origin of the names by which these localities are known.

The hanging rocks are merely huge masses of stratified conglomerate rocks, which present abrupt and mural precipices towards the sea, and in some points of view appear to overhang the shore. The white sandy beaches which here form a barrier to the wild ocean's waves, are frequented by strangers and by the people, for the sake of the grandeur of the scenery, and in pleasant weather they present suitable places for sea bathing, and afford a delightful ride. Much as I might wish to expatiate on the beauty and interest of these places, I feel that I ought not to spare time from my more serious duties in describing the geological contour of the country.

"Ktaadn"
by Henry David Thoreau

From The Union Magazine of Literature & Art *(1848)*

Most famous for dwelling in a small house he built himself at Walden Pond and the book based on that experience, Henry David Thoreau (1817–1862) spent most of his life in his hometown of Concord, Massachusetts. Graduating from Harvard in 1837, he returned home to teach school, later becoming a skilled surveyor and working in his father's pencil-making business. Befriended and mentored by Ralph Waldo Emerson, Thoreau styled himself "a mystic, a transcendentalist, and a natural philosopher to boot."

At Emerson's suggestion, he began keeping a journal shortly after returning from college. Into it he poured his ideas and observations, and tested his writing skill. An inveterate walker through fields and forests, he gave special attention to recording the phenomena of nature, which over time became increasingly precise and scientific. The beauty, exactitude, humor, and poetry in his prose has endured and gained readership over time. It is hardly an exaggeration to acknowledge that all subsequent nature writing may be a footnote to Thoreau.

Thoreau published two books in his lifetime, A Week on the Concord and Merrimack Rivers *(1849) and his masterpiece* Walden *(1854), as well as a smattering of poems, essays, and translations. The vast bulk of his work was published posthumously, including the two-million-word journal. Here we have an ecstatic excerpt from the "Ktaadn" essay published first in a magazine and later in* The Maine Woods *(1864).*

"Ktaadn"

Setting out on our return to the river, still at an early hour in the day, we decided to follow the course of the torrent, which we supposed to be Murch Brook, as long as it would not lead us too far out of our way. We thus traveled about four miles in the very torrent itself, continually crossing and recrossing it, leaping from rock to rock, and jumping with the stream down falls of seven or eight feet, or sometimes sliding down on our backs in a thin sheet of water. This ravine had been the scene of an extraordinary freshet in the spring, apparently accompanied by a slide from the mountain. It must have been filled with a stream of stones and water, at least twenty feet above the present level of the torrent. For a rod or two, on either side of its channel, the trees were barked and splintered up to their tops, the birches bent over, twisted, and sometimes finely split, like a stable-broom; some, a foot in diameter, snapped off, and whole clumps of trees bent over with the weight of rocks piled on them. In one place we noticed a rock, two or three feet in diameter, lodged nearly twenty feet high in the crotch of a tree. For the whole four miles, we saw but one rill emptying in, and the volume of water did not seem to be increased from the first. We traveled thus very rapidly with a downward impetus, and grew remarkably expert at leaping from rock to rock, for leap we must, and leap we did, whether there was any rock at the right distance or not. It was a pleasant picture when the foremost turned about and looked up the winding ravine, walled in with rocks and the green forest, to see, at intervals of a rod or two, a red-shirted or green-jacketed mountaineer against the white torrent, leaping down the channel with his pack on his back, or pausing upon a convenient rock in the midst of the torrent to mend a rent in his clothes, or unstrap the dipper at his belt to take a draught of the water. At one place we were startled by seeing, on a little sandy shelf by the side of the stream, the fresh print of a man's foot, and for a moment realized how Robinson Crusoe felt in a similar case; but at last we remembered that we had struck this stream on our way up, though we could not have told when, and one had descended into the ravine for a drink. The cool air above and the continual bathing of our bodies in mountain water, alternate foot, sitz, douche, and plunge baths, made this walk exceedingly refreshing, and we had traveled only a mile or two, after leaving the torrent before every thread of our clothes was as dry as usual, owing perhaps to a peculiar quality in the atmosphere.

After leaving the torrent, being in doubt about our course, Tom threw down his pack at the foot of the loftiest spruce-tree at hand, and shinned up the bare trunk some twenty feet, and then climbed through the green tower, lost to our sight, until he held the topmost spray in his hand. McCauslin, in his younger days, had marched through the wilderness with a body of troops, under General Somebody, and with one other man did all the scouting and spying service. The General's word was, "Throw down the top of that tree," and there was no tree in the Maine woods so high that it did not lose its top in such a case. I have heard a story of two men being lost once in these woods, nearer to the settlements than this, who climbed the loftiest pine they could find, some six feet in diameter at the ground, from whose top they discovered a solitary clearing and its smoke. When at this height, some two hundred feet from the ground, one of them became dizzy, and fainted in his companion's arms, and the latter had to accomplish the descent with him, alternately fainting and reviving, as best he could. To Tom we cried,—Where away does the summit bear? where the burnt lands? The last he could only conjecture; he descried, however, a little meadow and pond, lying probably in our course, which we concluded to steer for. On reaching this secluded meadow, we found fresh tracks of moose on the shore of the pond, and the water was still unsettled as if they had fled before us. A little farther, in a dense thicket, we seemed to be still on their trail. It was a small meadow, of a few acres, on the mountain side, concealed by the forest, and perhaps never seen by a white man before, where one would think that the moose might browse and bathe, and rest in peace. Pursuing this course, we soon reached the open land, which went sloping down some miles toward the Penobscot.

Perhaps I most fully realized that this was primeval, untamed, and forever untamable *Nature*, or whatever else men call it, while coming down this part of the mountain. We were passing over "Burnt Lands," burnt by lightning, perchance, though they showed no recent marks of fire, hardly so much as a charred stump, but looked rather like a natural pasture for the moose and deer, exceedingly wild and desolate, with occasional strips of timber crossing them, and low poplars springing up, and patches of blueberries here and there. I found myself traversing them familiarly, like some pasture run to waste, or partially reclaimed by man; but when I reflected what man, what brother or sister or kinsman of our race made it and claimed it, I expected the proprietor to rise up and dispute my passage. It is difficult to conceive of a region uninhabited by man. We habitually presume his presence and influence everywhere. And yet we have not seen pure Nature, unless we have seen her thus vast and drear and inhuman, though in the midst of cities. Nature was here something savage and awful, though beautiful. I looked with awe at the ground I trod on, to see what the Powers had made there, the form and fashion and material of their work. This was that Earth of which we have heard, made out of Chaos and Old Night. Here was no man's garden, but the unhandseled globe. It was not lawn, nor pasture, nor mead, nor woodland, nor lea, nor arable, nor waste land. It was the fresh and natural surface of the planet Earth, as it was made forever and ever,—to be the dwelling of man, we say,—so Nature made it, and man may use it if he can. Man was not to be associated with it. It was Matter, vast, terrific,—not his Mother Earth that we have heard of, not for him to tread on, or be buried in,—no, it were being too familiar even to let his bones lie there,—the home, this, of Necessity and Fate. There was clearly felt the presence of a force not bound to be kind to man. It was a place for heathenism and superstitious rites,—to be inhabited by men nearer of kin to the rocks and to wild animals than we. We walked over it with a certain awe, stopping, from time to time, to pick the blueberries which grew there, and had a smart and spicy taste. Perchance where *our* wild pines stand, and leaves lie on their forest floor, in Concord, there were once reapers, and husbandmen planted grain; but here not even the surface had been scarred by man, but it was a specimen of what God saw fit to make this world. What is it to be admitted to a museum, to see a myriad of particular things, compared with being shown some star's surface, some hard matter in its home! I stand in awe of my body, this matter to which I am bound has become so strange to me. I fear not spirits, ghosts, of which I am one,—*that* my body might,—but I fear bodies, I tremble to meet them. What is this Titan that has possession of me? Talk of mysteries! Think of our life in nature,—daily to be shown matter, to come in contact with it,—rocks, trees, wind on our cheeks! the *solid* earth! the *actual* world! The *common sense! Contact! Contact! Who* are we? *where* are we?

"The Great Stone Face"
by Nathaniel Hawthorne

From The Snow-Image, and Other Twice-Told Tales (1850)

*Born in Salem, Massachusetts, Nathaniel Hawthorne (1804–1864) gradu-
ated from Bowdoin College in 1825, found work as a customhouse agent, and
began to write. After marrying Sophia Peabody in 1842 and moving to the
Old Manse, he explored the fields and woods of Concord with Emerson and
Thoreau and the wilds of the Berkshires with Herman Melville.*

*Hawthorne's ideas about nature were not as direct as some of those contem-
poraries. Instead, they emerged through his popular fiction, where nature was
often metaphorical, with a rosebush symbolizing hope in* The Scarlet Letter *and
the wilderness serving as an allegory for doubt in "Young Goodman Brown."
In the long introduction to "The Great Stone Face," he describes this natural
phenomenon in the White Mountains as a sign of the weaknesses and failures
of those human faces that are inevitably compared to it. Perceiving nature as a
symbol is something that today may seem passé or reductionist to literary crit-
ics and environmentalists alike, but is still something that every single person
cannot help but do, in at least some of our interactions with the natural world.*

"THE GREAT STONE FACE"

One afternoon, when the sun was going down, a mother and her little boy
sat at the door of their cottage, talking about the Great Stone Face. They

had but to lift their eyes, and there it was plainly to be seen, though miles away, with the sunshine brightening all its features.

And what was the Great Stone Face?

Embosomed amongst a family of lofty mountains, there was a valley so spacious that it contained many thousand inhabitants. Some of these good people dwelt in log-huts, with the black forest all around them, on the steep and difficult hillsides. Others had their homes in comfortable farmhouses, and cultivated the rich soil on the gentle slopes or level surfaces of the valley. Others, again, were congregated into populous villages, where some wild, highland rivulet, tumbling down from its birthplace in the upper mountain region, had been caught and tamed by human cunning, and compelled to turn the machinery of cotton factories. The inhabitants of this valley, in short, were numerous, and of many modes of life. But all of them, grown people and children, had a kind of familiarity with the Great Stone Face, although some possessed the gift of distinguishing this grand natural phenomenon more perfectly than many of their neighbors.

The Great Stone Face, then, was a work of Nature in her mood of majestic playfulness, formed on the perpendicular side of a mountain by some immense rocks, which had been thrown together in such a position as, when viewed at a proper distance, precisely to resemble the features of the human countenance. It seemed as if an enormous giant, or a Titan, had sculptured his own likeness on the precipice. There was the broad arch of the forehead, a hundred feet in height; the nose, with its long bridge; and the vast lips, which, if they could have spoken, would have rolled their thunder accents from one end of the valley to the other. True it is, that if the spectator approached too near, he lost the outline of the gigantic visage, and could discern only a heap of ponderous and gigantic rocks piled in chaotic ruin one upon another. Retracing his steps, however, the wondrous features would again be seen; and the further he withdrew from them, the more like a human face, with all its original divinity intact, did they appear; until, as it grew dim in the distance, with the clouds and glorified vapor of the mountains clustering about it, the Great Stone Face seemed positively to be alive.

It was a happy lot for children to grow up to manhood or womanhood with the Great Stone Face before their eyes, for all the features were noble, and the expression was at once grand and sweet, as if it were the glow of a vast, warm heart, that embraced all mankind in its affections, and had room for more. It was an education only to look at it. According to the belief of many people, the valley owed much of its fertility to this benign aspect that was continually beaming over it, illuminating the clouds, and infusing its tenderness into the sunshine.

As we began with saying, a mother and her little boy sat at their cottage-door, gazing at the Great Stone Face, and talking about it. The child's name was Ernest.

"Mother," said he, while the Titanic visage smiled on him, "I wish that it could speak, for it looks so very kindly that its voice must needs be pleasant. If I were to see a man with such a face, I should love him dearly."

"If an old prophecy should come to pass," answered his mother, "we may see a man, some time or other, with exactly such a face as that."

"Nature"
by Ralph Waldo Emerson

From The Boston Book *(1850)*

The leading light of American transcendentalism, Ralph Waldo Emerson (1803–1882) was born in Boston, graduated from Harvard, and became a Unitarian minister, only to leave the pulpit to pursue life as a writer and phi-losopher. His first book, Nature *(1836), had enormous influence on the nature writing genre, though it is more philosophical than specific in its call to "enjoy an original relation to the universe." Nevertheless, it expressed a deep affection and connection to the natural world.*

In 1835 Emerson settled in Concord, Massachusetts, where he was leader of a literary renaissance that included Bronson Alcott, Margaret Fuller, Nathaniel Hawthorne, and Henry David Thoreau, among others. Emerson's influence on nature writers, however, extends well beyond his Concord neighbors to John Muir, to John Burroughs, and to contemporary writers.

Although entitled "Nature," the piece below is not from the 1836 book of the same name, but from a rarely reprinted essay that appeared in The Boston Book *(1850), an anthology that also included works by Henry Wadsworth Longfellow, John Greenleaf Whittier, and other leading writers of the day. Here Emerson urges us to explore the natural world immediately around us.*

"NATURE"

There are days which occur in this climate, at almost any season of the year, wherein the world reaches its perfection, when the air, the heavenly bodies, and the earth, make a harmony, as if nature would indulge her offspring; when, in these bleak upper sides of the planet, nothing is to desire that we have heard of the happiest latitudes, and we bask in the shining hours of Florida and Cuba; when everything that has life gives sign of satisfaction, and the cattle that lie on the ground seem to have great and tranquil thoughts. These halcyons may be looked for with a little more assurance in that pure October weather, which we distinguish by the name of the Indian Summer. The day, immeasurably long, sleeps over the broad hills and warm wide fields. To have lived through all its sunny hours, seems longevity enough. The solitary places do not seem quite lonely. At the gates of the forest, the surprised man of the world is forced to leave his city estimates of great and small, wise and foolish. The knapsack of custom falls off his back with the first step he makes into these precincts. Here is sanctity which shames our religions, and reality which discredits our heroes. Here we find nature to be the circumstance which dwarfs every other circumstance, and judges like a god all men that come to her. We have crept out of our close and crowded houses into the night and morning, and we see what majestic beauties daily wrap us in their bosom. How willingly we would escape the barriers which render them comparatively impotent, escape the sophistication and second thought, and suffer nature to entrance us. The tempered light of the woods is like a perpetual morning, and is stimulating and heroic. The anciently reported spells of these places creep on us. The stems of pines, hemlocks, and oaks, almost gleam like iron on the excited eye. The incommunicable trees begin to persuade us to live with them, and quit our life of solemn trifles. Here no history, or church, or state, is interpolated on the divine sky and the immortal year. How easily we might walk onward into the opening landscape, absorbed by new pictures, and by thoughts fast succeeding each other, until by degrees the recollection of home was crowded out of the mind, all memory obliterated by the tyranny of the present, and we were led in triumph by nature.

These enchantments are medicinal, they sober and heal us. These are plain pleasures, kindly and native to us. We come to our own, and make friends with matter, which the ambitious chatter of the schools would persuade us to despise. We never can part with it; the mind loves its old home; as water to our thirst, so is the rock, the ground, to our eyes, and hands, and feet. It is firm water; it is cold flame: what health, what affinity! Ever an old friend, ever like a dear friend and brother, when we chat affectedly with strangers, comes in this honest face, and takes a grave liberty with us, and shames us out of our nonsense. Cities give not the human senses room enough. We go out daily and nightly to feed the eyes on the horizon, and require so much scope, just as we need water for our bath. There are all degrees of natural influence, from these quarantine powers of nature, up to her dearest and gravest ministrations to the imagination and the soul. There is the bucket of cold water from the spring, the wood-fire to which the chilled traveler rushes for safety,—and there is the sublime moral of autumn and of noon. We nestle in nature, and draw our living as parasites from her roots and grains, and we receive glances from the heavenly bodies, which call us to solitude, and foretell the remotest future. The blue zenith is the point in which romance and reality meet. I think, if we should be rapt away into all that we dream of heaven, and should converse with Gabriel and Uriel, the upper sky would be all that would remain of our furniture.

It seems as if the day was not wholly profane, in which we have given heed to some natural object. The fall of snowflakes in a still air, preserving to each crystal its perfect form; the blowing of sleet over a wide sheet of water, and over plains, the waving rye-field, the mimic waving of acres of houstonia, whose innumerable florets whiten and ripple before the eye; the reflections of trees and flowers in glassy lakes; the musical steaming odorous south wind, which converts all trees to wind-harps; the crackling and spurting of hemlock in the flames; or of pine logs, which yield glory to the walls and faces in the sitting-room,—these are the music and pictures of the most ancient religion. My house stands in low land, with limited outlook, and on the skirt of the village. But I go with my friend to the shore of our little river, and with one stroke of the paddle, I leave the village politics and personalities, yes, and the world of villages and personalities behind, and pass into a delicate realm of sunset and moonlight, too bright almost for spotted man to enter without novitiate and probation. We penetrate bodily this incredible beauty: we dip our hands in this painted element: our eyes are bathed in these lights and forms. A holiday, a villeggiatura, a royal revel, the proudest, most heart-rejoicing festival that valor and beauty, power and taste, ever decked and enjoyed, establishes itself on the instant. These sunset clouds, these delicately emerging stars, with their private and ineffable glances, signify it and proffer it. I am taught the poorness of our invention, the ugliness of towns and palaces. Art and luxury have early learned that they must work as enhancement and sequel to this original beauty. I am over instructed for my return. Henceforth I shall be hard to please. I cannot go back to toys. I am grown expensive and sophisticated. I can no longer live without elegance: but a countryman shall be my master of revels. He who knows the most, he who knows what sweets and virtues are in the ground, the waters, the plants, the heavens, and how to come at these enchantments, is the rich and royal man. Only as far as the masters of the world have called in nature to their aid, can they reach the height of magnificence. This is the meaning of their hanging-gardens, villas, garden-houses, islands, parks, and preserves, to back their faulty personality with these strong accessories. I do not wonder that the landed interest should be invincible in the state with these dangerous auxiliaries. These bribe and invite; not kings, not palaces, not men, not women, but these tender and poetic stars, eloquent of secret promises. We heard what the rich man said, we knew of his villa, his grove, his wine, and his company, but the provocation and point of the invitation came out of these beguiling stars. In their soft glances, I see what men strove to realize in some Versailles, or Paphos, or Ctesiphon. Indeed, it is the magical lights of the horizon, and the blue sky for the background, which save all our works of art, which were otherwise baubles. When the rich tax the poor with servility and obsequiousness, they should consider the effect of men, reputed to be the possessors of nature, on imaginative minds. Ah! if the rich were rich as the poor fancy riches! A boy hears a military band play on the field at night, and he has kings and queens, and famous chivalry palpably before him. He hears the echoes of a horn in a hill country, in the Notch Mountains, for example, which converts the mountains into an Aeolian harp, and this supernatural *tiralira* restores to him the Dorian mythology, Apollo, Diana, and all divine hunters and huntresses. Can a musical note be so lofty, so haughtily beautiful? To the poor young poet, thus fabulous is his picture of society; he is loyal; he respects the rich; they are rich for the sake of his imagination; how poor his fancy would be, if they were not rich! That they have some high-fenced grove, which they call a park; that they live in larger and better garnished saloons than he has visited, and go in coaches, keeping only the society of the elegant, to watering-places, and to distant cities, are the groundwork from which he has delineated estates of romance, compared with which their actual possessions are shanties and paddocks. The muse herself betrays her son, and enhances the gifts of wealth and well born beauty, by a radiation out of the air, and clouds, and forests that skirt the road,—a certain haughty favor, as if from patrician genii to patricians, a kind of aristocracy in nature, a prince of the power of the air.

The moral sensibility which makes Edens and Tempes so easily, may not be always found, but the material landscape is never far off. We can find these enchantments without visiting the Como Lake, or the Madeira Islands. We exaggerate the praises of local scenery. In every landscape, the point of astonishment is the meeting of the sky and the earth, and that is seen from the first hillock as well as from the top of the Alleghanies. The stars at night stoop down over the brownest, homeliest common, with all the spiritual magnificence which they shed on the Campagna, or on the marble deserts of Egypt. The uprolled clouds and the colors of morning and evening, will transfigure maples and alders.

The difference between landscape and landscape is small, but there is great difference in the beholders. There is nothing so wonderful in any particular landscape, as the necessity of being beautiful under which every landscape lies. Nature cannot be surprised in undress. Beauty breaks in everywhere.

"Descriptive and Physical Geography" by Zadock Thompson

From Natural History of Vermont *(1853)*

Born to humble circumstances in Bridgewater, Vermont, Zadock Thompson (1796–1856) graduated from the University of Vermont in 1823 and taught there for many years. He served as assistant state geologist from 1845 to 1848 and as state naturalist from 1853 to 1856. He was also an Episcopal priest.

Thompson is said to have begun his career as an author by writing and publishing almanacs which he sold by traveling on foot. He later became the first person to write about Vermont's history and environment. An early champion of protecting rare species and conserving natural resources, his interest in nature covered all facets from geology to entomology. Among his books are Gazetteer of the State of Vermont *(1824),* History of the State of Vermont *(1833),* Geography and Geology of Vermont *(1848), and* Natural History of Vermont *(1853).*

This excerpt from Natural History of Vermont *illustrates Thompson's concern about the impact on water resources caused by cutting forests, establishing mills on streams, and general development. Although this book is a factual survey of Vermont's natural history, his cautions about the limits of natural resources presage George Perkins Marsh's* Man and Nature, *published less than a decade after Thompson's death.*

"DESCRIPTIVE AND PHYSICAL GEOGRAPHY"

No country in the world is better supplied with pure and wholesome water than Vermont. There are scarcely any farms in the state which are not well watered by springs, or brooks; and none, with the exception of those upon the islands in Lake Champlain, which are not in the vicinity of one, or more, considerable mill stream. It is a common remark that the streams in this state have diminished very much in size, since the country began to be cleared and settled, and it is doubtless true to some extent. Many mill sites, which were once thought valuable, have, from the same cause, become entirely useless. One of the principal causes of this diminution of our streams is supposed to be the cutting down of the forests, which formerly threw off immense quantities of vapor into the atmosphere, which was again precipitated upon the earth in rain and snow. But it is believed that the quantity of water which annually passes off in our streams is not so much less than formerly as is generally imagined. Before the country was cleared, the whole surface of the ground was deeply covered with leaves, limbs, and logs, and the channels of all the smaller streams were much obstructed by the same. The consequence was that, when the snows dissolved in the spring, or the rains fell in the summer, the waters were retained among the leaves, or retarded by the other obstructions, so as to pass off slowly, and the streams were kept up, nearly uniform as to size, during the whole year. But since the country has become settled, and the obstructions, which retarded the water, removed by freshets, when the snows melt or the rains fall, the waters run off from the surface of the ground quickly, the streams are raised suddenly, run rapidly, and soon subside. In consequence of the water being thus carried off more rapidly, the streams would be smaller than formerly during a considerable part of the year, even though the quantity of water be the same. It is a well-known fact that the freshets in Vermont are more sudden and violent than when the country was new.

Swamps.—These are hardly of sufficient importance to deserve a separate notice. Though considerably numerous, they are, in general, of small extent, and, in many cases, have been, or may be drained and converted into excellent lands. They are most common in the northern and northeastern parts of the state. In the county of Essex are several unsettled townships, which are said to be made up of hills and mountains with swamps lying between them, which render them to a great extent incapable of settlement. There is a considerable tract of swampy land at the south end of Memphremagog lake, and another in Highgate about the mouth of Missisco river. When the country was new, there were many stagnant coves along the margin and among the islands of Lake Champlain, which, during the hotter parts of the summer, generated intermittent and bilious fevers. But, since the clearing of the country, these have been, to a considerable extent, filled up, and, with the causes which produced them, those disorders have nearly disappeared.

Medicinal Springs.—There are in Vermont springs which are more or less impregnated with mineral, or gaseous substances, but none which have yet acquired a very general or permanent celebrity for their curative properties. Along the shore of Lake Champlain, in the counties of Addison and Rutland, the waters generally are impregnated with Epsom salts (sulphate of magnesia). Some of the springs are so highly charged with these salts, in the dryer parts of the year, that a pail full of the water will produce a pound of the salts. They have been manufactured, for medicinal purposes, in some quantities, and, did the price of the article make it an object, they might be made here to almost any extent. The medicinal properties of most of the waters in this state, which have acquired any notoriety, are derived from gaseous and not from mineral substances. In different towns in the northeastern part of the state, are springs of cold, soft and clear water, which are strongly impregnated with sulphuretted hydrogen gas, and said to resemble the Harrow-Gate waters in England, and those of Ballcastle and Castlemain in Ireland. These waters are found to be efficacious in scrofulous and many other cutaneous complaints, and the springs at Newbury, Tunbridge, Hardwick, &c, have been much resorted to by valetudinarians in their vicinity.

Of medicinal springs on the west side of the Green Mountains, those of Clarendon and Alburgh have acquired the greatest notoriety. It is now about 16 years since the springs at Clarendon began to be known beyond their immediate neighborhood. Since that time their reputation has been annually extending, and the number of visitors increasing, till they have at length become a place of considerable resort for the afflicted from various parts of the country. They are situated in a picturesque and beautiful region, 7 miles southwest from Rutland, and have, in their immediate vicinity, good accommodations for 500 visitors. The waters are found to be highly efficacious in affections of the liver, dyspepsia, urinary and all cutaneous complaints, rheumatism, inveterate sore eyes, and many others, and they promise fair to go on increasing in notoriety and usefulness.

"Pleasures of Winter"
by Lydia Sigourney

From Past Meridian *(1854)*

Lydia Huntley (1791–1865) was born in Norwich, Connecticut, where she later ran a school for young women at only 20 years of age. She moved to Hart-ford, married Charles Sigourney in 1819, and after he suffered financial losses, began to write as a way to support her family. She wrote poetry and prose on education, Native American rights, and nature, becoming the popular and beloved "Sweet Singer of Hartford" and inspiring a generation of women to take up the pen.

Many of Sigourney's poems were in the new Romantic style, engaging with nature and its relationship with human emotions and ideas. The follow-ing essay takes the bane of New Englanders since the Little Ice Age—winter—and tries to get people to think about it in a different way. If people were to care about nature, they had to care about all of it, even the traditionally unpleasant parts, and she takes this "ill-treated season" and lauds its many virtues.

"PLEASURES OF WINTER"

What a singular subject! The pleasures of winter. And what may they be? Some, with whom the imagery of frost and snow predominates, will be ready to say that it has none.

Surely it has been the most ill-treated season, decried by almost every one that could wield a pen or weave a couplet. The poets have been in league against it from time immemorial. Still it has some very respectable, shall I say desirable characteristics? It has not the fickleness of spring, whose blossoms so soon fall, nor the enervation of summer, when the strong men bow themselves, nor the imperious exactions of autumn, when the in-gathering is a weariness, and may be a disappointment.

Do not speak with too much scorn of a wintry landscape. The wreaths of smoke rising high into the clear, blue skies, the pure, white covering under which nature reposes, the sparkling of the sinuous streams, where the graceful skaters glide, the groups of children, gathering rosier cheeks and merrier spirits from the heightened oxygen of the atmosphere, give to a winter morning in our sunny latitude cheering excitement.

Did you ever chance to look upon the glorious Niagara in the garniture of winter? And did not its solemn, solitary majesty, impress you more deeply, than when the green, waving woods, and the busy, gazing throngs, divided the absorbing sentiment?

Is not the wintry eve sweet, with its warm fires and bright lights, when families gather in a closer circle, and better love each other? Heart springs to heart, with fewer obstacles than in the more discursive seasons, when the foot is tempted to roam and the eye to wander. The baby crows louder after its father because it can sit longer on his knee. The youth has a lengthened tale for his lady-love, and the storm passes by unheard. Pleasant talk, and sweet song, and loud reading, vary the scene of household delights. Added cheerfulness and love are among the treasures of the wintry evening.

Shall we not avail ourselves of these hints, when the winter of life comes? Shall we not light up the cheerful lamp, and put more fuel on the flame in our cold hearts? They need not go out, though some are gone who were wont to feed them with fresh oil. We will keep love to our race, alive, till the last. Let its embers throw their warmth even into the dark valley. Yes, we will carry those embers with us, and relight them where they can never wane or expire.

The young are said to love winter. Let us strive to make them love us, when we become the personification of winter. We will redouble our offices of kindness, and our powers of entertainment, and see if we cannot melt the ice that has collected between us.

"Young men," says Lord Bacon, "are to be happy by hope, and the old by memory." Yes, with us, are the pictures of the past, the winter gallery, whose landscapes fade not, and whose fountains still freshly murmur. Memory! she who hath sifted and winnowed the harvest of life, that she may know the true wheat. Memory, who hath stood by us when Hope and Love have so often rung the death-knell, and forsaken us, may we be happy through her? The Lord be thanked if it is so. If, in looking back on all the way wherein He hath led us, she presents a predominance of correct motive, of earnest obedience, of forgiven sin, let us strike that keytone of praise which shall re-echo through eternity.

Among the prominent joys of life's winter, are those of faith; a nearness, and shadowing forth of things unseen. It was at a festal gathering of the old and young, that the question was once proposed, which season of human life was the happiest. It was freely discussed, with varying opinions. Then the guests decided that their host, a man of four score, should be the umpire. Pointing to a neighboring grove, he replied, "When vernal airs call forth the first buds, and yonder trees are covered with blossoms, I think how beautiful is spring. When summer clothes them with rich foliage, and birds sing among the branches, I say how beautiful is summer. When they are loaded with fruit, or bright with the hues of early frost, I feel how beautiful is autumn. But in sere winter, when there are neither verdure or fruit, I look through the leafless boughs as I could never do before, and see the stars shine."

Stars of our God! beam more brightly into our souls, through this wintry atmosphere. For our home is near. And notwithstanding the Great Philosopher hath said that the old can be happy only through memory, we will be happy through hope also, yea, through that hope which hath no mixture of earth, the "hope that maketh not ashamed, and which is as an anchor to the soul."

"The Fairy Flower"
by Louisa May Alcott

From Flower Fables *(1854)*

Daughter of transcendentalist Amos Bronson Alcott, Louisa May Alcott (1832–1888) grew up amongst the giants of nineteenth-century philosophy. Ralph Waldo Emerson instructed her in abolitionism, and Henry David Thoreau took her on nature walks. However, her father was not a good provider, and she began to write novels and stories to support her family. She became a household name with Little Women *(1868), which has never since gone out of print.*

The following selection comes from her first work, Flower Fables *(1854), written for Ellen Emerson and other children. This sort of fanciful or magical perception of the natural world is how most children in the nineteenth century first encountered it, and influenced generations of nature-lovers far more than the scientific thought of Darwin or Agassiz.*

"THE FAIRY FLOWER"

Autumn flowers were dead and gone, yellow leaves lay rustling on the ground, bleak winds went whistling through the naked trees, and cold, white Winter snow fell softly down; yet now, when all without looked dark and dreary, on little Annie's breast the fairy flower bloomed more beautiful than ever. The memory of her forest dream had never passed away, and through trial and temptation she had been true, and kept her resolution still unbroken; seldom now did the warning bell sound in her ear, and seldom did the flower's fragrance cease to float about her, or the fairy light to brighten all whereon it fell.

So, through the long, cold Winter, little Annie dwelt like a sunbeam in her home, each day growing richer in the love of others, and happier in herself; often was she tempted, but, remembering her dream, she listened only to the music of the fairy bell, and the unkind thought or feeling fled away, the smiling spirits of gentleness and love nestled in her heart, and all was bright again.

So better and happier grew the child, fairer and sweeter grew the flower, till Spring came smiling over the earth, and woke the flowers, set free the streams, and welcomed back the birds; then daily did the happy child sit among her flowers, longing for the gentle Elf to come again, that she might tell her gratitude for all the magic gift had done.

At length, one day, as she sat singing in the sunny nook where all her fairest flowers bloomed, weary with gazing at the far-off sky for the little form she hoped would come, she bent to look with joyful love upon her bosom flower; and as she looked, its folded leaves spread wide apart, and, rising slowly from the deep white cup, appeared the smiling face of the lovely Elf whose coming she had waited for so long.

"Dear Annie, look for me no longer; I am here on your own breast, for you have learned to love my gift, and it has done its work most faithfully and well," the Fairy said, as she looked into the happy child's bright face, and laid her little arms most tenderly about her neck.

"And now have I brought another gift from Fairy-Land, as a fit reward for you, dear child," she said, when Annie had told all her gratitude and love; then, touching the child with her shining wand, the Fairy bid her look and listen silently.

And suddenly the world seemed changed to Annie; for the air was filled with strange, sweet sounds, and all around her floated lovely forms. In every flower sat little smiling Elves, singing gayly as they rocked amid the leaves. On every breeze, bright, airy spirits came floating by; some fanned her cheek with their cool breath, and waved her long hair to and fro, while others rang the flower-bells, and made a pleasant rustling among the leaves. In the fountain, where the water danced and sparkled in the sun, astride of every drop she saw merry little spirits, who plashed and floated in the clear, cool waves, and sang as gayly as the flowers, on whom they scattered glittering dew. The tall trees, as their branches rustled in the wind, sang a low, dreamy song, while the waving grass was filled with little voices she had never heard before. Butterflies whispered lovely tales in her ear, and birds sang cheerful songs in a sweet language she had never understood before. Earth and air seemed filled with beauty and with music she had never dreamed of until now.

"O tell me what it means, dear Fairy! is it another and a lovelier dream, or is the earth in truth so beautiful as this?" she cried, looking with wondering joy upon the Elf, who lay upon the flower in her breast.

"Yes, it is true, dear child," replied the Fairy, "and few are the mortals to whom we give this lovely gift; what to you is now so full of music and of light, to others is but a pleasant summer world; they never know the language of butterfly or bird or flower, and they are blind to all that I have given you the power to see. These fair things are your friends and playmates now, and they will teach you many pleasant lessons, and give you many happy hours; while the garden where you once sat, weeping sad and bitter tears, is now brightened by your own happiness, filled with loving friends by your own kindly thoughts and feelings; and thus rendered a pleasant summer home for the gentle, happy child, whose bosom flower will never fade. And now, dear Annie, I must go; but every Springtime, with the earliest flowers, will I come again to visit you, and bring some fairy gift. Guard well the magic flower, that I may find all fair and bright when next I come."

Then, with a kind farewell, the gentle Fairy floated upward through the sunny air, smiling down upon the child, until she vanished in the soft, white clouds, and little Annie stood alone in her enchanted garden, where all was brightened with the radiant light, and fragrant with the perfume of her fairy flower.

"Sounds of Inanimate Nature"
by Wilson Flagg

From Studies in the Field and Forest *(1857)*

Born in Beverly, Massachusetts, Thomas Wilson Flagg (1805–1884) gradu-
ated from Phillips Andover Academy before studying medicine. He never
became a practicing physician, and instead began contributing articles to the
Boston Weekly Magazine *and later to* The Atlantic Monthly. *A trip to New*
Hampshire sparked his interest in natural history in what he later described as
a "religious conversion."

His collections of essays like The Woods and Byways of New England *(1872) and* A Year Among the Birds *(1881) were well received by*
a nineteenth-century audience who loved sentimentality. During his lifetime
Flagg was often compared to Thoreau, often favorably, though he was also criti-
cized both for over-romanticizing and somewhat contradictorily for his lack
of passion for the subject. The following essay comes from his first collection,
Studies in the Field and Forest, *and though Flagg is largely forgotten in the*
twenty-first century, we can see why his contemporaries thought him one of the
most important nature writers of his day.

"SOUNDS OF INANIMATE NATURE"

Nature in every scene and situation has established certain sounds which
are indicative of its character. The sounds we hear in the hollow dells
among the mountains are unlike those of the open plains; and the echoes

of the sea-shore repeat sounds that are never reverberated among the inland valleys. There are many species of singing birds within the solitudes of a forest, which are seldom heard or seen in our orchards or gardens. In the mind of one who has been early accustomed to the wild woods, the warbling of these solitary birds is pleasantly connected with their stillness and their grandeur. Besides the singing of birds and the chirping of insects, there are voices from inanimate nature, which are full of pleasing suggestions. The murmuring of winds and the rustling of foliage, the gurgling of streams and the bubbling of fountains, come to our ears like the music of our early days, accompanied by many agreeable fancies. A stream rolling over a rough declivity, a fountain bubbling up from a subterranean hollow, produce sounds suggestive of fragrant summer arbors, of cool retreats, and all their delightful accompaniments.

The roar of a waterfall, when constantly near us, is disagreeable; but the purling of a rill, if not music, is something very nearly allied to it. The most agreeable expression of the noise of waters is their animation. They give life to the scenes around us, like the voices of birds and insects. In winter, especially, they make an agreeable interruption of the stillness; and remind us, that during the slumber of all visible things, some hidden powers are still guiding the operations of nature. The rapids produced by a small stream flowing over a gentle declivity of rocks yield, perhaps, the most expressive sound of waters, unless we except the distant roar of waves, as they are dashed upon the shore of the sea. The last, being intermittent, is preferable to the roar of a waterfall, which is tiresomely incessant. Nearly all the sounds made by water are agreeable, and cannot be multiplied without increasing the delightful influences of the place and the season.

Besides the pleasant sounds that come from water, in all its variety of shapes and movements, we must not omit to mention those which are produced by winds, as they pass through the branches and foliage of trees and shrubbery. The colors of their leaves, and the glittering light from their more or less refractive surfaces, do not differ more than the modifications of sound produced from them by the passing breezes. Every tree may be said, when agitated by the winds, to have a voice peculiar to itself, and capable of exciting the most agreeable sensations. The lofty branches of pines, when swayed by the wind, emit a sound like the murmuring of distant waters, and inspire a soothing melancholy like that inspired by the continual twilight that reigns within their solitudes. The leaves of the poplar, proverbial for their tremulous motion, produce a more cheerful sound, corresponding with the gayety of summer, and harmonizing with the more lively scenes around them. Every tree and shrub is a delicate musical instrument, whose notes remind us of the character of their foliage, and of the season of the year,—from the mellow harmony of the willow trees in summer, to the sharp rustling of the dry oak leaf that tells us of the arrival of winter.

Each season of the year has its peculiar melodies, besides those proceeding from the animated creation. In the opening of the year, when the leaves are tender and pliable, there is a mellowness in the sound of the breezes, as if they felt the voluptuous influence of spring. Nature then softens all the sounds from inanimate things, as if to avoid making any harsh discords with the anthem that issues from the streams and wood lands, vocal with the songs of millions of happy creatures. The echoes also repeat less distinctly the multitudinous notes of birds, insects, and other creeping things. To the echoes, spring and summer are seasons of comparative rest, save those which reside among the rocks of the desert, or among the dells of the craggy sea-shore. Here, sitting invisibly in their retreats, are they ever responding to those sorrowful sounds that are borne upon the waves, as they sullenly recount the perils and accidents of the great deep.

After the severe frosts of autumn, the winds become shriller, as they pass over the naked reeds and rushes, and through the leafless branches of the trees, and there is a familiar sadness in their murmurs, as they whirl among the dry rustling leaves. When winter has arrived and enshrouded all the landscape in a winding sheet of snow, the echoes once more venture out upon the open plain, and repeat, with unusual distinctness, the miscellaneous sounds from wood, village, and farm. During winter they enjoy a long holiday of freedom, and show no sympathy with the desolate appearance of nature. They hold a laughing revelry in the haunts of the Dryad, who sits sad and disconsolate in her now unsheltered retreats, where the leafless boughs scarcely protect her from the shivering wind, or shade her from the cold icy beams of the moon.

I believe that the majority of agreeable sounds from the inanimate world owe their charm to their power of gently exciting the emotion of melancholy. Our minds are constructed with such a benevolent regard to our happiness, that all the feelings of the heart, including even those of a painful sort, are capable, under certain states or degrees of excitement, of becoming a source of agreeable sensations. Such is the memory of past pleasures, that brings with it a species of melancholy which is a luxury to all persons of refined sensibility. The murmur of gentle gales among the trembling aspen leaves, or the noise of the hurricane upon the seashore, the roar of distant waters, the sighing of the wind as it flits by our windows or moans through the casement, have the power of exciting just enough of this sentiment to produce an agreeable state of the mind. Along with the melancholy they excite, there is something that tranquillizes the soul and exalts it above the mere pleasures of sense.

It is this power of producing the sentiment of melancholy that causes the sound of rain to yield pleasure to the majority of minds. The pattering of rain upon the windows, but more particularly on the roof of a house under which we are sitting, is attended with a singular charm. The more violent the rain, if its violence be not sufficient to cause alarm, the more profound is the emotion that springs from it. There are few persons who do not recollect, with a most agreeable sense of past delight, some adventure of a shower that obliged them, on a journey, to take shelter under a rustic roof by the way-side. The pleasure produced by the sight and sound of the rain, under this retreat, often comes more delightfully to our remembrance than all the sun shiny adventures of the day. But in order to be affected in the most agreeable manner by the sound of rain, it is necessary to be in the company of those whom we love, and to know at the same time that the objects of our care are within doors, and to be ignorant of any one's exposure to its violence. From this consciousness of security comes perhaps half the pleasure awakened by the sound of rain; but this I am confident would not account for the whole effect.

It is evident that the charm of all these sounds proceeds from the imagination. A person who has not cultivated this faculty is dead to a thousand pleasures from this source, that form a considerable portion of the happiness of the man of superior intellect. Music has no advantage over other sounds, except in its greater power to act upon the imagination. To appreciate the charm of musical notes, or to perceive the beauty of an elegant building or of splendid tapestry, requires but little mental culture. But to be susceptible of pleasure from what are commonly regarded as indifferent sounds, or indifferent sights, is the meed of those who have cherished the higher faculties and the better feelings of their nature. To such persons the world is full of suggestive sounds as well as of suggestive sights, and not the whisper of a breeze or the murmur of a wave but is in unison with some chord in their memory or their imagination.

"Katahdin"
by Theodore Winthrop

From Life in the Open Air and Other Papers *(1863)*

A Connecticut native and descendant of a seventeenth-century governor, Theodore Winthrop (1828–1861) graduated from Yale in 1848 and later earned a law degree. His career included work as a tutor, in company accounting offices, and the practice of law in St. Louis and New York. Despite uncertain health, he excelled at outdoor activities and was an expert canoeist and horseman. He loved adventure travel, which seemed to have a restorative effect. His journeys included trips to the Pacific Northwest, the Maine woods, and Panama, sometimes involving daring and risky exploits. Eagerly enlisting in the Civil War, he rose to the rank of major and was killed at the battle of Big Bethel, one of the first Union officers to die in the conflict.

Novelist, poet, and essayist, Winthrop benefited posthumously from his sister, Laura Winthrop Johnson, through whose diligence almost all of her brother's work was published after his death. Among his novels are Cecil Dreeme *(1861), a tale of sexual ambiguity set around Manhattan's Washington Square, and* John Brent *(1862), a story of western life. His travel books are* The Canoe and the Saddle *(1863), mostly about the Pacific Northwest, and* Life in the Open Air *(1863), in which he relates experiences in Maine. This piece about Mount Katahdin conveys his crisp, energetic style and longing for adventure.*

"KATAHDIN"

To write an epic or climb a mountain is merely a dogged thing; the result is more interesting to most than the process. Mountains, being cloud-compellers, are rain-shedders, and the shed water will not always flow with decorous gayety in dell or glen. Sometimes it stays bewildered in a bog, and here, the climber must plunge. In the moist places great trees grow, die, fall, rot, and barricade the way with their corpses. Katahdin has to endure all the ills of mountain being, and we had all the usual difficulties to fight through doggedly. When we were clumsy, we tumbled and rose up torn. Still we plodded on, following a path blazed by the Bostonians, Cancut's late charge, and we grumblingly thanked them.

Going up, we got higher and drier. The mountain-side became steeper than it could stay, and several land-avalanches, ancient or modern, crossed our path. It would be sad to think that all the eternal hills were crumbling thus, outwardly, unless we knew that they bubble up inwardly as fast. Posterity is thus cared for in regard to the picturesque. Cascading streams also shot by us, carrying light and music. From them we stole refreshment, and did not find the waters mineral and astringent, as Mr. Turner, the first climber, calumniously asserts.

The trees were still large and surprisingly parallel to the mountain wall. Deep soft moss covered whatever was beneath, and sometimes this would yield and let the foot measure a crevice. Perilous pitfalls; but we clambered unharmed. The moss, so rich, deep, soft, and earthily fragrant, was a springy stair-carpet of a steep stairway. And sometimes when the carpet slipped and the state of heels overhead seemed imminent, we held to the baluster-trees, as one after wassail clings to the lamp-post.

Even on this minor mountain the law of diminishing vegetation can be studied. The great trees abandoned us, and stayed indolently down in shelter. Next the little wiry trees ceased to be the comrades of our climb. They were no longer to be seen planted upon jutting crags, and, bold as standard-bearers, inciting us to mount higher. Big spruces, knobby with balls of gum, dwindled away into little ugly dwarf spruces, hostile, as dwarfs are said to be always, to human comfort. They grew man-high, and hedged themselves together into a dense thicket. We could not go under, nor over, nor through. To traverse them at all, we must recall the period when we were squirrels or cats, in some former state of being.

Somehow, we pierced, as man does ever, whether he owes it to the beast or the man in him. From time to time, when in this struggle we came to an open point of rock, we would remember that we were on high, and turn to assure ourselves that nether earth was where we had left it. We always found it *in situ*, in belts green, white, and blue, a tricolor of woods, water, and sky. Lakes were there without number, forest without limit. We could not analyze yet, for there was work to do. Also, whenever we paused, there was the old temptation, blueberries. Every outcropping ledge offered store of tonic, ozone-fed blueberries, or of mountain-cranberries, crimson and of concentrated flavor, or of the white snowberry, most delicate of fruits that grow.

As we were creeping over the top of the dwarf wood, Cancut, who was in advance, suddenly disappeared; he seemed to fall through a gap in the spruces, and we heard his voice calling in cavernous tones. We crawled forward and looked over. It was the upper camp of the Bostonians. They had profited by a hole in the rocks, and chopped away the stunted scrubs to enlarge it into a snug artificial abyss. It was snug, and so to the eye is a cell at Sing-Sing. If they were very misshapen Bostonians, they may have succeeded in lying there comfortably. I looked down ten feet into the rough chasm, and I saw, *Corpo di Bacco!* I saw a cork.

To this station our predecessors had come in an easy day's walk from the river; here they had tossed through a night, and given a whole day to finish the ascent, returning hither again for a second night. As we purposed to put all this travel within one day, we could not stay and sympathize with the late tenants. A little more squirrel-like skipping and cat-like creeping over the spruces, and we were out among bulky boulders and rough *debris* on a shoulder of the mountain. Alas! the higher, the more hopeless. Katahdin, as he had taken pains to inform us, meant to wear the veil all day. He was drawing down the white drapery about his throat and letting it fall over his shoulders. Sun and wind struggled mightily with his sulky fit; sunshine rifted off bits of the veil, and wind seized, whirled them away, and, dragging them over the spruces below, tore them to rags. Evidently, if we wished to see the world, we must stop here and survey, before the growing vapor covered all. We climbed to the edge of Cloudland, and stood fronting the semicircle of southward view.

Katahdin's self is finer than what Katahdin sees. Katahdin is distinct, and its view is indistinct. It is a vague panorama, a mappy, unmethodic maze of water and woods, very roomy, very vast, very simple—and these are capital qualities, but also quite monotonous. A lover of largeness and scope has the proper emotions stirred, but a lover of variety very soon finds himself counting the lakes. It is a wide view, and it is a proud thing for a man six feet or less high, to feel that he himself, standing on something he himself has climbed, and having Katahdin under his feet a mere convenience, can see all Maine. It does not make Maine less, but the spectator more, and that is a useful moral result. Maine's face, thus exposed, has almost no features; there are no great mountains visible, none that seem more than green hillocks in the distance. Besides sky, Katahdin's view contains only the two primal necessities of wood and water. Nowhere have I seen such breadth of solemn forest, gloomy, were it not for the cheerful interruption of many fair lakes, and bright ways of river linking them.

Far away on the southern horizon we detected the heights of Mount Desert, our old familiar haunt. All the northern semicircle was lost to us by the fog. We lost also the view of the mountain itself. All the bleak, lonely, barren, ancient waste of the bare summit was shrouded in cold fog. The impressive gray ruin and Titanic havoc of a granite mountain-top, the heaped boulders, the crumbling crags, the crater-like depression, the long stern reaches of sierra, the dark curving slopes channeled and polished by the storms and fine drifting mists of aeons, the downright plunge of precipices, all the savageness of harsh rock, unsoftened by other vegetation than rusty moss and the dull green splashes of lichen, all this was hidden, except when the mist, white and delicate where we stood, but thick and black above, opened whimsically and delusively, as mountain mists will do, and gave us vistas into the upper desolation. After such momentary rifts the mist thickened again, and swooped forward as if to involve our station; but noon sunshine, reverberated from the plains and valleys and lakes below, was our ally; sunshine checked the overcoming mist, and it stayed overhead, an unwelcome parasol, making our August a chilly November. Besides what our eyes lost, our minds lost, unless they had imagination enough to create it, the sentiment of triumph and valiant energy that the man of body and soul feels upon the windy heights, the highest, whence he looks far and wide, like a master of realms, and knows that the world is his; and they lost the sentiment of solemn joy that the man of soul recognizes as one of the surest intimations of immortality, stirring within him, whenever he is in the unearthly regions, the higher world.

We stayed studying the pleasant solitude and dreamy breadth of Katahdin's panorama for a long time, and every moment the mystery of the mist above grew more enticing. Pride also was awakened. We turned from sunshine and Cosmos into fog and Chaos. We made ourselves quite miserable for naught. We clambered up into Nowhere, into a great, white, ghostly void. We saw nothing but the rough surfaces we trod. We pressed along crater-like edges, and all below was filled with mist, troubled and rushing upward like the smoke of a volcano. Up we went—nothing but granite and gray dimness. Where we arrived we know not. It was a top, certainly: that was proved by the fact that there was nothing within sight. We cannot claim that it was the topmost top; Kimchinjinga might have towered within pistol-shot; popgun-shot was our extremest range of vision, except for one instant, when a kind-hearted sunbeam gave us a vanishing glimpse of a white lake and breadth of forest far in the unknown North toward Canada.

When we had thus reached the height of our folly and made nothing by it, we addressed our-selves to the descent, no wiser for our pains. Descent is always harder than ascent, for divine ambitions are stronger and more prevalent than degrading passions. And when Katahdin is befogged, descent is much more perilous than ascent. We edged along very cautiously by remembered landmarks the way we had come, and so, after a dreary march of a mile or so through desolation, issued into welcome sunshine and warmth at our point of departure. When I said "we," I did not include the gravestone peddler. He, like a sensible fellow, had determined to stay and eat berries rather than breathe fog. While we wasted our time, he had made the most of his. He had cleared Katahdin's shoulders of fruit, and now, cuddled in a sunny cleft, slept the sleep of the well-fed. His red shirt was a cheerful beacon on our weary way. We took in the landscape with one slow, comprehensive look, and, waking Cancut suddenly, (who sprang to his feet amazed, and cried "Fire!") we dashed down the mountain-side.

It was long after noon; we were some dozen of miles from camp; we must speed. No glissade was possible, nor plunge such as travelers make down through the ash-heaps of Vesuvius; but, having once worried through the wretched little spruces, mean counterfeits of trees, we could fling ourselves down from mossy step to step, measuring off the distance by successive leaps of a second each, and alighting, sound after each, on moss yielding as a cushion.

On we hastened, retracing our footsteps of the morning across the avalanches of crumbled granite, through the bogs, along the brooks; undelayed by the beauty of sunny glade or shady dell, never stopping to botanize or to classify, we traversed zone after zone, and safely ran the gantlet of the possible bears on the last level. We found lowland Nature still the same; Ayboljockameegus was flowing still; so was Penobscot; no pirate had made way with the birch; we embarked and paddled to camp.

The first thing, when we touched *terra firma*, was to look back regret-fully toward the mountain. Regret changed to wrath, when we perceived its summit all clear and mistless, smiling warmly to the low summer's sun. The rascal evidently had only waited until we were out of sight in the woods to throw away his night-cap.

"Water Lilies"
by Thomas Wentworth Higginson

From Out-door Papers *(1863)*

Born in Cambridge, Massachusetts, and graduated from Harvard in 1841, Thomas Wentworth Higginson (1823–1911) was a Unitarian minister, an advocate for women's rights, an ardent abolitionist, and a colonel in the 1st South Carolina Volunteers, the first federally authorized black regiment. He was friends with many in the transcendentalist circles of Concord, and after the Civil War he spent much of his time in literary pursuits, producing poems, biographies, fiction, essays, and histories. Higginson was the first to publicly encourage and recognize the genius of Emily Dickinson and coedited two volumes of her poems in the early 1890s.

He had a deep love of nature, which is evident in his writing. This essay on water lilies is typical of his work in the genre and follows the poet–naturalist style of Thoreau rather than a more analytical, scientific approach.

"WATER LILIES"

The inconstant April mornings drop showers or sunbeams over the glistening lake, while far beneath its surface a murky mass disengages itself from the muddy bottom, and rises slowly through the waves. The tasseled alder-branches droop above it; the last year's blackbird's nest swings over it in the grape-vine; the newly-opened Hepaticas and Epigaeas on the neighboring bank peer down modestly to look for it; the water-skater

(Gerris) pauses on the surface near it, casting on the shallow bottom the odd shadow of his feet, like three pairs of boxing-gloves; the Notonecta, or water-boatman, rows round and round it, sometimes on his breast, sometimes on his back; queer caddis-worms trail their self-made home-steads of leaves or twigs beside it; the Dytiscus, dorbug of the water, blunders clumsily against it; the tadpole wriggles his stupid way to it, and rests upon it, meditating of future frogdom; the passing wild-duck dives and nibbles at it; the mink and muskrat brush it with their soft fur; the spotted turtle slides over it; the slow larvae of gauzy dragon-flies cling sleepily to its sides and await their change: all these fair or uncouth creatures feel, through the dim waves, the blessed longing of spring; and yet not one of them dreams that within that murky mass there lies a treasure too white and beautiful to be yet intrusted to the waves, and that for many a day the bud must yearn toward the surface, before, aspiring above it, as mortals to heaven, it meets the sunshine with the answering beauty of the Water-Lily.

Days and weeks have passed away; the wild-duck has flown onward, to dive for his luncheon in some remoter lake; the tadpoles have made themselves legs, with which they have vanished; the caddis-worms have sealed themselves up in their cylinders, and emerged again as winged insects; the dragon-flies have crawled up the water-reeds, and, clinging with heads upturned, have undergone the change which symbolizes immortality; the world is transformed from spring to summer; the lily-buds are opened into glossy leaf and radiant flower, and we have come for the harvest.

We visitors lodged, last night, in the old English phrase, "at the sign of the Oak and Star." Wishing, not, indeed, like the ancient magicians, to gather magic berry and bud before sunrise, but at least to see these treasures of the lake in their morning hour, we camped last night on a little island, which one tall tree almost covers with its branches, while a dense undergrowth of young chestnuts and birches fills all the intervening space, touching the water all around the circular, shelving shore. Yesterday was hot, but the night was cool, and we kindled a gypsy fire of twigs, less for warmth than for society. The first gleam made the dark, lonely islet into a cheering home, turned the protecting tree to a starlit roof, and the chestnut-sprays to illuminated walls. To us, lying beneath their shelter, every fresh flickering of the fire kindled the leaves into brightness and banished into dark interstices the lake and sky; then the fire died into embers, the leaves faded into solid darkness in their turn, and water and heavens showed light and close and near, until fresh twigs caught fire and the blaze came up again. Rising to look forth, at intervals, during the peaceful hours,—for it is the worst feature of a night out-doors, that sleeping seems such a waste of time,—we watched the hilly and wooded shores of the lake sink into gloom and glimmer into dawn again, amid the low plash of waters and the noises of the night.

Precisely at half past three, a song-sparrow above our heads gave one liquid trill, so inexpressibly sudden and delicious, that it seemed to set to music every atom of freshness and fragrance that Nature held; then the spell was broken, and the whole shore and lake were vocal with song. Joining in this jubilee of morning, we were early in motion; bathing and breakfast, though they seemed indisputably in accordance with the instincts of the Universe, yet did not detain us long, and we were promptly on our way to Lily Pond. Will the reader join us?

"Destructiveness of Man"
by George Perkins Marsh

From Man and Nature *(1864)*

Born into a prominent Vermont family, George Perkins Marsh (1801–1882) was a frail and serious child. It's said that at age seven he almost damaged his eyesight by too much reading. He was the top scholar in his Dartmouth College class of 1820. A polymath and linguistic genius, Marsh became a congressman and later ambassador to Turkey and then Italy.

Marsh is often considered the nation's first environmentalist because his 1864 book Man and Nature *was the first to warn of the destructive impact humankind was having on the natural world. Lewis Mumford called him "the fountainhead of the conservation movement." He was the inspiration for the creation of forest reserves in this country and elsewhere.*

Most of Marsh's books were about language, but he is most remembered today for his notions that humans are agents of environmental change and that the physical earth was not just the result of natural factors, but of cultural ones as well. The excerpt below states Marsh's principal thesis in unambiguous terms.

"DESTRUCTIVENESS OF MAN"

Man has too long forgotten that the earth was given to him for usufruct alone, not for consumption, still less for profligate waste. Nature has provided against the absolute destruction of any of her elementary matter, the raw material of her works; the thunderbolt and the tornado, the most convulsive throes of even the volcano and the earthquake, being only phenomena of decomposition and recomposition. But she has left it within the power of man irreparably to derange the combinations of inorganic matter and of organic life, which through the night of æons she had been proportioning and balancing, to prepare the earth for his habitation, when, in the fulness of time, his Creator should call him forth to enter into its possession.

Apart from the hostile influence of man, the organic and the inorganic world are, as I have remarked, bound together by such mutual relations and adaptations as secure, if not the absolute permanence and equilibrium of both, a long continuance of the established conditions of each at any given time and place, or at least, a very slow and gradual succession of changes in those conditions. But man is everywhere a disturbing agent. Wherever he plants his foot, the harmonies of nature are turned to discords. The proportions and accommodations which insured the stability of existing arrangements are overthrown. Indigenous vegetable and animal species are extirpated, and supplanted by others of foreign origin, spontaneous production is forbidden or restricted, and the face of the earth is either laid bare or covered with a new and reluctant growth of vegetable forms, and with alien tribes of animal life. These intentional changes and substitutions constitute, indeed, great revolutions; but vast as is their magnitude and importance, they are, as we shall see, insignificant in comparison with the contingent and unsought results which have flowed from them.

The fact that, of all organic beings, man alone is to be regarded as essentially a destructive power, and that he wields energies to resist which, nature—that Nature whom all material life and all inorganic substance obey—is wholly impotent, tends to prove that, though living in physical nature, he is not of her, that he is of more exalted parentage, and belongs to a higher order of existences than those born of her womb and submissive to her dictates.

There are, indeed, brute destroyers, beasts and birds and insects of prey—all animal life feeds upon, and, of course, destroys other life,—but this destruction is balanced by compensations. It is, in fact, the very means by which the existence of one tribe of animals or of vegetables is secured against being smothered by the encroachments of another; and the reproductive powers of species, which serve as the food of others, are always proportioned to the demand they are destined to supply. Man pursues his victims with reckless destructiveness; and, while the sacrifice of life by the lower animals is limited by the cravings of appetite, he unsparingly persecutes, even to extirpation, thousands of organic forms which he cannot consume.

The earth was not, in its natural condition, completely adapted to the use of man, but only to the sustenance of wild animals and wild vegetation. These live, multiply their kind in just proportion, and attain their perfect measure of strength and beauty, without producing or requiring any change in the natural arrangements of surface, or in each other's spontaneous tendencies, except such mutual repression of excessive increase as may prevent the extirpation of one species by the encroachments of another. In short, without man, lower animal and spontaneous vegetable life would have been constant in type, distribution, and proportion, and the physical geography of the earth would have remained undisturbed for indefinite periods, and been subject to revolution only from possible, unknown cosmical causes, or from geological action.

But man, the domestic animals that serve him, the field and garden plants the products of which supply him with food and clothing, cannot subsist and rise to the full development of their higher properties, unless brute and unconscious nature be effectually combated, and, in a great degree, vanquished by human art. Hence, a certain measure of transformation of terrestrial surface, of suppression of natural, and stimulation of artificially modified productivity becomes necessary.

This measure man has unfortunately exceeded. He has felled the forests whose network of fibrous roots bound the mould to the rocky skeleton of the earth; but had he allowed here and there a belt of woodland to reproduce itself by spontaneous propagation, most of the mischiefs which his reckless destruction of the natural protection of the soil has occasioned would have been averted. He has broken up the mountain reservoirs, the percolation of whose waters through unseen channels supplied the fountains that refreshed his cattle and fertilized his fields; but he has neglected to maintain the cisterns and the canals of irrigation which a wise antiquity had constructed to neutralize the consequences of its own imprudence. While he has torn the thin glebe which confined the light earth of extensive plains, and has destroyed the fringe of semi-aquatic plants which skirted the coast and checked the drifting of the sea sand, he has failed to prevent the spreading of the dunes by clothing them with artificially propagated vegetation. He has ruthlessly warred on all the tribes of animated nature whose spoil he could convert to his own uses, and he has not protected the birds which prey on the insects most destructive to his own harvests.

Purely untutored humanity, it is true, interferes comparatively little with the arrangements of nature, and the destructive agency of man becomes more and more energetic and unsparing as he advances in civilization, until the impoverishment, with which his exhaustion of the natural resources of the soil is threatening him, at last awakens him to the necessity of preserving what is left, if not of restoring what has been wantonly wasted. The wandering savage grows no cultivated vegetable, fells no forest, and extirpates no useful plant, no noxious weed. If his skill in the chase enables him to entrap numbers of the animals on which he feeds, he compensates this loss by destroying also the lion, the tiger, the wolf, the otter, the seal, and the eagle, thus indirectly protecting the feebler quadrupeds and fish and fowls, which would otherwise become the booty of beasts and birds of prey. But with stationary life, or rather with the pastoral state, man at once commences an almost indiscriminate warfare upon all the forms of animal and vegetable existence around him, and as he advances in civilization, he gradually eradicates or transforms every spontaneous product of the soil he occupies.

"Hiding in the Woods"
by James Mars

From The Life of James Mars *(1864)*

James Mars (1790–1880) was born into slavery in Canaan, Connecticut, just after the state outlawed the importation of new slaves, and began a gradual emancipation. When the town's minister who owned him tried to take him to Virginia in order to prevent his liberation, he refused to follow and escaped, only to be put into slavery again in Norfolk, Connecticut. He escaped again and finally made a deal to secure his freedom. He worked in Hartford, served as deacon at a local church, and joined the local free African American community. He married, and after his wife had eight children, they moved to Pittsfield, Massachusetts, then back to Norfolk, where he wrote his memoir in order to shine a light on Connecticut's own shameful relationship with slavery.

For escaped slaves, the wilderness could be a terrifying place, as they made their way between the lonely stops of the Underground Railroad. But as this piece from Mars's memoir demonstrates, it could also be a refuge, providing space to hide from slave-hunters, to join with other fugitives, and to plan a way to freedom. When civilization is organized against you, where else can you turn?

"HIDING IN THE WOODS"

When father came back, we set off for the woods pointed out by our friends; we went across the lots and came to a road, and crossed that into another open field. The woods were in the backside of the field. As we went on, we ascended a ridge of land, and we could see the road that led from Canaan to Norfolk. The road then went past the burying-ground, and we could see it from where we were. We saw fourteen men on horse-back; they were men we knew; the parson was one of them. We hid behind a log that was near us until they got out of sight; we then went into the woods, and there we found my mother and sister; they had been sent there by the man that had told us of the parson's information of where I was. We all remained there. This I should think was about two or three o'clock in the afternoon. Very soon the thought of night came to mind; how we were to spend the night, and what we should do for something to eat; but between sundown and dark a man passed along by the edge of the woods, whistling as he went. After he had passed on, father went up where the man went along, and came back with a pail or basket, and in it was our supper. We sat down and ate. The man we saw no more that night, but how were we to spend the night I could not tell; it was starlight, yet it was out in the woods, but father and mother were there, and that was a comfort to us children, but we soon fell asleep and forgot all our troubles, and in the morning we awoke and were still in the woods. In due time the man that passed along the night before, came again with more food for us, and then went his way; his name was Walter. We spent several days in the woods—how many I do not remember. I think it was the fore part of the week when we went into the woods; we were there over the Sabbath, for I well remember a man by the name of Bishop had a shop where he fulled and dressed cloth not very far from where we were, and he came to the back door of his shop and stood and looked out a while, and went in and shut the door. I felt afraid he would see us. We kept very still, but I think he did not know that we were there; if he did, it did us no hurt. We were fed by kind friends all the time we were in the woods.

One afternoon, or towards night, it was thought it would be safe to go to a barn and sleep. After it was dark we went to a barn belonging to Mr. Munger and slept, but left it while the stars were shining, and so for a few nights, and then it was thought we might sleep in the house. The next night after dark, we went in the house of Mr. Munger for the night. My sister and myself were put up in a back chamber, behind barrels and boxes, closely put together, out of sight for safe keeping. We had not been there long before mother came and told us we must get up, for Captain Lawrence, our friend, had sent word that the parson said he would have the boys at any rate, whether he got the parents or not. His pickets were going to search every house within a mile of the meeting-house that night, or search until he found them. But we went into the woods again; we were there awhile again; when it rained, we went sometimes into a barn when we dared. After a time it was rather still, and we were at one house and sometimes at another. We had pickets out as well as the parson. It was thought best that I should not be with the rest of the family, for the hunt seemed to be for the boys. My brother, I have said, was out of the State. I was sent to one family, and then to another, not in one place long at a time. The parson began to think the task harder than he had an idea; it rather grew worse and more perplexing; he did not know what to do. He was outwitted in all his attempts; every effort or trial he had made, had failed. He now thought of giving my father and mother and sister their freedom if they would let him have the boys to take with him; this they would not do.

After some time was spent, the parson or his pickets had an idea that we were all at Capt. Lawrence's house, shut up there; how to find out if we were there or not, was the puzzle. They contrived various plans, but did not succeed. Finally there was one thing yet. They knew that Mr. Lawrence loved money; they thought they would tempt him with that; so they came to his house and made trial. They met together one day and wanted to search his house; he would not consent for a time; they urged and he refused. He finally told them on certain conditions they might go into every room but one. They went into all the rooms but one. They then wanted to go into the room that they had not been into; they offered him money to let them go into the room—how much he did not tell, as I know of. He finally consented. The much-desired room was a chamber over the kitchen. Mr. Lawrence opened the door at the foot of the stairs, and called and said, "Jupiter! (for that was my father's first name,) you must look out for yourself now, for I cannot hide you any longer." He then told the parson's pickets they must take care, for Jupiter says he will kill the first man that lays hands on him. They hesitated some; they then went upstairs still, and stopped a short time, and then with a rush against the door, it gave way, and they all went in. They found the landlady sitting there as composed as summer, with her knitting-work, unconscious of an arrest to go south as a slave! But they found us not, although the room they last went into was the one we had occupied all the time we were in that house, sometimes one night, sometimes a week, and then in the woods or elsewhere, as was thought best to keep out of the way.

The pickets returned to the land of Canaan to see what was to be the next move. The parson then proposed to give my father and mother and sister their freedom, if they would let him have the boys. That they would not do; but the boys he said he must have. As my brother was away, it was thought best that I should be away. I was sent to Mr. Pease, well-nigh Canaan, and kept rather dark. I was there for a time, and I went to stay with a man by the name of Camp, and was with him a time, and then I went to stay with a man by the name of Akins, and stayed with him a few days, and went to a man by the name of Foot, and was with him a few days. I went to another man by the name of Akins, and was there some time. The parson was not gone south yet, for he could not well give up his prey. He then proposed to sell the boys until they were twenty-five, to somebody here that my parents would select, for that was as long as the law of Connecticut could hold slaves, and he would give the other members of the family their freedom. It was finally thought best to do that if the purchasers that were acceptable could be found. Some friends were on the lookout. Finally a man by the name of Bingham was found; it was a man that my father was once a slave to; he would take my brother, then a man by the name of Munger would buy me if they could agree. Mr. Bingham lived in Salisbury, Mr. Munger lived in Norfolk; the two men lived about fifteen miles apart, both in Connecticut.

The trade was made, and we two boys were sold for one hundred pounds a head, lawful money—yes, sold by a man, a minister of the gospel in Connecticut, the land of steady habits. It would seem that the parson was a worshiper with the Athenians, as Paul said unto them when he stood on Mars Hill, he saw an inscription on one of their altars; and it would seem that the parson forgot or passed over the instruction of the apostle that God made of one blood all nations of men for to dwell on all the face of the earth.

"Advertising in Nature"
by P. T. Barnum

From Humbugs of the World: An Account of
Humbugs, Delusions, Impositions, Quackeries,
Deceits and Deceivers Generally, in All Ages *(1865)*

*Born in Bethel, Connecticut, Phineas Taylor Barnum (1810–1891) became
one of the most famous and successful people of the nineteenth century. He pio-
neered advertising techniques still in use today, and created the modern culture
of celebrity. A consummate humbug in the world of entertainment, he was a
surprisingly honest politician, railing against quack doctors and fighting for the
voting rights of African Americans. He was also a proponent of Frederick Law
Olmsted's theories about parks, and created several in the city of Bridgeport.*

*In the following piece, Barnum condemns the common practice (even then)
of erecting billboards in natural spaces. As an early advocate of "all press is good
press," he used new technologies to draw crowds to his museum, to the tours of
General Tom Thumb, and to the larger, better circus that he founded. However, he saw that limits must be placed to prevent advertising from invading
ordinary life and ruining our human relationship to the spectacular American
landscape.*

"ADVERTISING IN NATURE"

No man ought to advertise in the midst of landscapes or scenery, in such a
way as to destroy or injure their beauty by introducing totally incongruous

and relatively vulgar associations. Too many transactions of the sort have been perpetrated in our own country.

The principle on which the thing is done is, to seek out the most attractive spot possible—the wildest, the most lovely, and there, in the most staring and brazen manner to paint up advertisements of quack medicines, rum, or as the case may be, in letters of monstrous size, in the most obtrusive colours, in such a prominent place, and in such a lasting way, as to destroy the beauty of the scene both thoroughly and permanently.

Any man with a beautiful wife or daughter would probably feel disagreeably, if he should find branded indelibly across her smooth white forehead, or on her snowy shoulder in blue and red letters such a phrase as this: "Try the Jigamaree Bitters!" Very much like this is the sort of advertising I am speaking of. It is not likely that I shall be charged with squeamishness on this question. I can readily enough see the selfishness and vulgarity of this particular sort of advertising, however.

It is outrageously selfish to destroy the pleasure of thousands, for the sake of a chance of additional gain. And it is an atrocious piece of vulgarity to flaunt the names of quack nostrums, and of the coarse stimulants of sots, among the beautiful scenes of nature. The pleasure of such places depends upon their freedom from the associations of everyday concerns and troubles and weaknesses. A lovely nook of forest scenery, or a grand rock, like a beautiful woman, depends for much of its attractiveness upon the attendant sense of freedom from whatever is low; upon a sense of purity and of romance. And it is about as nauseous to find "Bitters" or "Worm Syrup" daubed upon the landscape, as it would be upon the lady's brow.

Since writing this I observe that two legislatures—those of New Hampshire and New York—have passed laws to prevent this dirty misdemeanor. It is greatly to their credit, and it is in good season. For it is matter of wonder that some more colossal vulgarian has not stuck up a sign a mile long on the Palisades. But it is a matter of thankfulness too. At the White Mountains, many grand and beautiful views have been spoiled by these nostrum and bedbug-souled fellows.

It is worth noticing that the chief haunts of the city of New York, the Central Park, has thus far remained unviolated by the dirty hands of these vulgar advertisers. Without knowing anything about it, I have no doubt whatever that the commissioners have been approached often by parties desiring the privilege of advertising within its limits. Among the advertising fraternity it would be thought a gigantic opportunity to be able to flaunt the name of some bug-poison, fly-killer, bowel-rectifier, or disguised rum, along the walls of the Reservoir; upon the delicate stonework of the Terrace, or the graceful lines of the Bow Bridge; to nail up a tin sign on every other tree, to stick one up right in front of every seat; to keep a gang of young wretches thrusting pamphlet or hand bill into every person's palm that enters the gate; to paint a vulgar sign across every grey rock; to cut quack words in ditch-work in the smooth green turf of the mall or ball-ground. I have no doubt that it is the peremptory decision and clear good taste of the commissioners alone which have kept this last retreat of nature within our crowded city from being long ago plastered and daubed with placards, hand-bills, sign boards and paint, from side to side and from end to end, over turf, tree, rock, wall, bridge, archway, building and all.

"Natural History"
by James Gates Percival

From Life and Letters of James Gates Percival *(1866)*

Born in Berlin, Connecticut, James Gates Percival (1795–1856) graduated from Yale College medical school in 1820 and was appointed assistant surgeon in the U.S. Army, serving at West Point Military Academy as a chemistry professor. However, he resigned, practiced medicine in South Carolina, and then moved to New Haven, where he helped Noah Webster finish the American Dictionary. *He made a geological survey of Connecticut, and on the strength of that was hired to survey Wisconsin, where he eventually became state geologist.*

Parallel to Percival's career and writings in science, he composed poetry, published in small editions and in newspapers. His complete poetical works were published posthumously in 1859 to great acclaim. The following piece from his Life and Letters *makes an argument for the importance of studying natural history.*

"NATURAL HISTORY"

Next to the consideration of our destiny and duties, few employments are more useful to the young mind than the study of nature, or in more suitable language, of the works of creation and providence. Whether we consider it in its influences on the mind or heart, it will be found not only in the highest degree interesting and attractive, but equally ameliorating and instructive in its tendency. We do not now speak of the simple scientific investigation of natural things, the mere examination of their outward forms and internal organization, or even of the observation of their continued existence and all its manifold phenomena and changes, but rather of their relation to us and their Author. Even the first method of studying nature, coldly philosophical as it is, is not without its pleasures and attractions, as we see by the intense enthusiasm of those who are devoted to such pursuits, nor is it to be considered an idle play of the mind, without any useful results on the heart and conduct, for whatever employs our intellectual faculties on subjects elevated above moral debasement is in itself a means of purifying the character and giving it a spiritual tendency. We must indeed regret that so many among the first and wisest philosophers have paused as it were on the threshold of nature, without penetrating to the secret shrine of its Maker; but we should do injustice to them and the object of their pursuits if we supposed that their unwearied investigations had no salutary influence on their moral being, or that their irreligion was the result of their philosophy. If we examine their lives and deportment, we shall, in most instances, find that they have been better and more moral, if not more pious and devout, for their studies, and that their irreligion should not be attributed to the tendency of their own peculiar pursuits, but to some unhappy moral influences connected with society and education. True philosophy and true religion are indeed the same. If the one is more intellectual in its character, more a light which irradiates the head and less a fire that warms the heart, it is not for that reason adverse to, or incompatible with, the other. Both are alike the guides that conduct us up from the downward paths of life to the throne of the Deity and the regions where we alone can be happy. They aid and illustrate each other; and while philosophy is quickened and animated by religion, and filled with a devout and living energy, religion is rendered clearer and more certain by philosophy, and saved from the dangers of superstition and misguided enthusiasm.

But in the study of nature we should never forget that these visible things are but the manifestations of the One Invisible. Nature considered as a vast instrument, guided by an Almighty hand, is the perpetual source of the most devout and religious emotions. It then finds an entrance into the heart, and becomes a mover of the finest feelings and affections. The more it is studied the more it reveals of design and order, and the more it displays the presence of the Deity in all his works. Whether we consider the forms of things or the works of creation, or their ever-varying changes or the works of providence, wisdom and benevolence are everywhere presented to us: and while the mind is convinced, the heart is irresistibly impelled to acknowledge the great Author and Ruler of the universe. We cannot but hope that the prejudices which have existed in so many excellent minds against the study of natural science from its irreligious tendency will no longer find a place with those who have so great opportunities of usefulness, and who may have it so much in their power to correct any improper application of its truths, as the teachers of Sabbath schools. We have long been convinced that our happiness and even our security depend in a great degree on the truths of nature, and that in giving us a revealed and written law, the Deity did not abrogate the law which he had inscribed on our hearts and on the world around us, and we have therefore been anxious that those studies which can alone make known to us that older law should be freed from an odium which in the opinions of many has so long rested upon them. We have known, too, how much peace and innocent pleasure may be derived from those studies, how the mind is diverted from the control of debasing and depressing passions, and how often the heart is touched and warmed by exhibitions of benevolence and wisdom. These considerations have induced us to give some little time to the preparation of a few short articles on the study of Natural History, in its connection with Sabbath-school instruction. We propose to treat of it in its intellectual, moral, and religious bearings. In its intellectual character, we shall consider it as a means of developing and disciplining the understanding; in its moral character, as a corrector of the disposition and affections; and in its religious character, as a source of elevated and devout emotions, by revealing at once the greatness and the kindness of the Deity, in the immensity of his works as a whole, and in the minute design and nice adaptation of parts to their purposes, which pervade every portion of the universe.

"A Good Word for Winter"
by James Russell Lowell

From My Garden Acquaintance, and A
Good Word for Winter *(1871)*

Born in Cambridge, Massachusetts, to a distinguished family, James Russell Lowell (1819–1891) graduated from Harvard in 1838 as class poet and later earned a law degree from the institution. Early in life he was an ardent abolitionist and devoted his literary talents to the cause. He taught at Harvard from 1855 to 1877, served as minister to Spain from 1877 to 1880, and was appointed minister to England from 1880 to 1885.

Lowell published many volumes of poetry and essays. As a leading literary critic of his age, he exerted powerful sway over public taste. He was a founder and editor of magazines and literary journals, including first editor of The Atlantic Monthly. *Among his books are* Poems *(1844),* The Bigelow Papers *(1848),* Fireside Travels *(1864), and* The Old English Dramatists *(1892). In this piece, the citified and urbane Lowell demonstrates that one need not live in a rural area or travel to wild places in order to appreciate and write evocatively about natural phenomena.*

"A Good Word for Winter"

The preludings of Winter are as beautiful as those of Spring. In a gray December day, when, as the farmers say, it is too cold to snow, his numbed fingers will let fall doubtfully a few star-shaped flakes, the snow-drops and anemones that harbinger his more assured reign. Now, and now only, may be seen, heaped on the horizon's eastern edge, those "blue clouds" from forth which Shakespeare says that Mars "doth pluck the masoned turrets." Sometimes also, when the sun is low, you will see a single cloud trailing a flurry of snow along the southern hills in a wavering fringe of purple. And when at last the real snow-storm comes, it leaves the earth with a virginal look on it that no other of the seasons can rival,—compared with which, indeed, they seem soiled and vulgar.

And what is there in nature so beautiful as the next morning after such confusion of the elements? Night has no silence like this of busy day. All the batteries of noise are spiked. We see the movement of life as a deaf man sees it, a mere wraith of the clamorous existence that inflicts itself on our ears when the ground is bare. The earth is clothed in innocence as a garment. Every wound of the landscape is healed . . .

—⁓—

Poets have fancied the footprints of the wind in those light ripples that sometimes scurry across smooth water with a sudden blur. But on this gleaming hush the aerial deluge has left plain marks of its course; and in gullies through which it rushed torrent-like, the eye finds its bed irregularly scooped like that of a brook in hard beach-sand, or, in more sheltered spots, traced with outlines like those left by the sliding edges of the surf upon the shore. The air, after all, is only an infinitely thinner kind of water, such as I suppose we shall have to drink when the state does her whole duty as a moral reformer. Nor is the wind the only thing whose trail you will notice on this sensitive surface. You will find that you have more neighbors and night visitors than you dreamed of. Here is the dainty footprint of a cat; here a dog has looked in on you like an amateur watchman to see if all is right, slumping clumsily about in the mealy treachery. And look! before you were up in the morning, though you were a punctual courtier at the sun's levee, here has been a squirrel zigzagging to and fro like a hound gathering the scent, and some tiny bird searching for unimaginable food,—perhaps for the tinier creature, whatever it is, that drew this slender continuous trail like those made on the wet beach by light borderers of the sea.

—◦—

The snow that falls damp comes commonly in larger flakes from wind-less skies, and is the prettiest of all to watch from under cover. This is the kind Homer had in mind; and Dante, who had never read him, compares the *dilatate falde*, the flaring flakes, of his fiery rain, to those of snow among the mountains without wind. This sort of snowfall has no fight in it, and does not challenge you to a wrestle like that which drives well from the northward, with all moisture thoroughly winnowed out of it by the frosty wind. Burns, who was more out of doors than most poets, and whose barefoot Muse got the color in her cheeks by vigorous exercise in all weathers, was thinking of this drier deluge, when he speaks of the "whirling drift," and tells how

"Chanticleer
Shook off the powthery snaw."

But the damper and more deliberate falls have a choice knack at draping the trees; and about eaves or stone-walls, wherever, indeed, the evaporation is rapid, and it finds a chance to cling, it will build itself out in curves of wonderful beauty. I have seen one of these dumb waves, thus caught in the act of breaking, curl four feet beyond the edge of my roof and hang there for days, as if Nature were too well pleased with her work to let it crumble from its exquisite pause. After such a storm, if you are lucky enough to have even a sluggish ditch for a neighbor, be sure to pay it a visit. You will find its banks corniced with what seems precipitated light, and the dark current down below gleams as if with an inward lustre. Dull of motion as it is, you never saw water that seemed alive before. It has a brightness, like that of the eyes of some smaller animals, which gives assurance of life, but of a life foreign and unintelligible.

A damp snow-storm often turns to rain, and, in our freakish climate, the wind will whisk sometimes into the northwest so suddenly as to plate all the trees with crystal before it has swept the sky clear of its last cobweb of cloud. Ambrose Philips, in a poetical epistle from Copenhagen to the Earl of Dorset, describes this strange confectionery of Nature,—for such, I am half ashamed to say, it always seems to me, recalling the "glorified sugar-candy" of Lamb's first night at the theatre.

The damper snow tempts the amateur architect and sculptor. His Pentelicus has been brought to his very door, and if there are boys to be had (whose company beats all other recipes for prolonging life) a middle-aged Master of the Works will knock the years off his account and make the family Bible seem a dealer in foolish fables, by a few hours given heartily to this business. First comes the Sisyphean toil of rolling the clammy balls till they refuse to budge farther. Then, if you would play the statuary, they are piled one upon the other to the proper height; or if your aim be masonry, whether of house or fort, they must be squared and beaten solid with the shovel. The material is capable of very pretty effects, and your young companions meanwhile are unconsciously learning lessons in aesthetics.

Now look down from your hillside across the valley. The trees are leafless, but this is the season to study their anatomy, and did you ever notice before how much color there is in the twigs of many of them? And the smoke from those chimneys is so blue it seems like a feeder of the sky into which it flows. Winter refines it and gives it agreeable associations. In summer it suggests cookery or the drudgery of steam-engines, but now your fancy (if it can forget for a moment the dreary usurpation of stoves) traces it down to the fireside and the brightened faces of children. Thoreau is the only poet who has fitly sung it.

"Elm Trees"
by Oliver Wendell Holmes

From The Autocrat of the Breakfast-Table *(1873)*

Born in Cambridge, Massachusetts, Oliver Wendell Holmes Sr. (1809–1894) attended Phillips Academy and Harvard before studying to be a doctor, eventually helping to reform nineteenth-century medical practices. However, he would find more fame as a poet, published frequently in the magazine he named The Atlantic Monthly *and becoming friends with other titans of American literature. Though considered one of the most important poets of his day, Holmes has lasted longer as a prose writer, with his "table talk" books remaining popular well into the twentieth century.*

The following piece on elm trees is from Holmes's The Autocrat of the Breakfast-Table, *a dramatized, conversational essay in a form that he developed. He derides the scientific language of the day, saying that we should learn a tree's "character" and appreciate each as an individual. This is all the more poignant now, when the elm trees of New England have passed into history, with only a select few remaining, lone individuals amidst the wreck of their species.*

"Elm Trees"

I want you to understand, in the first place, that I have a most intense, passionate fondness for trees in general, and have had several romantic attachments to certain trees in particular. Now, if you expect me to hold forth in a "scientific" way about my tree-loves—to talk, for instance, of the

Ulmus Americana, and describe the ciliated edges of its samara, and all that—you are an anserine individual, and I must refer you to a dull friend who will discourse to you of such matters. What should you think of a lover who should describe the idol of his heart in the language of science, thus: Class, Mammalia; Order, Primates; Genus, Homo; Species, Europeus; Variety, Brown; Individual, Ann Eliza; Dental Formula

$$i \; \frac{2\text{-}2}{2\text{-}2} \quad c \; \frac{1\text{-}1}{1\text{-}1} \quad p \; \frac{2\text{-}2}{2\text{-}2} \quad m \; \frac{3\text{-}3}{3\text{-}3}$$

and so on?

No, my friends, I shall speak of trees as we see them, love them, adore them in the fields, where they are alive, holding their green sun-shades over our heads, talking to us with their hundred thousand whispering tongues, looking down on us with that sweet meekness which belongs to huge, but limited organisms—which one sees in the brown eyes of oxen, but most in the patient posture, the outstretched arms, and the heavy-drooping robes of these vast beings endowed with life, but not with soul—which outgrow us and outlive us, but stand helpless—poor things!—while Nature dresses and undresses them, like so many full-sized, but under-witted children.

—

Just think of applying the Linnæan system to an elm! Who cares how many stamens or pistils that little brown flower, which comes out before the leaf, may have to classify it by? What we want is the meaning, the character, the expression of a tree, as a kind and as an individual.

There is a mother-idea in each particular kind of tree, which, if well marked, is probably embodied in the poetry of every language. Take the oak, for instance, and we find it always standing as a type of strength and endurance. I wonder if you ever thought of the single mark of supremacy which distinguishes this tree from all our other forest-trees? All the rest of them shirk the work of resisting gravity; the oak alone defies it. It chooses the horizontal direction for its limbs, so that their whole weight may tell—and then stretches them out fifty or sixty feet, so that the strain

may be mighty enough to be worth resisting. You will find, that, in passing from the extreme downward droop of the branches of the weeping-
willow to the extreme upward inclination of those of the poplar, they
sweep nearly half a circle. At 90° the oak stops short; to slant upward
another degree would mark infirmity of purpose; to bend downwards,
weakness of organization. The American elm betrays something of both;
yet sometimes, as we shall see, puts on a certain resemblance to its sturdier
neighbor.

It won't do to be exclusive in our taste about trees. There is hardly
one of them which has not peculiar beauties in some fitting place for it.
I remember a tall poplar of monumental proportions and aspect, a vast
pillar of glossy green, placed on the summit of a lofty hill, and a beacon
to all the country round. A native of that region saw fit to build his house
very near it, and, having a fancy that it might blow down some time or
other, and exterminate himself and any incidental relatives who might
be "stopping" or "tarrying" with him—also laboring under the delusion
that human life is under all circumstances to be preferred to vegetable
existence—had the great poplar cut down. It is so easy to say, "It is only
a poplar!" and so much harder to replace its living cone than to build a
granite obelisk!

I must tell you about some of my tree-wives. I was at one period of my
life much devoted to the young lady-population of Rhode Island, a small,
but delightful State in the neighborhood of Pawtucket. The number of
inhabitants being not very large, I had leisure, during my visits to the
Providence Plantations, to inspect the face of the country in the intervals
of more fascinating studies of physiognomy. I heard some talk of a great
elm a short distance from the locality just mentioned. "Let us see the
great elm,"—I said, and proceeded to find it—knowing that it was on a
certain farm in a place called Johnston, if I remember rightly. I shall never
forget my ride and my introduction to the great Johnston elm.

I always tremble for a celebrated tree when I approach it for the first
time. Provincialism has no *scale* of excellence in man or vegetable; it never
knows a first-rate article of either kind when it has it, and is constantly

taking second and third rate ones for Nature's best. I have often fancied the tree was afraid of me, and that a sort of shiver came over it as over a betrothed maiden when she first stands before the unknown to whom she has been plighted. Before the measuring-tape the proudest tree of them all quails and shrinks into itself. All those stories of four or five men stretching their arms around it and not touching each other's fingers, if one's pacing the shadow at noon and making it so many hundred feet, die upon its leafy lips in the presence of the awful ribbon which has strangled so many false pretensions.

As I rode along the pleasant way, watching eagerly for the object of my journey, the rounded tops of the elms rose from time to time at the road-side. Wherever one looked taller and fuller than the rest, I asked myself, "Is this it?" But as I drew nearer, they grew smaller—or it proved, perhaps, that two standing in a line had looked like one, and so deceived me. At last, all at once, when I was not thinking of it—I declare to you it makes my flesh creep when I think of it now—all at once I saw a great, green cloud swelling in the horizon, so vast, so symmetrical, of such Olympian majesty and imperial supremacy among the lesser forest-growths, that my heart stopped short, then jumped at my ribs as a hunter springs at a five-barred gate, and I felt all through me, without need of uttering the words, "This is it!"

"Bird and Lighthouse"
by Celia Thaxter

From Among the Isles of Shoals *(1873)*

Born in Portsmouth, New Hampshire, Celia Thaxter (1835–1894) lived most of her life on the Isles of Shoals, those tiny islands shared by Maine and New Hampshire. At the hotel on Appledore Island, she acted as hostess to writers like Henry Wadsworth Longfellow and painters like William Morris Hunt, whose drowned body she discovered after his probable suicide. When she herself died in 1894, she was buried on Appledore, the place she immortalized in poetry and prose that reached far beyond the rocky coast of New England.

Along with many poems, Thaxter wrote essays and fiction. Her prose was picturesque, but as we can see in the following excerpt from Among the Isles of Shoals *(1873), her details could be insightful as well as scenic. Here we find birds that are suffering from their interaction with development. Much of her writing points out these small tragedies, as the idyll is shattered by the inevitable human failures that come with civilization.*

"BIRD AND LIGHTHOUSE"

Several snowy owls haunt the islands the whole winter long. I have never heard them cry like other owls; when disturbed or angry, they make a sound like a watchman's rattle, very loud and harsh, or they whistle with intense shrillness, like a human being. Their habitual silence adds to their ghostliness; and when at noonday they sit, high up, snow-white above the snowdrifts, blinking their pale yellow eyes in the sun, they are weird indeed. One night in March I saw one perched upon a rock between me and the "last remains of sunset dimly burning" in the west, his curious outline drawn black against the redness of the sky, his large head bent forward, and the whole aspect meditative and most human in its expression. I longed to go out and sit beside him and talk to him in the twilight, to ask of him the story of his life, or, if he would have permitted it, to watch him without a word. The plumage of this creature is wonderfully beautiful,—white, with scattered spots like little flecks of tawny cloud,—and his black beak and talons are powerful and sharp as iron; he might literally grapple his friend, or his enemy, with hooks of steel. As he is clothed in a mass of down, his outlines are so soft that he is like an enormous snowflake while flying; and he is a sight worth seeing when he stretches wide his broad wings, and sweeps down on his prey, silent and swift, with an unerring aim, and bears it off to the highest rock he can find, to devour it. In the summer one finds frequently upon the heights a little, solid ball of silvery fur and pure white bones, washed and bleached by the rain and sun; it is the rat's skin and skeleton in a compact bundle, which the owl rejects after having swallowed it.

Some quieter day, on the edge of a southerly wind, perhaps, boats go out over the gray, sad water after sea-fowl,—the murres that swim in little companies, keeping just out of reach of shot, and are so spiteful that they beat the boat with their beaks, when wounded, in impotent rage, till they are despatched with an oar or another shot; or kittiwakes,—exquisite creatures like living forms of snow and cloud in color, with beaks and feet of dull gold,—that come when you wave a white handkerchief, and flutter almost within reach of your hand; or oldwives, called by the natives *scoldenores*, with clean white caps; or clumsy eider-ducks, or coots, or mergansers, or whatever they may find. Black ducks, of course, are often shot. Their jet-black, shining plumage is splendidly handsome, set off with the broad, flame-colored beak. Little auks, stormy-petrels, loons, grebes, lords-and-ladies, sea-pigeons, sea-parrots, various guillemots, and all sorts of gulls abound. Sometimes an eagle sweeps over; gannets pay occasional visits; the great blue heron is often seen in autumn and spring. One of the most striking birds is the cormorant, called here "shag"; from it the rock at Duck Island takes its name. It used to be an object of almost awful interest to me when I beheld it perched upon White Island Head,—a solemn figure, high and dark against the clouds. Once, while living on that island, in the thickest of a great storm in autumn, when we seemed to be set between two contending armies, deafened by the continuous cannonading of breakers, and lashed and beaten by winds and waters till it was almost impossible to hear ourselves speak, we became aware of another sound, which pierced to our ears, bringing a sudden terror lest it should be the voices of human beings.

Opening the window a little, what a wild combination of sounds came shrieking in! A large flock of wild geese had settled for safety upon the rock, and completely surrounded us,—agitated, clamorous, weary. We might have secured any number of them, but it would have been a shameful thing. We were glad, indeed, that they should share our little foothold in that chaos, and they flew away unhurt when the tempest lulled. I was a very young child when this happened, but I never can forget that autumn night,—it seemed so wonderful and pitiful that those storm-beaten birds should have come crying to our rock; and the strange, wild chorus that swept in when the window was pried open a little took so strong a hold upon my imagination that I shall hear it as long as I live. The lighthouse, so beneficent to mankind, is the destroyer of birds,—of land birds particularly, though in thick weather sea-birds are occasionally bewildered into breaking their heads against the glass, plunging forward headlong towards the light, just as the frail moth of summer evenings madly seeks its death in the candle's blaze. Sometimes in autumn, always in spring, when birds are migrating, they are destroyed in such quantities by this means that it is painful to reflect upon. The keeper living at the island three years ago told me that he picked up three hundred and seventy-five in one morning at the foot of the lighthouse, all dead. They fly with such force against the glass that their beaks are often splintered. The keeper said he found the destruction greatest in hazy weather, and he thought "they struck a ray at a great distance and followed it up." Many a May morning have I wandered about the rock at the foot of the tower mourning over a little apron brimful of sparrows, swallows, thrushes, robins, fire-winged blackbirds, many-colored warblers and fly-catchers, beautifully clothed yellow-birds, nuthatches, cat-birds, even the purple finch and scarlet tanager and golden oriole, and many more beside,—enough to break the heart of a small child to think of! Once a great eagle flew against the lantern and shivered the glass. That was before I lived there; but after we came, two gulls cracked one of the large, clear panes, one stormy night.

The sea-birds are comparatively few and shy at this time; but I remember when they were plentiful enough, when on Duck Island in summer the "medrake's," or tern, made rude nests on the beach, and the little yellow gulls, just out of the eggs, ran tumbling about among the stones, hiding their foolish heads in every crack and cranny, and, like the ostrich, imagining themselves safe so long as they could not see the danger. And even now the sandpipers build in numbers on the islands, and the young birds, which look like tiny tufts of fog, run about among the bayberry bushes, with sweet, scared piping. They are exquisitely beautiful and delicate, covered with a down just like gray mist, with brilliant black eyes, and slender, graceful legs that make one think of grass-stems. And here the loons congregate in spring and autumn. These birds seem to me the most human and at the same time the most demoniac of their kind. I learned to imitate their different cries; they are wonderful!

At one time the loon language was so familiar that I could almost always summon a considerable flock by going down to the water and assuming the neighborly and conversational tone which they generally use: after calling a few minutes, first a far-off voice responded, then other voices answered him, and when this was kept up a while, half a dozen birds would come sailing in. It was the most delightful little party imaginable; so comical were they, so entertaining, that it was impossible not to laugh aloud,—and they could laugh too, in a way which chilled the marrow of one's bones. They always laugh, when shot at, if they are missed; as the Shoalers say, "They laugh like a warrior." But their long, wild, melancholy cry before a storm is the most awful note I ever heard from a bird. It is so sad, so hopeless,—a clear, high shriek, shaken, as it drops into silence, into broken notes that make you think of the fluttering of a pennon in the wind,—a shutter of sound. They invariably utter this cry before a storm.

"Bluefish off Nantucket"
by Samuel Adams Drake

From Nooks and Corners of the New England Coast *(1875)*

Educated in Boston public schools, Samuel Adams Drake (1833–1905) traveled in 1858 to Kansas, where he was employed as a telegraph agent for the New York Associated Press. He became a correspondent for papers in St. Louis, Missouri, and Louisville, Kentucky, and also edited the Leavenworth Times *in Kansas. He served in the Civil War and rose to the rank of brigadier general. Returning to Boston in 1871, he pursued a literary career, authoring over twenty books on history and travel. Among his books are* Old Landmarks of Boston *(1873),* Heart of the White Mountains *(1882),* New England Legends and Folk Lore *(1884),* The Pine Tree Coast *(1891),* Our Colonial Homes *(1894), and* The Myths and Fables of To-day *(1900).*

In the following piece from Nooks and Corners of the New England Coast *(1875), Drake writes in the style of the literate and urbane observer who takes note of both natural and cultural elements in nearby landscapes, weaving an integrated narrative of place. While not strictly nature writing, works such as these beckoned readers to see nature even in settled areas. Such place-based writing, with nature a critical constituent, would grow in popularity in the twentieth century.*

"Bluefish off Nantucket"

The sail across the Vineyard Sound is more than beautiful; it is a poem. Trending away to the west, the Elizabeth Islands, like a gate, ajar, half close the entrance into Buzzard's Bay. Among them nestles Cuttyhunk, where the very first English spade was driven into New England soil. Straight over in front of the pathway the steamer is cleaving, the Vineyard is looking its best and greenest, with oak-skirted highlands inclosing the sheltered harbor of Vineyard Haven, famous on all this coast. Edgartown is seen at the bottom of a deep indentation, its roofs gleaming like scales on some huge reptile that has crawled out of the sea, and is basking on the warm yellow sands. Chappaquiddick Island, with its sandy tentacles, terminates in Cape Poge, on which is a light-house.

Between the shores, and as far as eye can discern, the fleet that passes almost without intermission is hurrying up and down the Sound. One column stretches away under bellying sails, like a fleet advancing in line of battle, but the vanguard is sinking beneath the distant waves. Still they come and go, speeding on to the appointed mart, threading their way securely among islands, capes, and shoals. Much they enliven the scene. A sea without a sail is a more impressive solitude than a deserted city.

We ran between the two sandy points, long and low, that inclose the harbor into smoother water. The captain went on the guard. "Heave your bow-line." "Ay, ay, sir." "Back her, sir" (to the pilot). "Hold on your spring." "Stop her." "Slack away the bow-line there." "Haul in." It is handsomely done, and this is Nantucket.

It was a delicious afternoon that I set sail for the "Opening," as it is called, between Nantucket and Tuckanuck, an appanage of the former, and one of the five islands constituting the county of Nantucket. The tide runs with such swiftness that the boatmen do not venture through the Opening except with plenty of wind, and of the right sort. With a stiff breeze blowing, the breakers are superb, especially when wind and tide are battling with each other. With the wind blowing freshly over these shallow waters, it does not take long for the seas to assume proportions simply appalling to a landsman. It was a magnificent sight! Great waves erected themselves into solid walls of green, advancing at first majestically, then rushing with increased momentum across our course to crash in clouds of foam upon the opposite shore. It needs a skillful boatman at the helm. What with the big seas, the seething tide-rips, and the scanty sea-room, the sail is of itself sufficiently exciting.

But the fishing, what of that? We cast our lines over the stern, and, as the boat was going at a great pace, they were straightened out in a trice. At the end of each was a wicked-looking hook of large size, having a leaden sinker run upon the shank of it. Over this hook, called by the fishermen hereabouts a "drail," an eel-skin was drawn, though I have known the blue-fish to bite well at a simple piece of canvas or leather. Away bounded the boat, while we stood braced in the standing-room to meet her plunging. Twenty fathoms with a pound of lead at the end seems fifty, at least, with your boat rushing headlong under all she can bear. Half an acre of smooth water wholly unruffled is just ahead. "I'm going to put you right into that slick," said our helmsman. "Now look out for a big one."

I felt a dead weight at my line. At the end of it a shining object leaped clear from the water and fell, with a loud plash, a yard in advance. Now, haul in steadily; don't be flurried; but, above all, mind your line does not slacken. I lost one splendid fellow by too great precipitation. The line is as rigid as steel wire, and, if your hands are tender, cuts deep into the flesh. Ah! he is now near enough to see the boat. How he plunges and tries to turn! He makes the water boil, and the line fairly sing. I had as lief try to hold an old hunter in a steeple-chase. Ha! here you are, my captive, under the counter; and now I lift you carefully over the gunwale. I enjoin on the inexperienced to be sure they land a fish in the boat, and not lose one, as I did, by throwing him on the gunwale.

The fish shows fight after he is in the tub, shutting his jaws with a vicious snap as he is being unhooked. Look out for him; he can bite, and sharply too. The blue-fish is not unlike the salmon in looks and in action.

He is furnished with a backbone of steel, and is younger brother to the shark.

I looked over my shoulder. My companion, a cool hand ordinarily, was engaged in hauling in his line with affected nonchalance; but compressed lips, stern eye, and rigid figure said otherwise. There is a quick flash in the water, and in comes the fish. "Eight-pounder," says the boatman.

These "slicks" are not the least curious feature of blue-fishing. The fish seems to have the ability to exude an oil, by which he calms the water so that he may, in a way, look about him, showing himself in this an adept in applying a well-known principle in hydrostatics. A perceptible odor arises from the slicks, so that the boatmen will often say, "I smell blue-fish."

The boatman steered among the tide-rips, where each of us soon struck a fish, or, as the phrase here is, "got fast." The monster—I believe he was a ten-pounder at least—that took my hook threw himself bodily into the air, shaking his head as if he did not mean to come on board us. And he was as good as his threat: I saw the drail skipping on the top of the wave as my line came in empty.

In two hours we had filled a barrel with fish, and it was time to shape our course harborward. We saw the smoke of the Island Home, looking at first as if rising out of the Sound; then her funnel appeared, and at length her hull rose into view; but she was come within a mile of us before I could distinguish her walking-beam. Tuckanuck and Low Water Island were soon a-lee. Maddequet Harbor opened a moment for us, but we did not enter. We rounded Eel Point with a full sail, and shot past Whale Rock and the shoal of stranded blackfish I told you of. Ever and anon we had passed one adrift, stripped of his fatty epidermis, and now food for the sharks. They were grotesque objects, though now mere carrion, above which the tierce gulls screamed noisily. Here is Brant Point, and its light-house of red brick. We stand well over for Coatue, then about with her for the home stretch. "Fast bind fast find." Our bark is moored. With stiffened joints, but light hearts, we seek our lodgings. What do they say to us? In faith I am not sorry I went blue-fishing. Reader, are you?

"New England Weather"
by Mark Twain

From Mark Twain's Speeches *(1910, first spoken in 1876)*

When Samuel Clemens's (1835–1910) first book, The Innocents Abroad, *became a best seller, he and his wife Livy moved to the town many considered to be the most beautiful in America at the time—Hartford, Connecticut. He spent his happiest and most productive years as a New Englander, walking through the fields and forests with his friend Joseph Hopkins Twichell. In a billiards room on the top floor of his mansion on Farmington Avenue, he penned the immortal books that made his pseudonym "Mark Twain" synonymous with American literature.*

Twain often served as a gadfly, poking holes in our lofty ideas and hypocritical pretensions. Some of his work, such as Roughing It *or* Life on the Mississippi, *deals with humans' relationship with nature in a humorous way. And nothing he wrote makes the absurdity of our lack of control over the natural world clearer than "New England Weather." This lecture was given at the New England Society's 71st Annual Dinner on December 22, 1876. Amusingly, and perhaps tellingly, the dinner took place in New York.*

"NEW ENGLAND WEATHER"

I reverently believe that the Maker who made us all makes everything in New England but the weather. I don't know who makes that, but I think it must be raw apprentices in the weatherclerk's factory who experiment and learn how, in New England, for board and clothes, and then are pro-moted to make weather for countries that require a good article, and will take their custom elsewhere if they don't get it. There is a sumptuous variety about the New England weather that compels the stranger's admiration—and regret. The weather is always doing something there; always attending strictly to business; always getting up new designs and trying them on the people to see how they will go.

But it gets through more business in spring than in any other season. In the spring I have counted one hundred and thirty-six different kinds of weather inside of four-and-twenty hours. It was I that made the fame and fortune of that man that had that marvelous collection of weather on exhibition at the Centennial, that so astounded the foreigners. He was going to travel all over the world and get specimens from all the climes. I said, "Don't you do it; you come to New England on a favorable spring day." I told him what we could do in the way of style, variety, and quantity. Well, he came and he made his collection in four days. As to variety, why, he confessed that he got hundreds of kinds of weather that he had never heard of before. And as to quantity—well, after he had picked out and discarded all that was blemished in any way, he not only had weather enough, but weather to spare; weather to hire out; weather to sell; to deposit; weather to invest; weather to give to the poor.

The people of New England are by nature patient and forbearing, but there are some things which they will not stand. Every year they kill a lot of poets for writing about "Beautiful Spring." These are generally casual visitors, who bring their notions of spring from somewhere else, and cannot, of course, know how the natives feel about spring. And so, the first thing they know the opportunity to inquire how they feel has permanently gone by. Old Probabilities has a mighty reputation for accurate prophecy, and thoroughly well deserves it. You take up the paper and observe how crisply and confidently he checks off what to-day's weather is going to be on the Pacific, down South, in the Middle States, in the Wisconsin region. See him sail along in the joy and pride of his power till he gets to New England, and then see his tail drop. *He* doesn't know what the weather is going to be in New England. Well, he mulls over it, and by and by he gets out something about like this: Probable northeast to southwest winds, varying to the southward and westward and eastward, and points between, high and low barometer swapping around from place to place; probable areas of rain, snow, hail, and drought, succeeded or preceded by earthquakes, with thunder and lightning. Then he jots down this postscript from his wandering mind, to cover accidents: "But it is possible that the program may be wholly changed in the mean time."

Yes, one of the brightest gems in the New England weather is the dazzling uncertainty of it. There is only one thing certain about it: you are certain there is going to be plenty of it—a perfect grand review; but you never can tell which end of the procession is going to move first. You fix up for the drought; you leave your umbrella in the house and sally out, and two to one you get drowned. You make up your mind that the earthquake is due; you stand from under, and take hold of something to steady yourself, and the first thing you know you get struck by lightning. These are great disappointments; but they can't be helped. The lightning there is peculiar; it is so convincing, that when it strikes a thing it doesn't leave enough of that thing behind for you to tell whether— Well, you'd think it was something valuable, and a Congressman had been there. And the thunder. When the thunder begins to merely tune up and scrape and saw, and key up the instruments for the performance, strangers say, "Why, what awful thunder you have here!" But when the baton is raised and the real concert begins, you'll find that stranger down in the cellar with his head in the ash-barrel.

Now as to the *size* of the weather in New England—lengthways, I mean. It is utterly disproportioned to the size of that little country. Half the time, when it is packed as full as it can stick, you will see that New England weather sticking out beyond the edges and projecting around hundreds and hundreds of miles over the neighboring states. She can't hold a tenth part of her weather. You can see cracks all about where she has strained herself trying to do it. I could speak volumes about the inhuman perversity of the New England weather, but I will give but a single specimen. I like to hear rain on a tin roof. So, I covered part of my roof with tin, with an eye to that luxury. Well, sir, do you think it ever rains on that tin? No, sir; skips it every time. Mind, in this speech I have been trying merely to do honor to the New England weather—no language could do it justice.

But, after all, there is at least one or two things about that weather (or, if you please, effects produced by it) which we residents would not like to part with. If we hadn't our bewitching autumn foliage, we should still have to credit the weather with one feature which compensates for all its bullying vagaries—the ice-storm: when a leafless tree is clothed with ice from the bottom to the top—ice that is as bright and clear as crystal; when every bough and twig is strung with ice-beads, frozen dewdrops, and the whole tree sparkles cold and white, like the Shah of Persia's diamond plume. Then the wind waves the branches and the sun comes out and turns all those myriads of beads and drops to prisms that glow and burn and flash with all manner of colored fires, which change and change again with inconceivable rapidity from blue to red, from red to green, and green to gold—the tree becomes a spraying fountain, a very explosion of dazzling jewels; and it stands there the acme, the climax, the supremest possibility in art or nature, of bewildering, intoxicating, intolerable magnificence. One cannot make the words too strong.

"The Sugar Camp"
by Charles Dudley Warner

From Being a Boy *(1877)*

Born in Plainfield, Massachusetts, Charles Dudley Warner (1829–1900) traveled and lived around the United States, until returning to New England in 1861 to become an editor for the Hartford Press *and then the* Hartford Courant. *He became friends with Mark Twain, and they coauthored a novel,* The Gilded Age *(1873), which gave its name to the late nineteenth century in American history. He edited* Harper's *Magazine, wrote many books on travel and literature, and became the first president of the National Institute of Arts and Letters.*

Warner's love for outdoor pursuits runs through all his writing, from My Summer in the Garden *(1870) to* Our Italy *(1891). The following piece, "The Sugar Camp," from the book* Being a Boy *(1877), describes his experiences in Charlemont, Massachusetts, as a child, enjoying one of New England's greatest pleasures, taking part in the ritual of maple sugaring.*

"THE SUGAR CAMP"

I think there is no part of farming the boy enjoys more than the making of maple sugar; it is better than "blackberrying," and nearly as good as fishing. And one reason he likes this work is, that somebody else does the most of it. It is a sort of work in which he can appear to be very active, and yet not do much.

And it exactly suits the temperament of a real boy to be very busy about nothing. If the power, for instance, that is expended in play by a boy between the ages of eight and fourteen could be applied to some industry, we should see wonderful results. But a boy is like a galvanic battery that is not in connection with anything; he generates electricity and plays it off into the air with the most reckless prodigality. And I, for one, wouldn't have it otherwise. It is as much a boy's business to play off his energies into space as it is for a flower to blow, or a catbird to sing snatches of the tunes of all the other birds.

In my day maple-sugar-making used to be something between picnicking and being shipwrecked on a fertile island, where one should save from the wreck tubs and augers, and great kettles and pork, and hen's eggs and rye-and-indian bread, and begin at once to lead the sweetest life in the world. I am told that it is something different nowadays, and that there is more desire to save the sap, and make good, pure sugar, and sell it for a large price, than there used to be, and that the old fun and picturesqueness of the business are pretty much gone. I am told that it is the custom to carefully collect the sap and bring it to the house, where there are built brick arches, over which it is evaporated in shallow pans, and that pains is taken to keep the leaves, sticks, and ashes and coals out of it, and that the sugar is clarified; and that, in short, it is a money-making business, in which there is very little fun, and that the boy is not allowed to dip his paddle into the kettle of boiling sugar and lick off the delicious sirup. The prohibition may improve the sugar, but it is cruel to the boy.

As I remember the New England boy (and I am very intimate with one), he used to be on the *qui vive* in the spring for the sap to begin running. I think he discovered it as soon as anybody. Perhaps he knew it by a feeling of something starting in his own veins—a sort of spring stir in his legs and arms, which tempted him to stand on his head, or throw a handspring, if he could find a spot of ground from which the snow had melted. The sap stirs early in the legs of a country-boy, and shows itself in uneasiness in the toes, which get tired of boots, and want to come out and touch the soil just as soon as the sun has warmed it a little. The country-boy goes barefoot just as naturally as the trees burst their buds, which were packed and varnished over in the fall to keep the water and the frost out. Perhaps the boy has been out digging into the maple-trees with his jack-knife; at any rate, he is pretty sure to announce the discovery as he comes running into the house in a great state of excitement—as if he had heard a hen cackle in the barn—with "Sap's runnin'!"

And then, indeed, the stir and excitement begin. The sap-buckets, which have been stored in the garret over the wood-house, and which the boy has occasionally climbed up to look at with another boy, for they are full of sweet suggestions of the annual spring frolic—the sap-buckets are brought down and set out on the south side of the house and scalded. The snow is still a foot or two deep in the woods, and the ox-sled is got out to make a road to the sugar camp, and the campaign begins. The boy is everywhere present, superintending everything, asking questions, and filled with a desire to help the excitement.

It is a great day when the cart is loaded with the buckets and the procession starts into the woods. The sun shines almost unobstructedly into the forest, for there are only naked branches to bar it; the snow is soft and beginning to sink down, leaving the young bushes spindling up everywhere; the snowbirds are twittering about, and the noise of shouting and of the blows of the axe echoes far and wide. This is spring, and the boy can scarcely contain his delight that his out-door life is about to begin again.

In the first place, the men go about and tap the trees, drive in the spouts, and hang the buckets under. The boy watches all these operations with the greatest interest. He wishes that sometime, when a hole is bored in a tree, the sap would spout out in a stream as it does when a cider-barrel is tapped; but it never does, it only drops, sometimes almost in a stream, but on the whole slowly, and the boy learns that the sweet things of the world have to be patiently waited for, and do not usually come otherwise than drop by drop.

Then the camp is to be cleared of snow. The shanty is re-covered with boughs. In front of it two enormous logs are rolled nearly together, and a fire is built between them. Forked sticks are set at each end, and a long pole is laid on them, and on this are hung the great caldron kettles. The huge hogsheads are turned right side up, and cleaned out to receive the sap that is gathered. And now, if there is a good "sap run," the establishment is under full headway.

The great fire that is kindled up is never let out, night or day, as long as the season lasts. Somebody is always cutting wood to feed it; somebody is busy most of the time gathering in the sap; somebody is required to watch the kettles that they do not boil over, and to fill them. It is not the boy, however; he is too busy with things in general to be of any use in details. He has his own little sap-yoke and small pails, with which he gathers the sweet liquid. He has a little boiling-place of his own, with small logs and a tiny kettle. In the great kettles the boiling goes on slowly, and the liquid, as it thickens, is dipped from one to another, until in the end kettle it is reduced to sirup, and is taken out to cool and settle, until enough is made to "sugar off." To "sugar off" is to boil the sirup until it is thick enough to crystallize into sugar. This is the grand event, and is done only once in two or three days.

But the boy's desire is to "sugar off" perpetually. He boils his kettle down as rapidly as possible; he is not particular about chips, scum, or ashes; he is apt to burn his sugar; but if he can get enough to make a little wax on the snow, or to scrape from the bottom of the kettle with his wooden paddle, he is happy. A good deal is wasted on his hands, and the outside of his face, and on his clothes, but he does not care; he is not stingy.

To watch the operations of the big fire gives him constant pleasure. Sometimes he is left to watch the boiling kettles, with a piece of pork tied on the end of a stick, which he dips into the boiling mass when it threatens to go over. He is constantly tasting of it, however, to see if it is not almost sirup. He has a long round stick, whittled smooth at one end, which he uses for this purpose, at the constant risk of burning his tongue. The smoke blows in his face; he is grimy with ashes; he is altogether such a mass of dirt, stickiness, and sweetness, that his own mother wouldn't know him.

He likes to boil eggs in the hot sap with the hired man; he likes to roast potatoes in the ashes, and he would live in the camp day and night if he were permitted. Some of the hired men sleep in the bough shanty and keep the fire blazing all night. To sleep there with them, and awake in the night and hear the wind in the trees, and see the sparks fly up to the sky, is a perfect realization of all the stories of adventures he has ever read. He tells the other boys afterwards that he heard something in the night that sounded very much like a bear. The hired man says that he was very much scared by the hooting of an owl.

The great occasions for the boy, though, are the times of "sugaring-off." Sometimes this used to be done in the evening, and it was made the excuse for a frolic in the camp. The neighbors were invited; some-times even the pretty girls from the village, who filled all the woods with their sweet voices and merry laughter and little affectations of fright. The white snow still lies on all the ground except the warm spot about the camp. The tree branches all show distinctly in the light of the fire, which sends its ruddy glare far into the darkness, and lights up the bough shanty, the hogsheads, the buckets on the trees, and the group about the boiling kettles, until the scene is like something taken out of a fairy play. If Rembrandt could have seen a sugar party in a New England wood, he would have made out of its strong contrasts of light and shade one of the finest pictures in the world. But Rembrandt was not born in Massachusetts; people hardly ever do know where to be born until it is too late. Being born in the right place is a thing that has been very much neglected.

At these sugar parties everyone was expected to eat as much sugar as possible; and those who are practiced in it can eat a great deal. It is a peculiarity about eating warm maple sugar, that though you may eat so much of it one day as to be sick and loathe the thought of it, you will want it the next day more than ever. At the "sugaring-off" they used to pour the hot sugar upon the snow, where it congealed, without crystallizing, into a sort of wax, which I do suppose is the most delicious substance that was ever invented. And it takes a great while to eat it. If one should close his teeth firmly on a ball of it, he would be unable to open his mouth until it dissolved. The sensation while it is melting is very pleasant, but one cannot converse.

The boy used to make a big lump of it and give it to the dog, who seized it with great avidity, and closed his jaws on it, as dogs will on anything. It was funny the next moment to see the expression of perfect surprise on the dog's face when he found that he could not open his jaws. He shook his head; he sat down in despair; he ran round in a circle; he dashed into the woods and back again. He did everything except climb a tree, and howl. It would have been such a relief to him if he could have howled. But that was the one thing he could not do.

"Going A-Chestnutting"
by Harriet Beecher Stowe

From Poganuc People *(1878)*

Born in Litchfield, Connecticut, Harriet Beecher (1811–1896) grew up in a family of high achievers. She enrolled in the Hartford Female Seminary, run by her older sister Catharine, and at age 21 accompanied her father, Reverend Lyman Beecher, to Ohio. While there she met her future husband, Calvin Stowe, and they married in 1836. She also encountered slavery up close during those years, and she and her husband supported the Underground Railroad before moving to Brunswick, Maine. In 1850 she reacted with horror to the Fugitive Slave Law and began to write a novel on the topic, finishing Uncle Tom's Cabin *over the next two years. It was an instant success and educated hundreds of thousands of people about the evils of slavery in the years leading up to the Civil War.*

Beecher Stowe continued her writing career after the war, completing a number of fiction and nonfiction books about rural New England life, including The Pearl of Orr's Island: A Story of the Coast of Maine *(1862) and* Oldtown Folks *(1869). The following excerpt comes from* Poganuc People *(1878), which is based on her childhood in Litchfield. It describes the ritual of chestnut harvesting, and the passing away of such traditions due to new laws and customs.*

"Going A Chestnutting"

Our fathers came to New England from a country where the poor man was everywhere shut out from the bounties of nature by game-laws and severe restrictions. Though his children might be dying of hunger he could not catch a fish, or shoot a bird, or snare the wild game of the forest, without liability to arrest as a criminal; he could not gather the wild fruits of the earth without danger of being held a trespasser, and risking fine and imprisonment. When the fathers took possession of the New England forest it was in the merciful spirit of the Mosaic law, which commanded that something should always be left to be gathered by the poor. From the beginning of the New England life till now there has been poor people, widows and fatherless children, who have eked out their scanty living by the sale of the fruits and nuts which the custom of the country allowed them freely to gather on other people's land. Within the past fifty years, while this country has been filling up with foreigners of a different day and training, these old customs have been passing away. Various fruits and nuts, once held free, are now appropriated by the holders of the soil and made subject to restriction and cultivation.

In the day we speak of, however, all the forest hills around Poganuc were a free nut-orchard, and one of the chief festive occasions of the year, in the family at the parsonage, was the autumn gathering of nuts, when Dr. Cushing took the matter in hand and gave his mind to it. On the present occasion, having just finished four sermons which completely cleared up and reconciled all the difficulties between the doctrines of free agency and the divine decrees, the doctor was naturally in good spirits. He declared to his wife, "There! my dear, *that* subject is disposed of. I never before succeeded in really clearing it up; but now the matter is done for all time." Having thus wound up the sun and moon, and arranged the courses of the stars in celestial regions, the doctor was as alert and light hearted as any boy, in his preparations for the day's enterprise.

"Boys," he said, "we'll drive over to Poganuc Ledge; up there are those big chestnuts that grow right out of the rock; there's no likelihood of anybody's getting them—but I noticed the other day they were hanging full."

"Oh, father, those trees are awful to climb."

"Of course they are. I won't let you boys try to climb them—mind that; but I'll go up myself and shake them, and you pick up underneath."

No Highland follower ever gloried more in the physical prowess of his chief than the boys in that of their father. Was there a tree he could not climb—a chestnut, or walnut, or butternut, however exhausted in fastnesses of the rock, that he could not shake down? They were certain there was not. The boys rushed hither and thither with Spring barking at their heels, leaving open doors and shouting orders to each other concerning the various pails and baskets necessary to contain their future harvest. Mrs. Cushing became alarmed for the stability of her household arrangements.

"Now, father, *please* don't take all my baskets this time," pleaded she, "just to let me arrange—"

"Well, my dear, have it all your own way; only be sure to provide things enough."

"Well, surely, they can all pick in pails or cups, and then they can be emptied into a bag," said Mrs. Cushing. "You won't get more than a bushel, certainly."

"Oh yes, we shall—three or four bushels," said Will triumphantly.

"There's no end of what we shall get when father goes," said Bob. "Why, you've no idea how he rattles 'em down."

Meanwhile Mrs. Cushing and the Nabby were packing a hamper with bread and butter, and tea-rusks, and unlimited gingerbread, and doughnuts crisp and brown, and savory ham, and a bottle of cream, and coffee all ready for boiling in the pot, and teacups and spoons—everything, in short, ready for a gypsy encampment, while the parson's horse stood meekly absorbing an extra ration of oats in that contemplative attitude which becomes habitual to good family horses, especially of the ministerial profession. Mrs. Cushing and the doctor, with Nabby and Dolly, and the hamper and baskets, formed the load of the light wagon, while Will and Bob were both mounted upon "the colt"—a scrawny ewe-necked beast, who had long outgrown this youthful designation. The boys, however, had means best known to themselves of rousing his energies and keeping him ahead of the wagon in a convulsive canter, greatly to the amusement of Nabby and Dolly.

Our readers would be happy could they follow the party along the hard, stony roads, up the winding mountain paths, where the trees, flushing in the purple, crimson, and gold, seemed to shed light on their paths; where beds of fringed gentian seemed, as the sunlight struck them, to glow like so many sapphires, and every leaf of every plant seemed to be passing from the green of summer into some quaint new tint of autumnal Splendor. Here and there groups of pines or tall hemlocks, with their heavy background of solemn green, threw out the flamboyant tracery of the forest in startling distinctness. Here and there, as they passed a bit of low land, the swamp maples seemed really to burn like crimson flames; and the clumps of black alder, with their vivid scarlet berries, exhausted the effect of color to the very highest and most daring result. No artist ever has ventured to put on canvas the exact copy of the picture that nature paints for us every year in the autumn months. There are things the Almighty Artist can do that no earthly imitator can more than hopelessly admire.

As to Dolly, she was like a bird held in a leash, full of exclamations and longings, now to pick "those leaves," and then to gather "those gentians," or to get "those lovely red berries," but was forced to resign herself to be carried by.

"They would all fade before the day is through," said her mother; "wait till we come home at night, and then, if you're not too tired, you may gather them." Dolly sighed and resigned herself to wait.

We shall not tell the joys of the day; how the doctor climbed the trees victoriously, how the brown, glossy chestnuts flew down in showers as he shook the limbs, and how fast they were gathered by busy fingers below. Not merely chestnuts, but walnuts, and a splendid butternut-tree, that grew in the high cleft of a rocky ledge, all were made to yield up their treasures till the bags were swelled to a most auspicious size. Then came the nooning, when the boys delighted in making a roaring hot fire, and the coffee was put on to boil, and Nabby spread the tablecloth and unpacked the hamper on a broad, flat rock around which a white foam of moss formed a soft, elastic seat. The doctor was most entertaining, and related stories of the fishing and hunting excursions of his youth, of the trout he had caught and the ducks he had shot. The boys listened with ears of emulation, and Dolly sighed to think she never was to be a man and do all these fine things that her brothers were going to do.

"Sea Urchins"
by Elizabeth Cabot Cary Agassiz

From A First Lesson in Natural History *(1879)*

Born into a leading Boston family, Elizabeth Cabot Cary Agassiz (1822–1907) was a naturalist, writer, and educator. As a girl, fragile health required that she be educated at home. In 1850 she married prominent Swiss scientist Louis Agassiz, a widower with three children who had come to Harvard to teach. In addition to raising Louis's children and managing the household, she provided invaluable assistance to her husband in his scientific efforts. Between 1856 and 1863 she ran a school for girls out of the couple's Cambridge home, at which Louis and some of his fellow Harvard faculty taught. She became the cofounder and first president of Radcliffe College.

Among Elizabeth Agassiz's writings are A First Lesson in Natural History *(1859),* Seaside Studies in Natural History *(1865, with her stepson Alexander), and* A Journey in Brazil *(1867, with her husband). An excerpt from an 1879 edition of her first book demonstrates a mastery of clear description and a remarkable ability to present science in an easily understandable manner.*

"SEA URCHINS"

The Sea-Urchin has one very peculiar habit. He bores for himself a hole in the rocks, which just fits him, and makes a very snug and comfortable retreat.

I have seen a dead Sea-Urchin, about as large round as a five-cent piece, packed away as closely as possible in its hole, that fitted him as neatly as if it had been cut with the nicest instrument. Their mode of making these holes is not known; and as they are found in all kinds of rocks whether hard or soft, where Sea-Urchins exist, in granite or basalt as well as in limestone or sandstone, it is difficult to understand how animals not furnished with any sharp and powerful instruments can produce such an effect. There is, however, no doubt that these holes are made by the animals themselves, not only because the Sea-Urchins are found in them, but because they fit their inhabitants so perfectly that no animal not exactly of the same shape and size could have produced them; and they are of all sizes, from that of the young Sea-Urchin to the full-grown one.

It has been supposed by some naturalists that they were made by the constant friction of a fringe that is in unceasing motion, called the vibrating cilia; this fringe, though invisible to the naked eye, covers the spines of the Sea-Urchin, and, by the constant turning of the animal over and over in the same spot, may wear a hole in the rock. It seems difficult to believe that a substance so soft and delicate as the vibrating fringes on these animals should produce any effect on a substance hard as granite; yet we know that the constant dropping of water wears away a stone, and it maybe that the continual friction even of the soft parts of the Sea-Urchin would be equally effectual.

The common Sea-Urchin of Nahant is one of those that make these singular holes, and you may have an opportunity of seeing them in the rocks there. I hope you will try to find some Sea-Urchins for your Aquarium next summer, and watch them in their living condition. I dare say you have often seen them dead and dry on the beaches, but you cannot then judge at all of their appearance when living. They look very pretty when dried in that way, because, though they have lost all their spines and suckers, the spots where these appendages were attached form a sort of pattern in regular rows or zones over the surface of the animal, and you can trace in this pattern the lines along which the spines and suckers were arranged when the animal was living.

There is a great variety among the Sea-Urchins, as well as among the Star-Fishes. They do not all burrow in the rocks. Some of them are flat in form, and live on sandy flats, burying themselves in the sand; so that they are only discovered when left bare after storms, or in very still days, when, in changing their place, they have left tracks along the sand.

There is another animal, which, though it differs strikingly in appearance from the Sea-Urchin and the Star-Fish, is yet constructed on the same plan. It is commonly called, from its form, the Sea-Cucumber. It may be a little difficult to show you how this soft elongated animal, resembling a worm more than anything else, is related to the Star-Fish with its extended rays, or to the Sea-Urchin with its round outline; but I will try to explain it to you. Imagine that the Sea-Urchin were elastic, and that taking him at the mouth on one side, and at the spot just opposite to the mouth where the rays meet on the other side, you could stretch him out till, instead of being a round, compressed ball, he would have a long cylindrical form like a large worm: you would then have an animal like the one of which I speak. The rays would of course be stretched out also, and would extend from one end of the body to the other. This is the case with the Sea-Cucumber. It has no spines, being soft throughout; but the suckers are arranged in rows along the body, alternating with spaces having no appendages, but corresponding to those on which the spines are arranged in Star-Fishes and Sea-Urchins. The mouth is at one end of the body, and is surrounded by a wreath of tentacles; and the animal, resting on one side, moves along like the Star-Fish and the Sea-Urchin, by means of the suckers, always turning that end of the body at which the mouth is placed in the direction of its motion. Its body is, as I have said, soft throughout, and can contract and expand, making itself broader and shorter, or longer and narrower, by taking in or letting out the sea-water, which enters at the opening opposite the mouth, at the other end of the body. The main tubes for the circulation of food and water throughout the body, answering to those which in the Star-Fish run along the arms, and in the Sea-Urchins along the rows of suckers, extend in the Sea-Cucumber from one end of the body to the other, while the sieve through which the water is filtered is within the body instead of being on the outside, as in the two others. The animals of this kind found on our coast are very small. Larger kinds, however, abound in the Bay of Fundy and upon the mud-flats of the Reef of Florida. Some of those from Florida are as large as your arm, and more than a foot long.

This curious animal furnishes a very important article of food to the Chinese. They call it the Trepang, and they send every year large fishing fleets to the islands in the Pacific, and to the coasts of New Holland, for the express purpose of collecting it. When dried and preserved in a particular way, they find it a great delicacy, though I doubt whether you or I would like it very much.

As there is one general name, that of Polyps, including all animals of the kind which I first described, like the Sea-Anemone, and another, that of Medusa or Acalephs, including all of the second kind, like the Jelly-Fishes, so there is also a general name for all animals like the Star-Fishes, Sea-Urchins, and Sea-Cucumbers, that of Echinoderms. Each of these, the Polyps, the Acalephs or Medusae, and the Echinoderms, form what is called by naturalists a class, and these three classes are included under another name, that of Radiates. In other words, Radiates form one great division of animals, embracing Polyps, Acalephs or Medusae, and Echinoderms. Now, if you look in your dictionary for the definition of the verb "to radiate," you will find this: "To send out rays from a center." This explains the structure of all the animals belonging to this division, and the reason why they are called by this name. Whether they are round or long or star-shaped, they are all so constructed that their parts diverge from a center; and at that center is an opening, which is the mouth.

"Hunting for Nests"
by Amanda Bartlett Harris

From How We Went Birds'-Nesting:
Field, Wood and Meadow Rambles *(1880)*

Born in Warner, New Hampshire, Amanda Bartlett Harris (1824–1917) began writing when she was only a girl, despite caring for her younger siblings and father after her mother's death. She published for decades under a pen name in local newspapers and magazines until her father's passing in 1875. Only then did she start her real career, publishing over 150 stories and ten books, many of them for young readers and children. Nevertheless, she never left Warner, spending her days in quiet rambles around her home and at her writing desk.

Harris's books include Wildflowers and Where They Grow *(1882),* Dooryard Folks *(1883), and* Pleasant Authors for Young Folks *(1884). The following excerpt from her* How We Went Birds'-Nesting *is both inspirational and instructional, giving children the information they needed to know on how to find birds. One of the reasons she focuses so much on the nests, however, is that it was common practice for naturalists of the time to harvest eggs for their collections. Our ethics about doing so may have changed, but at the time it was seen as a normal and necessary part of scientific inquiry.*

"The Cuckoo, the Vireo, the Catbird, and the Sandpiper"

We had a great day of it hunting for nests on that thirty-first of May. I am particular about giving the date, because we meant to be accurate and so we noted down everything on the spot, not only the day of the month, but all about the place, the birds, the nests, and the eggs.

We went equipped for our business, wearing strong dresses and shoes, and shade hats securely tied down; and we each carried a basket, one containing lunch enough for all day, for going on such a tramp was hungry work; the other was to bring things home in—"things" meaning roots, mosses, vines, flowers, and any decorative bits we chose. It also held the rubber over-shoes which we took along for emergencies, as there was no knowing where we might venture, going through swamps or even wading a river; also into it I always slipped a jack-knife and some strings, for which I was invariably laughed at, especially about the strings, which, nevertheless, were sure to come handy; finally something which must by no means be left out of this record, viz: a transplanting trowel, which "had been in the family," as they say of jewels, more than fifty years. It had been lost and found as many times, consequently it had become highly valued, insomuch that our sole anxiety in all our excursions was about this precious relic, and our only worry was from the fear that we might lose it.

On that eventful day we first went to the tangled wood I have spoken of, where we discovered the whip-poor-will. It was hardly a mile from the village, and it not only bordered on the main thoroughfare but was within a stone's throw of two houses, and close by were cornfields where men were often at work; so that in one sense it was a very exposed place, although in another it was a very secluded one. The railroad was back of it, just where the ground made an abrupt descent into a strip of marsh; then the river fringed with alders and willows; then a belt of meadow.

This little wild, being a useless piece, neither field nor pasture nor woodland, had been left to itself in the midst of cultivation; and if it had been made for the sole use of birds it could not have served its purpose better. There were only three or four acres of it, bog and all, but as Thoreau once said about Concord, that he could find everything worth knowing within its limits, so we began to think before the season was over that there was at least a possibility of getting a sight of almost any inland bird of New England within that circumscribed district.

Both land and water-birds built there, undismayed by the sounds of life going on so near them—the carriages on the highway, or the rush of the cars which fairly shook them in their nests; and our experience seemed to justify us in the conclusion that the place to find the nests of even some shy birds is near the haunts of men, and further, that where we found one we were pretty sure of many others in the neighborhood. At any rate there seemed to be a gregarious spirit in this matter, even with varieties whose habits are supposed to be solitary. It was astonishing how much family life was being lived there, and equally a surprise to us that each separate pair were attending to their own business as if there were no others in the world; and it was so still there! The birds that were not brooding over their nests slipped about quietly, as if intent on business which demanded the utmost silence and mystery.

There were not only cat-birds, cuckoos, thrushes, yellow-birds, vireos, brown-and-white creepers and sparrows, but king-birds, sandpipers and bank-swallows, besides many others whose names were unknown to us; and even a scarlet tanager came; and on that same day in May we started up a pair of Blackburnian warblers from the darkest covert on the bank, but though we waited long and wore ourselves out in struggling through the briary thicket they were too crafty for us, and in following where their flame-bright plumage showed in the green gloom we strayed hopelessly away from their nesting-place which we were never able to find.

"Hunting and Trapping" by Fred C. Barker and John S. Danforth

From Hunting and Trapping on the Upper
Magalloway River and Parmachenee Lake:
First Winter in the Wilderness *(1882)*

*Born in Bristol, New Hampshire, John Samuel Danforth (1847–1913)
worked in his father's tannery, but also learned how to hunt and track game.
In 1870 he opened one of the first sports lodges in America, Camp Caribou, on
Parmachenee Lake in Maine. This operation expanded throughout the area,
and he eventually sold it at a profit. In 1892 he built a 125-foot paddleboat as
a floating hotel, but after he took it to Florida it was looted and sunk. He eventually left Maine permanently and built the Danforth Hotel on the St. Lucie
River in Florida, which became a destination in the early twentieth century.*

*Danforth's friend and coauthor, Fred C. Barker (1852–1937), was born
in Andover, Maine, and spent his childhood hunting and fishing the Rangeley
Lakes. He became a guide and log driver, and learned how to captain steamboats. He bought and ran a series of steamboats on Mooselookmeguntic Lake,
and eventually went on to build three hotels. After the book he wrote with
Danforth,* Hunting and Trapping on the Upper Magalloway River and
Parmachenee Lake: First Winter in the Wilderness *(1882), he went on to
write* Lake and Forest as I Knew Them *(1903).*

*The book from which this excerpt is taken was originally a journal of the
winter of 1876, when the two hunted and trapped the isolated northwestern
lakes of Maine. In a jolly tone, they describe the prevailing attitude toward
nature of their day, which was a full exploitation of its resources. It is in stark*

contrast to what they called the "flowery" nature writing of the day, "a plain record of facts."

"HUNTING AND TRAPPING"

Our load was not heavy, and we could march along at a good jog, because the morning was cold, making us feel like moving briskly. When we reached Rump Pond we went to our meat, and with an axe cut from one of the caribou as much as we thought we should need. We did not stop for skin, but chopped the animal as we would a log.

In one of the traps near the meat was a sable, which we took out and tied to a tree, as we did not want to take it up river. After leaving Rump Pond we found the valley narrow and the river crooked. First a high bank on one side of the river, then on the other, covered with spruce and fir-trees, while the opposite bank would be low and covered with alders and scattering elms. At almost every high bank springs came out nearly on a level with the river; around these we had to step with care, as they were not frozen over; and the river-ice in their vicinity was thin and treacherous.

But the beaver and otter were of a different mind, for around nearly every one of the springs they had played; and near one of them was a number of half-eaten fish which the otter had caught. After eating what they wanted, they had left the rest for owls and hawks, which are always hovering about on the water for such chances.

In some of the best spring-holes we set traps as we went along, to look to when we came back.

At noon we stopped on a high bank covered with spruce and fir-trees. There we made a fire and broiled some of our meat. After dinner we resumed our journey. The valley grew narrower and the river quicker, as we went farther up; and at four o'clock we reached a place where it was so rapid that it was not frozen hard enough to travel on. This put a stop to our further progress that day.

On the east side of the river was a thicket, where we concluded to spend the night. We built a bough-camp, cut a lot of fire-wood, and as the wind did not blow, we had a very comfortable night. In the morning we thought best to cruise round and not try to go farther with our sled. So with our rifles, and a good-sized piece of broiled caribou in our pockets, we started up river, going round the open and dangerous places.

Soon we saw that the valley was about to end in the northerly direction, for big mountains were just before us. Still the river must come through somewhere; so we pushed on to find the opening. We had not gone far when we came to a place where two streams of about the same size joined, one coming from the north, the other from the east.

The valley to the east was low, and the stream, as far as we could see, was covered on both sides with alders. But the one from the north came tumbling over coarse boulders, and its banks were covered with forest trees to the very water's edge.

We took this northern one, although we could not walk on the ice. But the woods were better than the thick alder bushes along the eastern stream. We had not ascended far when we heard the roar of water above the rattle caused by the current over the rough boulders. When we reached the place whence proceeded the roar, a magnificent spectacle met our view.

On each side of a deep pool were ledges running upward in irregular shapes; and the water pouring in between them over a drop of several feet, caused the ice to form over them in fancy shapes. Down into that curious-shaped and glittering cistern the water disappeared with a dull roar.

"Moose Hunting"
by Thomas Sedgwick Steele

From Paddle and Portage, from Moosehead
Lake to the Aroostook River, Maine *(1882)*

*Artist, author, and naturalist Thomas Sedgwick Steele (1845–1903) was born
in Hartford, Connecticut, and attended local schools. He studied art in Paris,
France, and was admitted to the National Academy of Design in 1877. His
specialty was painting and drawing fish and game, fruits, and flowers.*

*Long harboring a passion for wild places, Steele traveled to Maine and
wrote two books of backwoods adventure,* Canoe and Camera *(1880) and*
Paddle and Portage *(1882), both lavishly illustrated by the author. He was
among the earliest urban dwellers to document a canoe trip to the solitude and
wild forests of the area. Many would follow using his writings as a guide.*

*The selection is from the later book, where Steele with companions and
an Indian guide travel in birch bark canoes. After describing the "wild, desolate" countryside, the travelers here encounter a moose, an animal they thought
nearly extinct. Though moose are now relatively common in the area, the fascination of travelers persists, and we can feel Steele's excitement from almost a
century and a half ago.*

"MOOSE HUNTING"

On arriving the same difficulties which prevented our embarking delayed
our landing, and at one time it looked as if each man would make his

canoe his camp for the night. But just as the sun set we managed to land, and pitched our tents in the dark. Mud Pond Stream being almost dry, we were forced the next morning to carry our canoes and kit almost a mile, depositing them at last in the stream which flows through the moose barren bordering on Chamberlin Lake.

Here we found ourselves in a wild, desolate country. The stream along which we moved ran through an immense tract of bog, which was dotted here and there with old stumps reaching for a quarter of a mile in every direction. This was bounded in the dim distance by a dead wood forest, which enclosed it completely like a *chevaux de frise*. Within this was presented a most lugubrious landscape. It was the picture of a region dead to the world and to itself. The old grey stumps scattered about seemed like storm-beaten tombstones which marked the resting-places of perished souls, and the naked, bleached forms of the trees in the palisade like sentinel skeletons guarding a death ground.

Soon with our three canoes in line we entered the waters of Chamberlin Lake. There we were suddenly startled by hearing a loud splash in the water, and greeted with the vision of an immense bull caribou, which sprang up and instantly disappeared in the woods before we could tender him the slightest compliment at the pleasure of the meeting.

"Confound the luck!" yelled John, throwing aside a rifle in exasperating disappointment.

"Exceedingly impolite of the beast to decamp so suddenly" said the Colonel, as we examined the animal's tracks; "he would have weighed three hundred pounds, if an ounce!"

Chamberlin Lake is eighteen miles long, three miles wide, and is one of the largest bodies of water in Maine. At this point, the preceding year, I turned south through the East Branch of the Penobscot, and landed at Mattawamkeag on the European and North American Railroad. This year our course lay directly to the north.

At Chamberlin Farm we made a brief stay, and purchased an extra supply of hard tack, sugar, and molasses, as our stores were running short. Then turning our backs on the lovely peaks of Mt. Katahdin and the

Soudahaunk range, which lay to the southwest, we buffetted the waves of the lake for six miles, landing at the locks which divide its waters from those of Eagle Lake below.

Here we went into camp, and the Tourograph was brought into important requisition while a benign and smiling sun was at its best. And here we were delayed for three days afterwards, through a go-as-you-please rainstorm, during which we tried the camera while the aforesaid benign and smiling sun was at its worst, hidden away like an unfortunate trade-dollar during the storm of repudiation.

When the weather grew favorable, we followed the current of Chamberlin River one mile down to Eagle Lake below. Some people think of Maine as a state containing only one large lake with an innumerable number of smaller ponds within its borders, but the tourist visiting these regions for the first time is daily surprised by bodies of water which fairly compete with the area of Moosehead. Eagle Lake is thirteen miles long, with an average measurement of three wide. Within its bosom it nurses two islands, while the horizon of its northern extremity is broken by the cone-shaped peak of Soper Mountain.

Our next camp was made at the mouth of a beautiful stream near here, which writhes under the opprobrious title of Smith Brook. This innocent sheet of water, which I am certain has done naught to merit the ignominy it suffers, presents most picturesque beauties in its windings as far as Haymoak Falls.

There we discovered the skull of a large moose, and extracted the great teeth, fearing they would be the only souvenirs we should obtain of that almost extinct animal.

"My!" said the Colonel, as he pried out one of the grinders; "what a surface for a tooth-ache!"

There, also, we had splendid fishing, and captured many large trout.

— ·—

"If moose so near," said Nichols, one day, "me better make horn and call moose to-night; no try, no get him."

We thought this a good scheme, and with the approval of all, the Indian tramped off into the woods, and soon returned with a large piece of birch bark. Shaving the edges with his knife, he warmed it over the fire, and proceeded to roll it up into a great horn two feet in length, tapering it from six inches to one in diameter, and fastening the edges with wooden pegs.

Nichols and I were the only ones who went out on the hunt. Preparing ourselves after the evening repast, we stepped into our canoes at 7.30 o'clock. It was not a remarkably severe night, but as I knew I should be obliged to remain for a long time in almost motionless position, I took precautions to wrap up extremely well, and before I returned, the night chill had penetrated through it all to the very vicinity of my bones.

"Most ready?" asked the Indian, as in this clumsy and uncomfortable attire I rolled, rather than seated, myself in the bottom of the canoe.

"Yes; all ready, Nichols!" and throwing the birch moose horn into the craft we paddled out into the lake, with the best wishes of the rest of the party from the shore.

"If we hear a shot," yelled the Colonel, with a look of dubiousness, "we will add an extra log to the fire."

"And cut up the balance of our salt pork," added Hiram, "for moose steak is a little dry without it."

It was a clear night, and so still that the sound of voices and the blows of an axe at camp could be easily heard two miles across the lake. The bright October moon was gradually creeping down the western sky, but shone enough to light us on our way many miles.

The tall hemlocks that fringed the shore threw their shadows far out into the lake, and in these reflections the guide paddled from point to point.

A slight rustle behind me and the Indian draws forth the long birch horn, dips it noiselessly in the water, and for the first time in my existence I listen to the weird sound of the moose call.

Ugh—ugh—ugh—OO—OO—OO—OO—OO—ugh—ugh!

Three plaintive "ughs," then a prolonged bellow, commencing in a low tone, increasing in power and volume to the end, and followed by two notes like the first.

It rolled across the lake in every direction, was tossed from mountain tops to the inmost depths of the forests, echoing and re-echoing. Then all was hushed, and we waited in silence the result. The stillness was something overpowering. We held our breaths. At times, however, it was harshly broken. Away toward the distant shore some sportive animal would splash in his gambols at the water's edge, or a muskrat could be distinctly heard gathering his evening meal; then the prow of the canoe would graze the rushes or the lily-pads with a suddenness that was startling.

Noiselessly the Indian plied his paddle, and we crept silently on in the shadows. Again the horn was raised to his lips, and there came forth that strange midnight call so melodious to my ears. This was repeated again and again for six successive hours, neither of us exchanging a word during the entire time.

At last the stars alone cast their reflections in the glassy lake, and although from a distant mountain side we at last received an answer to our call, we could not draw the animal to the water's edge.

We had paddled over ten miles. It was now 2 o'clock in the morning, and we returned to camp. I was too stiff to move, and the Indian lifted me from the canoe to the shore, while I realized that I had experienced all the pleasures of moose hunting—save the moose.

"Loons" by Lucius Hubbard

From Woods and Lakes of Maine: A Trip from Moosehead Lake to New Brunswick in a Birch-bark Canoe *(1884)*

Lucius L. Hubbard (1849–1933) grew up in Cincinnati, Ohio; graduated from Harvard in 1872; and afterwards received a law degree from Boston University. Following several years practicing law in Boston, he went to Germany, where he received a PhD in mineralogy. In 1890 he left New England to join the Michigan Geological Survey and the Michigan College of Mines. He was the Michigan state geologist from 1893 to 1899, later working for private mining companies.

Before leaving New England, Hubbard traveled extensively in the Maine woods and became an expert on the area, inspiring a generation of wilderness tourists, travelers, and rusticators. The excerpt here is from Woods and Lakes of Maine: A Trip from Moosehead Lake to New Brunswick in a Birch-bark Canoe *(1884), in which he describes an encounter with a loon, to this day a haunting symbol of New England wilderness.*

"LOONS"

Onward we floated over the unruffled surface of Pongokwahemook. From the top of an immense dead pine-tree on Pillsbury Island flew a bald eagle (*Ilaliactus leucocephalus*), which mounted in a graceful spiral higher and higher, until, a mere speck in the sky, it became scarcely distinguishable. Far out on the lake we heard the warning cry of a loon (*Colymbus torquatus*), whose white breast, unusually conspicuous above the smooth water, seemed twice its ordinary size—a phenomenon probably due to mirage.

The loon is one of the most interesting of the ordinary features of camp life that come under one's observation among the lakes of Maine. Every lake, and almost every pond not too small for its safety, contains one loon, at least, if not a family of them. We see them constantly, or hear their weird cries at all hours of the day, and at night too. At early morn they circle the shores in search of food, and at these times often come close to our camp. Or perhaps at mid-day, attracted by the unusual sight of an overturned canoe, or of a tent whose white canvas gleams through the trees, they approach to make a closer observation, for the loon is an inquisitive bird. Quietly they swim on, warily looking from side to side, now stopping in their course, or sheering off a little, then again advancing, until, satisfied, they go elsewhere about their proper business—whatever that may be. On a large lake the loon seems indifferent to the presence of man, or even of such noisy things as steamboats, unless perhaps it is accompanied by its young. Then it is always in a flutter, and we hear its anxious "Hoo-hoo-hoo, hoo-hoo-hoo!" as if it were in great alarm. This is especially true on a small pond. The din it then makes is incessant, and resounds from shore to shore, gaining strength as it goes.

Far from being a "foolish" bird, the loon often exhibits much cunning. When disturbed, the parent and its young swim off in different directions, the latter seeking seclusion near some reedy shore, while the former tries to draw attention to itself. When pursued it dives repeatedly, and on reappearing exposes only its head above water. Sometimes, too, it doubles on its pursuers, or rather *under* them, and often thus escapes most mysteriously from their sight. Undoubtedly the loon's reputation for being "silly" or "crazy" is due to its cry of alarm, which, oft repeated by a single bird, or in chorus by several of them, may sound to some ears maniacal. This cry is certainly at times exasperating to the hunter on the lookout for game, however little in fact the latter may be disturbed by it.

Subjectively the loon seems to have been little studied, but its different notes furnish us with abundant material to interpret its varying moods. Its cry of alarm, and its shrill note when on the wing, are probably by many persons supposed to be the only ones it utters, the expression of its joy and affection being entirely overlooked. Its notes are more significant than those of many other birds, at times merry, tender, dreary, or full of fear, but almost always musical. Take the most common cry, with its several variations, Hu-hu-hu! or Whu-u-hu-hu! each note short and crisp. This indicates surprise or alarm, while in Hu-hu-wey-u or Hu-hu-wey-i-ooo the alarm seems to be increased. At night the camper often hears, the second and third notes slurred, and often flat, Hu-loo-uh or Hu-loo-oo sometimes supplemented by Loo-eee!

These dreary night cries are startling, and sound like those of a child in distress. They may be plaintive utterings to the orb of night, or the outcome perhaps of the bird's disturbed slumbers. Weird enough they seem, thus breaking the solemn stillness of the forest aisles.

Again at night there comes softly over the water a single note, full of tenderness, like the cooing of a mother to its young, a short gentle "Hu!" or sometimes the longer "Hu-whu-oo!" in low, plaintive tones. These sounds the writer has heard repeatedly on ponds where there were known to be families of loons, and the sounds seemed too full and mature to come from other than the old birds.

By far the most interesting manifestation of the loon's feelings, however, is the cry, sometimes heard late in the summer, but oftener in the springtime, in that joyous season when all nature is bright, and our bird, happy in his old haunts perhaps, or with his mate or new-born offspring, rings forth with a merry swing his Oh-oo – whi-oo – hoo-wi, whi-oo – hoo-wi – hoo-wi!

Who will say, then, that the loon has no feelings kindred with our own, consign him to a place among the insensates, and let his only function be to serve as a target for the wandering bullets of summer tourists?

"The City and Rural Scenery" by Frederick Law Olmsted

From Notes on the Plan of Franklin Park and Related Matters *(1886)*

Best known for the 1858 design of New York's Central Park in collaboration with architect Calvert Vaux, Frederick Law Olmsted (1822–1903) is considered the father of American landscape architecture. Born in Hartford, he came to his calling late, having tried his hand as a merchant, farmer, publisher, writer, and magazine editor. He traveled extensively in the United States, Europe, Britain, and elsewhere. Between 1859 and 1861 he served as architect-in-chief of Central Park, and from 1863 to 1865 as director of the U.S. Sanitary Commission overseeing public health issues for Civil War soldiers.

Olmsted and his firm designed Boston's Emerald Necklace, the Stanford University campus, Montreal's Mount Royal Park, the U.S. Capitol grounds, and hundreds of public and private spaces. He was among the first commissioners appointed to manage the grant of Yosemite Valley and the Mariposa Big Tree Grove from Congress to California as a park.

Olmsted's designs can provide a sense of natural space even in dense urban places. He was skilled at transforming degraded city areas with naturalistic plantings and sitework. This excerpt from his Notes on the Plan of Franklin Park and Related Matters *touches on the meaning of rural scenery and its value to city dwellers.*

"The City and Rural Scenery"

A man's eyes cannot be as much occupied as they are in large cities by artificial things, or by natural things seen under obviously artificial conditions, without a harmful effect, first on his mental and nervous system and ultimately on his entire constitutional organization.

That relief from this evil is to be obtained through recreation is often said, without sufficient discrimination as to the nature of the recreation required. The several varieties of recreation to be obtained in churches, newspapers, theaters, picture galleries, billiard rooms, baseball grounds, trotting courses, and flower gardens, may each serve to supply a mitigating influence. An influence is desirable, however, that, acting through the eye, shall be more than mitigative, that shall be antithetical, reversive, and antidotal. Such an influence is found in what, in notes to follow, will be called the enjoyment of pleasing rural scenery.

But to understand what will be meant by this term as here to be used, two ideas must not be allowed to run together, that few minds are trained to keep apart. To separate them let it be reflected, first, that the word beauty is commonly used with respect to two quite distinct aspects of the things that enter visibly into the composition of parks and gardens. A little violet or a great magnolia blossom, the frond of a fern, a carpet of the fine turf of the form and size of a prayer rug, a block of carved and polished marble, a vase or a jet of water,—in the beauty of all these things unalloyed pleasure may be taken in the heart of a city. And pleasure in their beauty may be enhanced by aggregations and combinations of them, as it is in arrangements of bouquets and head-dresses, the decoration of the dinner-tables, window-sills and dooryards, or, in a more complex and largely effective way, in such elaborate exhibitions of high horticultural art as the city maintains in the Public Gardens.

But there is a pleasure-bringing beauty in the same class of objects— foliage, flowers, verdure, rocks, and water—not to be enjoyed under the same circumstances or under similar combinations; a beauty which appeals to *a different class of human sensibilities*, a beauty the art of securing which is hardly more akin with the art of securing beauty on a dinner-table, a window-sill, a dooryard, or an urban garden, than the work of the sculptor is akin with the work of a painter.

Let beauty of the first kind be called here urban beauty, not because it cannot be had elsewhere than in a city, but because the distinction may thus, for the sake of argument in this particular case, be kept in mind between it and that beauty of the same things which can only be had clear of the confinement of a city, and which it is convenient therefore to refer to as the beauty of rural scenery.

Now as to this term scenery, it is to be borne in mind that we do not speak of what may be observed in the flower and foliage decorations of a dinner-table, window-sill, or dooryard, scarcely of what may be seen in even a large urban garden, as scenery. Scenery is more than an object or a series of objects; more than a spectacle, more than a scene of series of landscapes. Moreover, there may be beautiful scenery in which not a beautiful blossom or leaf or rock, bush or tree, not a gleam of water or of turf shall be visible. But there is no beautiful scenery that does not give the mind an emotional impulse different from that resulting from whatever beauty may be found in a room, courtyard, or garden, within which vision is obviously confined by walls or other surrounding artificial constructions.

It is necessary to be thus and even more particular in defining the term used to denote the paramount purpose embodied in the plan of Franklin Park, because many men, having a keen enjoyment of certain forms of beauty in vegetation, and even of things found only in the country, habitually class much as rural that is not only not rural, but is even the reverse of rural as that term is to be here used.

For example: in a region of undulating surface with a meandering stream and winding valleys, with much naturally disposed wood, there is a house with outbuildings and enclosures, roads, walks, trees, bushes, and flowering plants. If the constructions are of the natural materials of the locality and not fashioned expressly to manifest the wealth or art of the builders, if they are of the texture and the grain and the hues that such materials will naturally become if not effort to hide or disguise them is made, if the lines of the roads and walks are adapted to curves of the natural surface, and if the trees and plants are of a natural character naturally disposed, the result will be congruous with the general natural rural scenery of the locality, its rural quality being, perhaps, enhanced by these unobtrusive artificial elements. But in such a situation it oftener than otherwise occurs that customs will be followed which had their origin in a desire to obtain results that should be pleasing, not through congruity with pleasing natural rural circumstances, but through incongruity with them. Why? Simply because those designing them had been oppressed by a monotony of rural scenery, and desired to find relief from it, and because also they desired to manifest the triumph of civilized forces over nature. And on account of the general association with rural scenery of things determined by fashions originating in those desires, they are carelessly thought of as rural things, and the pleasure to be derived from them is esteemed a part of the pleasure taken in rural scenery.

It thus happens that things come to be regarded as elements of rural scenery which are simply cheap and fragmentary efforts to realize something of the pleasingness which the countryman finds in the artificialness of the city. This is why, to cite a few examples familiar to everyone, wooden houses are fashioned in forms and with decorations copied from houses of masonry, and why the wood of them is not left of its natural color, or given a tint harmonious with natural objects, but for distinction's sake smeared over with glistening white lead. This is the reason why trees are transplanted from natural to unnatural situations about houses so treated, why they are formally disposed, why forms are preferred for them to be obtained only by artificial processes, as grafting, pruning, and shearing; why shrubs are worked into fantastic shapes that cannot possibly be mistaken for natural growths; why groups are made studiously formal, why the trunks of trees are sometimes whitewashed; why rocks too heavy to be put out of sight are cleared of their natural beauty, and even sometimes also whitewashed; why flowering plants are often arranged as artificially as the stones of a mosaic pavement; why pools are furnished with clean and rigid stone margins and jets of water thrown from them; why specimens of rustic work and of rock work are displayed conspicuously that have been plainly designed to signalize, not to subordinate or soften, the artificialness of artificial conveniences.

Defining the purpose of the plan of Franklin Park to be that of placing within the easy reach of the people of the city the enjoyment of such a measure as is practicable of rural scenery, all such misunderstanding of the term as has thus been explained must be guarded against.

"The White Rose Road"
by Sarah Orne Jewett

From The Atlantic Monthly *(1889)*

Born in South Berwick, Maine, Sarah Orne Jewett (1849–1909) suffered from rheumatoid arthritis from childhood onward, experiencing an invisible pain that few noticed. She had her first story published in The Atlantic Monthly *when she was only 19 years old, and soon became a popular novelist in the region and beyond. Today, she is mostly forgotten outside of New England, other than perhaps her most famous novel,* The Country of the Pointed Firs *(1896).*

Jewett's writing delves into the complexity and potential of women's lives, and also our changing relationship with the natural world. In this nonfiction piece, she reflects on the way most people interact with nature—from the road as we pass by. As she drives along the Maine road to a farm she had visited years earlier with her father, she describes the views, near and far, but also reflects on inevitable transformation and the way nature seems to signify both sorrow and hope.

"THE WHITE ROSE ROAD"

Being a New Englander, it is natural that I should first speak about the weather. Only the middle of June, the green fields, and blue sky, and bright sun, with a touch of northern mountain wind blowing straight toward the sea, could make such a day, and that is all one can say about it.

We were driving seaward through a part of the country which has been least changed in the last thirty years—among farms which have been won from swampy lowland, and rocky, stump-buttressed hillsides: where the forests wall in the fields, and send their outposts year by year farther into the pastures. There is a year or two in the history of these pastures before they have arrived at the dignity of being called woodland, and yet are too much shaded and overgrown by young trees to give proper pasturage, when they made delightful harbors for the small wild creatures which yet remain, and for wild flowers and berries. Here you send an astonished rabbit scurrying to his burrow, and there you startle yourself with a partridge, who seems to get the best of the encounter. Sometimes you see a hen partridge and her brood of chickens crossing your path with an air of comfortable door-yard security. As you drive along the narrow, grassy road, you see many charming sights and delightful nooks on either hand, where the young trees spring out of a close-cropped turf that carpets the ground like velvet.

Toward the east and the quaint fishing village of Ogunquit, I find the most delightful woodland roads. There is little left of the large timber which once filled the region, but much young growth, and there are hundreds of acres of cleared land and pasture-ground where the forests are springing fast and covering the country once more, as if they had no idea of losing in their war with civilization and the intruding white settler. The pine woods and the Indians seem to be next of kin, and the former owners of this corner of New England are the only proper figures to paint into such landscapes. The twilight under tall pines seems to be untenanted and to lack something, at first sight, as if one opened the door of an empty house. A farmer passing through with his axe is but an intruder, and children straying home from school give one a feeling of solicitude at their unprotectedness. The pine woods are the red man's house, and it may be hazardous even yet for the gray farmhouses to stand so near the eaves of the forest. I have noticed a distrust of the deep woods, among elderly people, which was something more than a fear of losing their way. It was a feeling of defenselessness against some unrecognized but malicious influence.

Driving through the long woodland way, shaded and chilly when you are out of the sun; across the Great Works River and its pretty elm-grown intervale; across the short bridges of brown brooks; delayed now and then by the sight of ripe strawberries in sunny spots by the roadside, one comes to a higher open country, where farm joins farm, and the cleared fields lie all along the highway, while the woods are pushed back a good distance on either hand. The wooded hills, bleak here and there with granite ledges, rise beyond. The houses are beside the road, with green door-yards and large barns, almost empty now, and with wide doors standing open, as if they were already expecting the hay crop to be brought in. The tall green grass is waving in the fields as the wind goes over, and there is a fragrance of whiteweed and ripe strawberries and clover blowing through the sunshiny barns, with their lean sides and their festoons of brown, dusty cobwebs; dull, comfortable creatures they appear to imaginative eyes, waiting hungrily for their yearly meal. The eave-swallows are teasing their sleepy shapes, like the birds which flit about great beasts; gay, movable, irreverent, almost derisive, those barn swallows fly to and fro in the still, clear air.

The noise of our wheels brings fewer faces to the windows than usual, and we lose the pleasure of seeing some of our friends who are apt to be looking out, and to whom we like to say good-day. Some funeral must be taking place, or perhaps the women may have gone out into the fields. It is hoeing-time and strawberry-time, and already we have seen some of the younger women at work among the corn and potatoes. One sight will be charming to remember. On a green hillside sloping to the west, near one of the houses, a thin little girl was working away lustily with a big hoe on a patch of land perhaps fifty feet by twenty. There were all sorts of things growing there, as if a child's fancy had made the choice—straight rows of turnips and carrots and beets, a little of everything, one might say; but the only touch of color was from a long border of useful sage in full bloom of dull blue, on the upper side. I am sure this was called Katy's or Becky's piece by the elder members of the family. One can imagine how the young creature had planned it in the spring, and persuaded the men to plough and harrow it, and since then had stoutly done all the work herself, and meant to send the harvest of the piece to market, and pocket her honest gains, as they came in, for some great end. She was as thin as a grasshopper, this busy little gardener, and hardly turned to give us a glance, as we drove slowly up the hill close by. The sun will brown and dry her like a spear of grass on that hot slope, but a spark of fine spirit is in the small body, and I wish her a famous crop. I hate to say that the piece looked backward, all except the sage, and that it was a heavy bit of land for the clumsy hoe to pick at. The only puzzle is, what she proposes to do with so long a row of sage. Yet there may be a large family with a downfall of measles yet ahead, and she does not mean to be caught without sage-tea.

Along this road every one of the old farmhouses has at least one tall bush of white roses by the door—a most lovely sight, with buds and blossoms, and unvexed green leaves. I wish that I knew the history of them, and whence the first bush was brought. Perhaps from England itself, like a red rose that I know in Kittery, and the new shoots from the root were given to one neighbor after another all through the district. The bushes are slender, but they grow tall without climbing against the wall, and sway to and fro in the wind with a grace of youth and an inexpressible charm of beauty. How many lovers must have picked them on Sunday evenings, in all the bygone years, and carried them along the roads or by the pasture footpaths, hiding them clumsily under their Sunday coats if they caught sight of any one coming. Here, too, where the sea wind nips many a young life before its prime, how often the white roses have been put into paler hands, and withered there!

"Canoeing on the Connecticut"
by John Boyle O'Reilly

From Athletics and Manly Sport *(1890)*

Irish born, John Boyle O'Reilly (1844–1890) was the son of a schoolteacher and as a young man worked for a couple newspapers before enlisting in the British army. Court-martialed for Fenian activities, he eventually was imprisoned in Australia, coming to America in 1869 following his escape. By 1870 he was in Boston, a correspondent and editor of the Pilot, *an influential Irish Catholic newspaper which he continued to edit until his death. He developed a national reputation and lectured around the country, especially on political and civic matters.*

O'Reilly wrote novels, nonfiction works, and volumes of poetry. "His charm," Walt Whitman is reputed to have said, "came out of his tremendous experiences which were always appearing somehow reflected in his speech and in his dress and in his attitudes of body and mind." "Canoeing on the Connecticut" demonstrates O'Reilly's passion for the outdoors and his equally vigorous use of language that practically puts readers in the boat with him. Like many paddlers today, getting out in a canoe was a way he found relief from the pressures of work and life.

"CANOEING ON THE CONNECTICUT"

The canoe is the American boat of the past and of the future. It suits the American mind: it is light, swift, safe, graceful, easily moved; and the occupant looks in the direction he is going, instead of behind as in the stupid old tubs that have held the world up to this time.

— ⁓ —

I shall never forget that first glorious morning. For an hour before rising, I had lain awake looking out at the river, and listening to the strange country sounds around me. All over the grass and low bushes the spider's webs were stretched, glistening with dew. What a wonderful night's industry! Those webs were nearly all, or quite all, new. The little night toilers had woven them over our olive bottle, over the gun, over ourselves. The field above us was white as snow with this incomparable cloth-of-silver.

As I lay and looked at one of those webs close to my face, I saw a strange thing. A little gray-and-black spider ran up a tall grass blade, rested a moment, and then ran off, through empty air, to another blade, six inches off. I looked closer; surely he must have a fine line stretched between those points, I thought. No; the closest scrutiny could find none. I watched him; he was soon off again, straight for another point, a foot above the ground, running on clear space, and turning down and hanging to it, like a monkey, but still going ahead. I called Guiteras, and he came and saw and examined, and smiled in his wise way when he doesn't know. We could not see the little fellow's cable, or railway, or bridge. He was as much finer than we as we are finer than mastodons.

And the birds, in that first rich morning speech of theirs, full of soft, bubbling joy, not singing, but softly and almost silently overflowing. Two little fellows flew rapidly down to a twig near us, and began bubble-bubbling as if in a great flutter and hurry; and immediately they flew far and high, as for a long journey; at which my philosophic friend moralized:

"Those little fellows are like some canoeists who wake up, and don't wait for breakfast; but bubble-bubble, hurry-hurry, get-afloat, we-have-a-long-way-to-go! Now, *we* don't do that."

— ⁓ —

From Hartford to Middletown is one of the finest stretches of the Connecticut, and it is by no means as low-banked or monotonous. One of the peculiarities of the river is that it is almost as wide and apparently as deep at Hanover as in this latest reach.

It is not necessary to go a great distance up the Connecticut to find splendid canoeing water. If one had only a week's time, and entered the river at Brattleboro, or below Turner's Falls, he would find enough beauty to remember for a lifetime.

The distances on the river appear to be quite unknown to residents on the banks, who evidently judge by road measurement. We found, in most cases, that the river distance was at least a third to a half longer than the road.

One of our rarest pleasures came from paddling for a few miles up the smaller rivers that run into the Connecticut. They are invariably beautiful, and the smaller ones are indescribable as fairyland.

One stream, particularly (I think it is a short distance below White River Junction, on the New Hampshire side), called Bromidon, was, in all respects, an ideal brook. It had the merriest voice; the brownest and most sun-flecked shallows; the darkest little nooks of deep, leafy pools; the most happy-looking, creeper-covered homesteads on its banks. We could hardly paddle into it, it was so shallow; or out of it, it was so beautiful. Guiteras wanted to write a poem about it. "The name is a poem in itself," he said; "anyone could write a poem about such a stream." All the way down the river his muttered "Bromidon!" was like the self-satisfied bubble-bubble of the morning birds.

This leads me to say that, in the rapid growth of canoeing, which is surely coming, it is to be hoped that the paddle will be the legitimate means of propulsion, and not the sail. If men want to sail, let them get keel boats and open water. The canoe was meant for lesser surfaces. Indeed, the smaller the river, the more enjoyable the canoeing. A few feet of surface is wide enough. With the quiet paddle, one can steal under the overhanging boughs, drift silently into the deep morning and afternoon shadows;

study the ever-changing banks, birds, even the splendid dragonflies and butterflies among the reeds and rushes.

Since this trip on the Connecticut, we have canoed many other rivers, some of them streams of much greater volume. We had in these the width of water, the calm greatness of the flow, and the splendid reaches unbroken by falls and rapids and dams; but we often missed the overhanging branches, the flash and twitter among the leaves, the shadows that made the river look deep as the sky, and the murmur of the little brown brooks that are lost in the great stream, leaving only their names, like Bromidon, clinging to the water like naiads.

"The Sea in a Snowstorm"
by Frank Bolles

From Land of the Lingering Snow: Chronicles of a Stroller in New England from January to June *(1891)*

A native of rural Winchester, Massachusetts, Frank Bolles (1856–1894) developed a deep appreciation of nature in his early years. His father was a lawyer and former secretary of the Commonwealth of Massachusetts who moved the family to Baltimore and then Washington, D.C., when he became U.S. Navy solicitor. Bolles studied law at Columbian College in Washington and at Harvard, where he founded the Daily Echo, *one of the first college dailies.*

Between 1883 and 1886 Bolles was an editorial writer for the Boston Advertiser, *the city's first daily newspaper. After leaving the* Advertiser *he became private secretary to Harvard president Charles Eliot, and later that year secretary of the university, a post he held until his death. He joined the Nuttall Ornithological Club (the nation's oldest organization devoted to birds) in 1887 and served as its secretary.*

Bolles wrote several nature-oriented volumes, with some emphasis on his beloved Sandwich Range in New Hampshire. Among his books are At the North of Bearcamp Water *(1893),* From Blomidon to Smoky and Other Papers *(1894), and* Chocorua's Tenants *(1895). The 247-acre Frank Bolles Nature Preserve at the foot of Mount Chocorua was established by his daughter in 1969. This excerpt from* Land of the Lingering Snow *demonstrates that Bolles could find nature's power and beauty in an urban environment, and beyond.*

"The Sea in a Snowstorm"

Sunday, February 8, showed winter in his true colors again. The day was, as regards snow-laden trees and drifted roads, a duplicate of the last Sunday in January. Instead of enjoying the snow pictures in the woods and pastures of Arlington, I traversed Crab Alley, Bread and Milk Streets, and that meandering marvel of old Boston, Batterymarch Street, and gained the harbor front at Rowe's Wharf. Some of these snow-covered haunts of trade are as free from footprints as the *savin* swamps of Arlington. In Crab Alley I came to tracks in the snow which made me wonder whether some of the quail from the Parker House toast had not escaped alive. Dainty little steps crossed and re-crossed the narrow lane, and formed a dense network of converging paths at the back door of a small chophouse. As I approached, two tame doves flew noisily from behind the barrel which graced the doorstep, and several English sparrows swung from a telephone wire overhead.

I looked up into the iron caps of the electric light lamps to see whether the sparrows had built in them. They had. In Boston and several adjoining cities the major part of these iron witch-caps contain sparrows' nests. Even the lamps which are suspended over the streets and drawn in daily by the linemen are not disdained by the birds.

From the deck of the Janus-natured ferryboat, which was pausing for the time between trips to the Revere Beach cars, I looked out upon a chilly sky and sea. The waters were restless, the wind fierce and cold, the snowflakes stinging. At anchor lay a large steamer, black and thin. The odd gearing at her stern showed that she was an ocean cable steamer. Beyond her was a four-masted schooner. I wondered what her sailors called her fourth mast. Suddenly my wandering eyes were fixed in astonishment upon a jaunty form floating on the water within less than fifty feet of the ferryboat. It had emerged from the cold and tossing waters with a bounce, shaken itself, and begun a bobbing career in the daylight and snowflakes. Pop! Down went its head, up went its tail and feet and it was gone again. During fifteen minutes it bobbed up six times in the same spot, staying afloat each time from fifteen to thirty seconds, and below about two minutes. It was black above, snowy white below, and formed in the likeness of a duck. It was a whistler, a duck common in the harbor and along our coast in winter. While diving, it was probably breakfasting upon small shell-fish found on the bottom.

On the way across to East Boston I saw seven or eight more whistlers and over fifty herring-gulls, many of them in the dark plumage peculiar to the immature birds. Twenty minutes later I stood on the narrow strip of sand left between the poplar walk in front of the Point of Pines Hotel and the angry ocean. The wind was northeast, and blowing a gale. The tide had turned half an hour before, but it was still unusually high. Behind me the Saugus marshes were wholly submerged. A few haystacks alone broke the monotony of gray water, foam and scudding snow. To the north ought to have been seen distant Lynn, but the eye was met only by stinging snow-flakes and cold wind. My train, before it had gone an eighth of a mile, had been swallowed up in steam and hurrying masses of snow. Where was Nahant? There was not a trace of it. The hungry waves broke ten ranks deep upon the flat sands across which they roared; but beyond them was no land, only the fury of gray and white hanging above a hissing, greenish gray and white below. The sand was brown, not a warm brown, but a cold, shining, grayish brown with no kindness in it.

There was nothing in the whole world which my eye could reach to suggest warmth or happiness. True, there were the empty buildings with padlocked doors among the snow-covered trees, but they were more desolate and soul-chilling than anything in nature. I walked among them until wearied by the mockery of their signs and broken paraphernalia. Hideous kiosks, whose blue and yellow paint was partly covered by the white pity of the storm, told in glaring letters of "Ice Water," "Red Hot Pop Corn," "Sunshades and Fans," and "Clam Chowder." The wind shrieked through their cracks and pelted wet snow against their windows. In the amphitheater where spectacular plays are given on summer evenings the tide dabbled with the rusty wheels of a sheet-iron car marked "Apache." Beyond it, canvas mountains and canons were swaying and creaking in the storm, their ragged edges humming in the wind. A sign offered "Seats for 50 cents, children 25." The seats were softly cushioned by six inches of snow, but the idle summer crowd had been blown away by the winter's breath. Only a flock of a dozen crows lent life to the arena.

A train emerged from the storm. I could see its dark outlines; its torn column of steam; the swift motion of its many wheels, then it was gone, engulfed in the dizzy vibration of the snow, its voice unheard amid the greater voices of the sky and sea. The tide was going down as I started towards home on the hard, shining sand of Crescent Beach. I think at least two hundred herring-gulls passed by me, flying slowly against the gale and keeping over the water, but parallel to the beach and about a hundred yards from it. They were silent. Their strong wings beat against the storm. Now and then one plunged into the foam of a breaking wave, or glided for a second along the trough of the sea. They did not seem like true birds, beings of the same race as hummingbirds, sweet-voiced thrushes, or keen-witted chickadees. They were rather creations of the salt waves and ocean tempests; cold-blooded, scaly things, incapable of those loves and fears, songs and quaint nesting ways of the birds of field and forest. Near Oak Island a flock of four snow buntings, which had been feeding among the bunches of seaweed, rose at my approach and flew toward and past me up the beach. They are among the most beautiful of our winter visitors, their white and brown plumage being a sight always welcome to the eyes of those who love the birds. At intervals flocks of English sparrows rose from the seaweed and shunned me. There seems to be no form of vegetable food-supply upon which our native birds depend, that this ravenous, non-migratory pest does not devour. From Point of Pines to Crescent Beach station the thunder of the breakers and the rush of the wind and snow were ceaseless. The storm hurried me along in its strong embrace and drove its chill through me. The tide had left the marshes, and the snow had claimed them. As the waves retreated from the beach the snow stuck to the gleaming pebbles, the snaky bits of kelp and the purple shells. Where two hours before, at high tide, the waves had dashed foam fifty feet into the air, now the breakwaters and the heaps of shingle and seaweed were covered with white from the drippings of the great roof of sky.

The whistlers were still in the harbor at three o'clock, but most of the gulls had gone. Snow clung to decks, masts, yards, furled sails and rigging. It whitened the water-front of the city, purified the docks, and made even Crab Alley seem picturesque as I ploughed through it homeward bound.

"Night Witchery"
by William Hamilton Gibson

From Strolls by Starlight and Sunshine *(1891)*

*Born in Sandy Hook, Connecticut, William Hamilton Gibson (1850–1896)
worked in life insurance, but as a hobby began an amateur study of natural
history, as so many did in the nineteenth century. He had always loved nature,
drawing mushrooms and flowers as a child, and eventually found work as an
illustrator, photographer, and wood engraver for publications like the* American Agriculturalist *and* Harper's Monthly.

*Gibson's illustrations and photographs led to lectures and eventually his
own books on natural history. This piece from* Strolls by Starlight and Sunshine *demonstrates a lush Romantic sensibility, but also the attention to detail
that served him well in his other arts. For some, nighttime is not the best time to
enjoy nature, but as Gibson illustrates so clearly, this is a regrettable oversight.*

"Night Witchery"

How are the senses piqued and sharpened in the total darkness of the
woods! For though the path of the midnight rambler, surprised beneath
the lantern's glare, reveals an unknown world among the freaks of dewy
vegetation—the nodding somnolence of leaf and blossom, the twinkling
earth-stars bursting into bloom beneath the brooding galaxy for soft-
winged nestling moths and poising murmurers—nevertheless, with all its
strange surprises, for a full appreciation of the night's true witchery one

must become a sympathetic element of its mysteries, and see the darkness unalloyed. With the light extinguished you now become a harmonious instead of a disturbing element.

In the total darkness the eager pupils are restless, and the eyes roll in "fine frenzy" at the new importance of their companion faculties. Their occupation is gone. The ear and the nostril now take the watch, seeming possessed of a retina of their own, picturing facts and surrounding events which the jealous eye strives in vain to prove. In the dark woods you are conscious as never before of tension and muscular movement in your ears; they loom up in importance, as it were, and are pricked forward and backward like those of other alert but humbler beings.

Unaided by the sight, they carry on a subtle analysis of sound which seems independent of your reason—a slight augmented rustle among the wind-stirred leaves! the creaking of a limb! the soft burst of applause among the aspen leaves! a capricious patter of falling dew from the tree-tops, a snap of twig not precisely timed to your footfall, or a few inches too far removed therefrom; a falling object from the tree—an acorn, perhaps, were it not that for an inanimate thing it has rolled a foot too far upon the leaves! What events!

And so with your nose: you see with it. Now, if never before, it warrants its conspicuous position in your physiognomy, and becomes a member of utility as well as a luxurious ornament. In these midnight woods you follow your nose like a hound. It pilots the senses. Could this eclipsed eye ever have pictured more vividly the pungent copse of spice-wood through which you have just pressed, or that drooping branch of aromatic hickory which touched your shoulder, or that plume of tansy that now brushes against your elbow? Does our midnight poet affirm, "I cannot see what flowers are at my feet?" And why not, pray? This mint at your foot—is it spearmint, or peppermint, or horsemint, or pennyroyal? Your nose will tell you at a glance. The texture of the vaporous vault of the still midnight woods seems to the hungry, desperate eye marbled or party-colored with floating incense of odors.

You may sit in the ambrosial current upon some jutting rock or log, and take your fragrant quaffs as they glide by, each in its season—a whiff of arbutus, perhaps? how pink it smells! or an odorous yellow hint of primrose soft and luscious—in the dark it seems to the nostril what melting marsh-mallow confection is to the tongue—or a spicy glimpse of colt'sfoot or wild-ginger. And so, the redolent procession passes, now a visible aroma of sweet-fern, followed by a perfumed vision of sweet-pyrolas, ground-nut, or smilacena, or a cool, phosphorescent scent of toadstool or soggy wood, or the brown smell of mouldy loam. A misty messenger from the swamp without the woods now finds its way thither, borne on the pink breath of sweet azalea or visioned in the fragrant hint of clethra. And now it is the sweet-fern again.

Yes, sweet-fern tinctured with a faint gamy scent that plays Tantalus to our taunted vision as we search the gloom for two beads of animated fox-fire, for Reynard has recently passed this way, or is even now threading through the fragrant underwood. And what is this—for let us be true to the integrity of these nocturnal zephyrs—this faint piquant suspicion which now sophisticates the wild bouquet, this pronounced acrimony—how the impetuous eyes now begin to roll!—this overwhelming, painful effluvium which now sweeps the wilds in annihilating conquest? How graphic! more real than life—caustic, saturating, mordant! Mephitis, I could trace thy shaggy portrait to a hair from that pictorial smell!

It is part of the poet's creed that all the sights and sounds of nature are, or ought to be, beautiful in their environment. Even the perfume of many a favorite blossom of the woods becomes unpleasantly oppressive indoors. "The saunterer's apple not even the saunterer can eat in the house." The distant midnight baying of a hound is to many a night rambler a pleasant sound, though few perhaps have yet learned to "bathe their being" therein as Thoreau did—a feat which would seem more logical in relation to the skunk's accompaniment, many a midnight traveler having waded through the acrid, saturated mist in its evil premonition or trail.

It is true, however, that when only faintly perceived, the odor of Hosea Bigelow's "essence peddler" is not unpleasant. Nay, nay, my dainty damosel! turn not aside thy fastidious nostril, nor raise the spurning palm. How many times on a blustering winter's day hast thou nursed the rosy tip of that same delicate nose in the warm "Alaska sable" muff and found a pleasant pungency therein! Thus, in highly diluted doses, the odor of the "Alaska sable" is a not unpleasant occasional ingredient in the nocturnal nosegay. It is a sort of spice which brings alert variety in our midnight stroll.

The odor of the fox is readily detected by a keen nostril, especially at night. The noisomeness of the warren is distinctly perceptible where unperceived by day, and the taint is carried abroad in the ambling fur, the contaminated wake held in equilibrium, as it were, in the heavy mist. Even the tiny emerald lace-wing fly or the caddis-moth will sometimes thus leave its malodorous trail threading the maze of redolence in the mist; and the bronzy scented beetle will challenge your nostril as you loiter in the dark woods, perhaps within the course of its recent droning flight or in the neighborhood of its haunt upon oozy tree-trunk nearby. Often have I trailed him like a hound, and captured him in his concealment in the fissured bark.

The bibulous convivialist welcomes a certain ambrosial nectar which mortals call a *pousse cafe*, but which is said to be of the gods, wherein the several tempting ingredients are so deftly decanted as to lie unblended in their fragrant equipoise for a full minute; how much longer, it has possibly never been permitted to reveal. Something of the same phenomenon is naturally demonstrated in the scented distillations of the dew. In the sheltered lowlands, when the night is still, the motley ingredients of this odorous tangle seem to find their equilibrium, and lie in strata, as it were. How the redolence of the witch-hazel revels in the mist, weaving itself into the pale fabric as it floats above the marsh! It is the most volatile incense which we shall meet in the moonlight glens, and seems to float like oil upon the denser air, laden with the heavy emanations of the swamp. You may walk with your nostrils tingling in its tide, and leave it high and dry as you sit to rest. I have noted the same fact with regard to the evening primrose, but fancy the perfume is less volatile than the Hamamaelis, and occupies a lower plane. Here are veritable zones of varying humidity and temperature, each with its haunting fragrance, often capricious, and yet again quite constant in its recurrence. In a certain well-known glen, for instance, you will always pass through a fugitive stratum of meadow-rue or linden, or other faithful perfume for each season; in another swampy fallow you may confidently expect the welcome of the elders or wild grape.

I remember a certain nook which in still August nights is redolent of clethra, that constant blossom of the swamp, though no shrubs are there to be seen by day: a tribute from the marshy pond far up the mist-hung brook, where the reedy borders are fringed with the densely blooming shrub, where the almond-scented fog floods the sedgy waters, and the herons wade among the grasses, half-veiled in the tinctured tide. Here, too, the floating pond-weed claims its lowly plain below the mist, anointing the lily-pads in its aromatic perfume as its yellow blossom-clusters dance upon the ripples.

In another narrow glen the heavy distillation from the sloping chestnut woods always seems to pour, with annihilation of all subtle midnight odors. On the pasture slope above the wood the cool, stimulating exhalations of the mint follow your path, and linger till morn in the foggy hollows, while high up on the hill one seems suddenly to leave the dews and greet a whiff which brings a vision of the day—that "stratum of warm air" which quickened the happy muse of Thoreau in his "Moonlight Walk"— "a blast which has come up from the sultry plains of noon. It tells of the clay, of sunny noontide hours and banks, of the laborer wiping his brow, and the bee humming amid flowers. It is an air in which work has been done—which men have breathed. It circulates about from wood-side to hill-side like a dog that has lost its master, now that the sun is gone."

"Clearwater and Woods Hospitality"
by Fannie Hardy Eckstorm

From Forest and Stream *(1891)*

A folklorist, ornithologist, historian, and authority on Penobscot Indians, Fannie Hardy Eckstorm (1865–1946) was born and grew up in Brewer, Maine, where her father, Manly Hardy, was the state's foremost fur trader and an authority on the state's backwoods. She frequently accompanied her father on fur trading and other trips into the region's wilderness, learning woodcraft, natural history, and Indian languages and customs. She was an 1888 graduate of Smith College. As superintendent of schools in Brewer from 1889 to 1891, she was among the first women in her native state to serve in that capacity.

At her father's urging, she authored two series of articles for Forest and Stream *magazine which, while evocative of Maine woods adventure, also called for reform of fish and game laws that favored out-of-state sport hunters over natives who hunted for subsistence.*

Through firsthand knowledge and scrupulous scholarship, Eckstorm established herself as a leading authority on traditional life in the Maine woods and Penobscot Indians. This 1891 excerpt from Forest and Stream *demonstrates her love of the woods, precision of description, and ability to quickly put a reader out among the waters and trees.*

"Clearwater and Woods Hospitality"

The peculiar feature of Pistol Green is the soft green sward and white clover which cover it. Grass is a rarity in the woods; the weeds come early, almost before the lumberman, but only the lapse of many years and the frequent presence of man will make these civilized grasses grow in the wilderness. Pistol Green from time immemorial has been a favorite ground for camping, and this is attested by its deserving the name of Green, which, in our State, is very uncommon. Another sign was a part of the thigh bone of some large animal, which we dug up from several inches beneath our camp floor. Moose, ox, horse?—We asked which it was, and all judged it to be moose; for it had been cracked Indian-fashion to obtain the marrow. It is a long time since there were any moose in this region, except as infrequent stragglers.

From the Green several paths diverge; most are drivers' paths used only in the spring; the central one is the carry to Pistol Lake—two miles if we go all the way by land, but on high water like that of this year, it is not necessary to carry beyond the head of the roughest water. I asked why Pistol Stream got its name, and was told that it was because "it went just as if it had been shot out of a little gun." An entire stranger would know it at once from this description. It is what woodsman call "smart water" with a good strong "spring" in it. (Has it never impressed any one unused to our Maine woods and ways that we have a very peculiar feeling toward running water, calling it "good," "bad," "mean," "wicked looking" and so forth with a seriousness which so far exceeds any figurative or rhetorical intention that it seems to impute personality and moral responsibility to the element? There is something Greek in this: so came the gods about.)

Abol has richer colors, more of the crystalline iridescence of the iceberg, as if it held an imprisoned rainbow, more of the translucent emeraldine tints of cold caverns brought with it from its birth out of the side of old Katahdin, more absolute purity; but Abol is not navigable. And Millinocket has the spring and the impetuosity, but without the same pellucidness. The charm of Pistol is that it is itself. We poled up it in the clear, cool air of the morning, as much delighted as if it were a fresh creation made for us alone. The stream came down like a highway through the trees, ferns on the shores, waving half-vines, which we call "buck bean," in the water, and the tall stalks of the cardinal flowers, now brown with ripeness that erewhile had lighted up the banks with their flames; clean gravel in the shallows where the water was clearest, a rock-ribbed channel where it flowed faster. Great granite boulders lay along the stream, worn concavely to the height of several feet by logs and spring freshets, and rocks in the bed of the stream made it give continual little hops and leaps to get over or around them as it ran from one side to the other along its devious course, like a Naiad pursued by the great god Pan.

The first Pistol is a beautiful, rounded lake, apparently about two miles long, with high wooded shores, partly pineland and partly hardwood, rising highest on the side toward Nicatowis. The edges, especially near the outlet, are set with great granites both above and beneath the water, which in a heavy sea would make canoeing difficult.

The carry to Side Lake, which is one of the Pistols, was partly bog, though most of the way good walking through tall growth, hemlock partly, I should say, with a vague remembrance of feathery saplings; but some of the undergrowth was beech. Near the end the carry divides, one part going to the Third Pistol and the new right-handed branch to Side Lake. With the sun in the quarter where it now was, Side Lake was softer in its color than the glowing gem of the morning, but even dearer in its transparency. It was absolutely calm, and looking down we could see the bottom for a long distance from the shore. A canoe and paddles lay near by but we would not ruffle its tranquility. To me such clear, still water suggests solidity more strongly than anything else, so that the comparison to glass or marble seems not only highly expressive, but the only allusion properly explanatory. It is not the surface of the water alone, Milton's "clear hyaline, the glassy sea," but its depth and body, so to speak, which, in proportion to the transparency of the water, gives it more and more this appearance of being a solid block of glass, an underworld in which the fish are imprisoned. Our clearest ice looks scarcely more impenetrable than such pure still water to which may be given the fine Horatian phrase, *splendidior vitro*, not of surface only but of depth. We tarried awhile, watching the little fishes, and tossing in bits of moss and dry twigs to see them rise and draw under the coveted but disappointing morsels. We wished we had something better to give them; but finding that they learned nothing from experience, gradually withdrew our repentance and kept up our sport. They were beautiful, both chub and breams, though the latter had put off their brilliant summer garb of green and copper color and scarlet, and were now but shadows of their former splendor, recognizable only by the black spots on their gill covers and their pretty motion. A fish out of water is a coarse, clumsy, limbless creature; in its element it is sylph-like.

"Fishing for Trout"
by William Cowper Prime

From Along New England Roads *(1892)*

Born in Cambridge, New York, William Cowper Prime (1825–1905) practiced law in New York City and married Mary Trumbull of Stonington, Connecticut. After a trip to Europe and the Middle East in 1855, he published two books on his experiences. They were parodied for their sentimentality by Mark Twain a few years later in The Innocents Abroad. *He continued to write, edit, and practice law, and was elected the first chair of the art history department at Princeton University.*

Though he lived mostly in New York, he owned a large tract of alpine land in New Hampshire's Franconia Notch, including Lonesome Lake. He and co-owner William Frederick Bridge built hunting cabins there, and Prime often fished in the lake. His later books include I Go A-Fishing *(1873) and* Along New England Roads *(1892), from which the following piece on trout-fishing is taken.*

"FISHING FOR TROUT"

My raft was not a very heavy one, and the rule is to use your pole without deep pushing on such ponds, rather dragging, with the end only a little way in the mud.

I had followed the edge of the old bed of the brook, and with patience and perseverance came within a hundred feet of the place where the last trout had risen. There was no perceptible motion in the air, but there was a motion, nevertheless, such as anglers are familiar with, indicated by the fact that your cast goes out more easily with than against it. My rod was good for long casting, and I could lay the white moth-tail fly down within a few feet of the spot I desired to reach. I laid it down there a dozen times, and nothing else disturbed the surface, which now reflected a rosy cloud in the south-west. The sun had gone down. The original impetus given the raft and the existing movement of the atmosphere were carrying me slowly towards the mouth of the brook, which came out, a rod wide, between high banks covered with dense sedges. Up in the stream I saw three or four times the lift of a trout's head as he rose gently to the surface and took in some floating insect. He was feeding, August fashion, on some very small gnat, too small for imitation. So I tried approximation, changing the tail-fly, and for the white moth substituting a minute black object, the smallest lure known to my book, or any one's book, being a tiny hook, smaller than any regular number, tied with a yellow body and a delicate sparse black hackle, not an eighth of an inch long. I had drifted to the very mouth of the brook by the time this was ready, and the first cast sent it far up the canal-like stream. As it struck the water there was a magnificent roll of the glassy surface, a flash of reflected blue and crimson and pink and white in the water. It was as if some gorgeous piece of fireworks had burst on the dark surface between the sedge banks.

How many pounds of trout flesh and force were now on the end of that gossamer leader I shall never be able to tell you, for when he felt the slight stroke which fixed the tiny hook in his mouth, he made one swift, short rush, and I found that the leader was fastened on something heavier than a trout. There was nothing to do but break it loose or pole up the stream and try to unfasten it. I broke it, for I wanted another cast over that water. Half of the leader came home, with one fly yet on. I looped the end, put on another of the same small black hackles, cast three times; at the third cast again saw the brilliant explosion of the water-surface, again struck a heavy fish, and was again fast to something immovable.

This time I poled up to the spot. I might have hooked a hundred fish there and should never have gotten one. For my tail-fly had fallen each time just about ten feet beyond a great tree-trunk—a smooth, round log, two feet thick—of which the two ends were embedded in the banks on either side, while the log itself stretched across the stream about six inches below the surface. Under it the water was ten feet deep, and the fish had risen from this hole and plunged back into it, patching the upper flies in the log.

Twilight was established by the time I had put on the small white moth which I proposed to use for the last few casts. You will observe that my raft would not go over the log, and I could go no farther up-stream. So, I sent the flies up again and again and again, while the night gathered rapidly. Our twilights grow short up here in August. The air was ringing with the voices of frogs, with indescribable variety of tone and annuncia-tion. The sharp cry of a night-bird in the air overhead pierced my ears. I saw a great Cecropia moth crossing the stream just beyond my cast, and a dozen smaller moths flitting over the sedges. Suddenly, behind me, a trout rose in the old place. I fixed the pole against the log, pushed the raft back, and dropped the tail-fly in the centre of the circle of waves. This time I struck my fish firmly, and he went for open water; it was an easy matter to bring him in; he was only a two-pounder. A two-pound trout is a small affair to the angler who has lost a four-pounder. And those two fish I lost were, of course, four-pounders—five-pounders; who can prove to me that they were not?

Whatever their weight, I was fully as content as if they were in my basket, which hung on my shoulder, or on the dry end of my raft if they were too large for the basket. I see your smile of in-credulity, my friend; but you are one of the miserably uneducated community who will never appreciate the fact that the joy of the angler's day is in the surroundings of his sport. The very regrets he may have for lost fish are pleasant, not pain-ful, if the day has been bountiful in the ordinary delights which attend the fisherman. My day had been exceedingly rich. As the horses came up the dark mountain road, guiding their own steps since I could not see to guide them, I recalled a score of beautiful scenes along the course of the mountain torrent, great boulders lying in the foam, fern-covered cliffs, under which the river ran swift and smooth, giant white birch-trees on the bank, the outposts of armies of mighty trees behind them, rank on rank as far as eye could penetrate their array. And the dark lagoon-like stream, on which the twilight came down till the stars were reflected in it; the swoop of the nighthawks overhead; the call of the whippoorwill sitting on the saw-mill roof and the answer of his kin on the hill-side beyond—where can one close the catalogue of sights and sounds and thoughts, which made the hour's delay at the mill-pond a charming episode at the close of an angler's August day?

"Trees and Their Leaves"
by Caroline Alathea Stickney Creevey

From Recreations in Botany *(1893)*

Raised in Rockville, Connecticut, where her father owned paper mills and a store, Caroline Alathea Stickney Creevey (1843–1920) developed a love of nature from an early age and wandered freely in the woods and fields around her home. She recalled a pine grove near Snipsic (Shenipsit) Lake where she would walk, sit, lie down, and read in "my Eden." She spent one of her high school years in Bangor, Maine, and later graduated from Wheaton Seminary (now Wheaton College). After working at a school in New Britain, Connecticut, she later moved to Brooklyn with her husband, but never forgot the natural beauty of her New England home.

Among Creevey's books are Flowers of Hill, Field and Swamp *(1897),* Harpers' Guide to Wild Flowers *(1912), and* At Random *(1920), a series of essays on nature, literary, and other topics. This discussion of trees and their leaves from* Recreations in Botany *(1893) reveals her skill as an evocative recorder of natural phenomena, her interest in a scientific approach, and an ongoing passion for teaching children.*

"TREES AND THEIR LEAVES"

They who live in the perpetual green of the tropics, where the leaves decay and are replaced imperceptibly by a constant renewal of the plant's activities, miss our two most delightful seasons—the budding spring with its pale green and bronze tints, and the autumn with its gorgeous reds and yellows. Beautiful as is the summer, we would not choose it all the year round. In the resting-time of nature, town and city life attract us, and our social instincts are most alive. But when the first breath of spring is felt, and a faint shimmer of green spreads over the shrubs and trees of the parks, then the country and its miracles of new growth irresistibly attract us. An unrest pervades our city homes, and we desire nothing so much as to close the shutters and leave the homes, seeking for a grove where we may swing our hammocks, where the birds and flowers and lightly moving branches may afford us companionship and entertainment.

Have we ever thought how much of the pleasure of country life is due to the trees and their leaves? Not only because they fan and shade us, but because they are beautiful with an endless variety of shape and size, they gratify our aesthetic fancies. In a single short walk one will see the oak leaves, stiff and hard; the hornbeam, deeply furrowed; the aspen, small and delicate, hung upon a stem flattened contrary to their own planes, and therefore shaking as if with palsy; the spreading horse-chestnut; the dark green, handsomely cut maple and poplar—all combined into heavy or light masses of waving green.

It goes almost without saying that we ought to know the names of our most common trees, and the general functions and purposes of leaves. If a good botany and microscope go into our trunk as part of the summer's outfit, we shall need no other teacher than our own observation.

Certain queries about leaves will naturally arise the moment we pluck and look at them with reference to exploring their secrets. What are they? Why are they necessary to the tree's life? What are their special functions? Why is the upper side a darker green than the lower? Why, if covered with dust, will they die? Why does drouth or lack of sunlight turn them yellow? Why do they fall in autumn? To answer, we must peep into the wonder-chambers of nature. They are hidden and small, but the microscope, the great revealer, will disclose movements, chemical transformations, wonderful adaptations of means to ends, that we have never dreamed of.

Every child may know the common facts about the exterior of a leaf. The terms used in describing its shape and outline are not arbitrary, but those which are naturally suggested.

Let the children make a leaf autograph book. Nothing can better combine pleasure with profit. Under a pressed leaf fastened upon a page may be written a complete description of the leaf, height of tree or shrub, color and smoothness of bark, where found, and when. A parallel-veined leaf indicates that the plant is endogenous, like the lily, corn, grasses, and plantains. A netted-veined leaf, according to the shape, is either feather-veined, where the veins all spring from the mid-rib, or palmately veined, where they spring from a common point, and radiate like the spread fingers of the hand.

In general outline they are narrow and long, varying to round. The terms linear, lance-shaped, oblong, elliptical, ovate, orbicular, mean in botany just what they do as plain English adjectives. When the base narrows, put the syllable "ob" before the term, signifying inverse; as oblanceolate, obovate. If the base has projecting lobes or ears, call it heart, arrow, halberd, or shield shaped. The apex is tapering, acute, blunt, truncate (as in the tulip-tree), etc. The edges are entire, serrate (like teeth of a saw), dentate (toothed), crenate (scalloped), wavy, smooth. When lobed, write how deeply, as lobed, parted, cleft, or divided. Leaflets are little leaves when the division extend to the petiole. Suppose the leaf of a sugar-maple be chosen to describe. The descriptions would run somewhat as follows: Arrangement on stem—opposite. Petiole—rather long. Stipules—none. Lobed—palmately. Divisions—3-5. Veins—netted, palmately. Outline—serrate. Base—truncate. Size of tree—large.

Let the description continue: "We held a picnic under this tree;" or, "I saw a squirrel or a bird's-nest on this tree."

Nothing will cultivate the faculty of observation in children like the leaf album, and useful knowledge is in such ways pleasantly acquired.

"A Song of Summer"
by Mabel Osgood Wright

From The Friendship of Nature *(1894)*

Born in New York, Mabel Osgood (1859–1934) moved to Fairfield, Connecticut, after marrying James Wright, beginning a career as an environmental steward, founding the Connecticut Audubon Society, and serving as its first president. She then became the director of what became the National Audubon Society for twenty-three years, pioneering avian protection by establishing the oldest private songbird sanctuary in America in 1914. Her nature writing began appearing as early as 1889, and she wrote some of the first field guides for birds, with color reproductions from John James Audubon.

The following piece, "A Song of Summer," appeared in Wright's first collection, The Friendship of Nature: A New England Chronicle of Birds and Flowers. *It demonstrates the flowery prose of turn-of-the-century nature writing, giving a lovely description of the season. Even though she argued for the protection of birds her entire life, she knew well that such arguments must be made with emotions as well as logic. Our sympathetic attitudes about birds today are a direct result of the work she and others did to melt our hearts.*

"A SONG OF SUMMER"

The south wind sweeps over the mignonette, passing through the hedged sweet peas into the wood gap. The reeds on the brink of the river tremble and the pendulous red-gold meadow lilies ring the midsummer in with their clamouring bronze tongues. It is not the sun-god's day of the Julian calendar, the summer solstice; not the festival of St. John the Baptist, when old English custom trimmed the doors with St. Johnswort and green branches, when a wheel bound with straw was taken to some neighbouring hill and set on fire and then rolled down to bear away harm and mark the sun's descent; but middle July, the New England midsummer, the half-way stile between the first cautious growth of June and September's ripening.

A haze drops between the sky and the earth, laden with oppressive heat; the deeply shadowed porch is airless, and under it the two dogs lie panting and exhausted. Ben-Uncas, a St. Bernard, who loves cold and snow, dreams of the river, and Colin, a veteran setter, thinks of the fern copse where the rabbits hide.

We two stand together out in the full sunshine, with the summer surrounding us, pulsing in the hot earth under our feet, and with summer in the heart. Spring is a restless season, the time of mating, planting, hoping. The sap flows into dry branches and the river leaps along madly, but summer, with its poppy-fringed cloak, brings the peace of fulfilment.

Standing in the sunlight, we listen and hesitate; the wind whispers as it passes and brings alluring messages. The trees call us to come to their shade and learn the birds' secrets, to rest on their moss-cushioned trunks, and listen to the music of the brook as it makes harp-strings of their pushing roots and sings the Song of Summer. So, persuaded, we go out through the midsummer ways, and the dogs reconnoitre before us as scouts.

On the hillside they are cradling rye. The long awned heads sway on the glistening stalks, the breeze ripples this golden sea, and billowing it, a wave of music passes across, as if Pan was blowing softly through his oaten pipe a gentle prelude to the jovial harvest dance. Behind the cradle lies the prostrate rye, screening the sharp stubble, and here and there the pink-purple corn-cockle blends its flowers with the gold. In the neighbouring trees and bushes the birds lurk, waiting for the noontime silence, that they may gather up the gleanings.

Back of the rye field, a round knoll is topped by blooming chestnut trees. All the light and fragrance of the day is meshed by their feathery stamened spikes, and sifting through the mass of restless leaves, it refracts and breaks in countless tints. Romping all down the hill like jolly Indian babes, are troops of black-eyed-Susans, gay in warm yellow gowns. Perched on the road bank, nod blue campanulas, one of a tribe of half-wild things that escaped from gardens to beautify the roads and fields; only they strayed away so many years ago, that they seem completely merged in their surroundings and quite to the manor born.

An herby odour rises from the path, and in a space of less than twenty steps, sweet mint, catnip, wild thyme, yarrow, camomile, and tansy yield a bunch of simples, such as once hung on the rafters of every country garret, ready to be brewed in teas for various aches and pains. History, even in science, still repeats itself, and the peppermint, steeped into the tea that Lydia Languish might have sipped for the vapours, is now distilled and ministers to the nerves under the name of menthol, and the leaves of winter-green, that gran'ther chewed for his rheumatics, still pursue the same complaint, wearing its Latin name, Gaultheria. But do not let us talk of ills and medicines in mellowing summer-time, when the sunshine draws stagnation from the blood and clears its channels. Today let the world slip, and let us live in a summer reverie.

The dogs are true philosophers. While we, absorbed, still look over the quivering field, heat-sickened, they go on before, and spying a wayside pool, scatter the prim, important geese, and rolling in the shallow water, drink and bathe at once. Again we welcome the trees; thick maples arch the road, turning up the silver lining of their leaves in every whiff of air. Yonder is the bank of elecampane and the old locusts, and here are the mossy bars that lead to welcome depths of shade. Ben bounds over, shaking his wet coat, and rolls headlong in the deep, wild grass beyond; the path goes to the river and he knows it very well, knows every deep cold spring and muskrat run, knows also that all day he may run wild, and in an ecstasy he leaps and dashes to and fro.

Colin once followed the track of every field-mouse, scented the birds when neither human eye nor ear could detect them, crossed the country straight, leaped ditches, swam streams, but now grown old he waits until the bars are dropped, pretends he does not scent the trails he may no longer explore, and trusting us to choose an easy way, follows, looking up and rubbing his soft ears against us, his great brown eyes mutely confident; turning to man, to his dog-brain a god, to spare his age. Now wading deep in a maze of grass, weeds, ferns, we press through the unkempt lot to a great band of trees, and from them toward the heated body comes a wave of coolness, grateful as a refreshing draught to the lips or as music to the heart.

The breeze revives, and the shadows, drawn in by noontide, drop to eastward; a fragrance wafts from the moss tufts and guides us to its giver,—the dainty pipsissewa,—growing in bunches and masses, sprouting from creeping rootstalks, with a stem of madder-lined dark leaves with creamy veinings, crowned by waxy white flowers, their petals reflexed, having flesh-coloured stamens and a willow-green centre. This is the last of the spring-tinted and scented flowers that carpet the woods, thriving in its shadows. Who can describe its perfume? It is a combination of all the wild, spicy wood-essences, refined and distilled by the various chemical changes from the autumn-dyed leaves to their mould, that rears the flower in its bosom. From a heap of slowly crumbling brown leaves, the Indian pipe protrudes its ice-white, scentless flowers, that blacken at the gentlest touch, and though of the pipsissewa's clan, they are a parasitic growth.

The old setter stretches and yawns, but his companion is always fresh and ecstatic, and bounds down the slope to the river, trampling through the sweet-fern bushes, snapping dead branches, heedless of briers, and leaving a path where we may follow. Coiled on a stump, sunning himself, but not at all sleepy, lies a flat-headed adder, of a brownish colour, patched with a darker brown, and with the upper lip horny and aggressive. Instantly there springs up the old grudge born in the Garden of Eden, but Eve cautiously holds aloof, fearing perhaps that she may be further tempted, and Adam, replacing the Biblical heel with a stone, promptly bruises the serpent's head. Whether they are hurtful or not, snakes always seem a token of evil, the sign of some sinister power, and doubly so when we come upon them amid birds and flowers.

Again the undergrowth changes, and grows bolder. Great bushes of meadow sweet appear,—the wild white spirea salicifolia,—burr-reeds, and flowering sedge, with thickets of spurred jewelweed, and feathers of the late meadow-rue. Parting the tall weeds, we pushed through, and the odour of peppermint, crushed by our tread, rises about us; butterflies hover in flocks above the purple milkweeds, and the river glistens between the shallows. It is not a great stream carrying a burden of traffic, but a sociable, gossiping sort of a river, bearing the small tattle of mill-wheels, hidden in byways and corners, bringing down some bark from the saw-mill, or a little meal-foam from the grist-mill; scolding the pebbles, but growing silent as it passes the pools where the pickerel, like motion less shadows, hide under projections. In a bit of curled bark, drifted into a shallow, a song-sparrow bathes, and chirps an answer to the babbling water. If he would, he might tell us the story of the river. We sit on the bank and watch as he preens and spatters and flies to a brier, warbling with a heaving breast, his heart-beats keeping the rhythm, until the meaning of the river is blended in his song. Ben half wades, half swims in the water; Colin renews his youth at the fresh draught he laps, while down the river races to the willows:—"Sing willow, willow, willow." Is there any other tree that sings the river's measure so truly? The name itself is music, and its pendulous branches sweep an accompaniment to the melody of the water.

All through the afternoon we follow the river bank; the stream divides, and branching, trails its beauty through an open field, but the deeper channel still keeps to the woods and meets the straggler in the mill-pond. The pond's edge is thickly hedged and the bushes are tied together by wiry dodder; the heart-leaved pickerel-weed, with its purple spikes, outlines the shallow water, and the lily pads, whose flowers are closed or closing, rock with the gentle motion.

A kingfisher perching in a sycamore, above the mill house, dives suddenly; his reflection is so distinct that he seems to wrestle with himself under the water. One by one the birds begin to warble as the sun slants behind the cedars that top the hill, and we sit in the enclosing shadows. The colours of the submerged clouds circle and eddy with all the shifting hues of a bubble, and blend in an endless prism. The dogs, unnoticed, have slipped away and gone home. The shadows lengthen and then cease, passing to dark reflections; a mistlike breath comes from the water. A nighthawk, with white-spotted wings, skirls high in the air, and others answer. We two wait with full hearts. Silent in the present content, as in an endless vista where the past and future meet in the present. A star flowers out, then another, heat lightning quivers at the horizon, a bat flaps low, the wind drops through the willows, and the pond grows black and glassy as we listen for the song of evening. From the clouds to the water the words come like an echo:—Rest is the even-song of summer.

"Up Tripyramid on Snow-Shoes"
by Isaac Chubbuck

From Appalachia: The Journal of the Appalachian
Mountain Club *(1895, first spoken in 1892)*

*Born in Roxbury, Massachusetts, Isaac Y. Chubbuck (1835–1919) was the
son of a successful Boston manufacturer of steam engines, boilers, and related
machinery for residential buildings, factories, and public structures. Eventually, Isaac and his brother joined the business. Along with his father and
brother, Isaac would hold patents, including one for steam engine pistons.*

*Chubbuck was an early and active member of the Appalachian Mountain
Club, the nation's oldest outdoor adventuring and conservation organization.
The following paper was read at a club meeting on March 9, 1892. It is a classic
outdoor trip report of the late nineteenth century, demonstrating the expansive
enjoyment that adventurous urban dwellers like Chubbuck derived from natural scenery, wildlife, and outdoor experience. From these kinds of mountain
excursions grew an appreciation of, and concern for, nature that would later
blossom into widespread public support for the environment.*

"UP TRIPYRAMID ON SNOW-SHOES"

Tracks of rabbit, squirrel, and ruffed-grouse crossed our path in every
direction, showing that there had been a lively skirmish for an early
breakfast by the forest denizens. I sighted a rabbit as he disappeared into
the end of a hollow log, and I heard the notes of several kinds of birds.

On either side of the path the hobble-bush (*Viburnum lantanoides*) was waiting for early spring. New shoots clad in rich russet hue, bearing the leaf and flower buds of the coming season, stood boldly out and defied the severest cold. From the "Outlook" we went down the long slope of the hill, crossed Cascade Brook, and commenced the laborious task of breaking out a new path. We lost the trail on account of wind-falls; but after a little beating around, we took an easterly course through quite a tract of small growth, and came out into an opening which was probably the old site of "Beckytown."

Up the stream and in the direction we intended to go, at no very great distance apparently, stood a lofty mountain, grand and inviting. It was the north peak of Tripyramid. The steep western slope was suggestive. We looked. All were of the same mind but we said "nothing at all." The river was covered with ice and snow, the ridges and hummocks of which showed plainly the best places for walking. Depressions were avoided, and air-holes were left at a safe distance. We soon reached Avalanche Brook. Here the swift waters of both streams uniting caused a large air-hole in the ice-crust, obliging us to hug the north shore closely. But with all our caution the snow-shoe of one of the ladies broke through the snow-arch, but with no serious results. Crossing to the right side of Avalanche Brook, we had quite a stretch of good walking. I was leading off here, when suddenly one of the party in the rear shouted "Look out!" which I immediately did—from an opening that I had dropped into. A portion of the ice-bridge had given way, and I stood on the river-bed. I scrambled out, and the others got over without any difficulty. Some distance above here, open water appeared again.

We left the brook, went into the woods, and came out on a bluff. Another stream coming down from the mountains empties into Avalanche Brook at this place. We let ourselves down from the bluff by a tree that hung very conveniently over the bank, crossed over, and again started up Avalanche.

An eighth of a mile above, we left the brook for good, entered the open woods, and began to rise rapidly. Another eighth of a mile and a mass of debris, covering acres of ground, appeared on our left. Tree-trunks by the thousand were piled up in the most promiscuous manner. This proved to be a large portion of the material that composed the great slide of August, 1885. A bend in the brook at this place caused the mass to lodge here, over a mile below the base of the slide, thereby preventing the terrible havoc that would have taken place had it continued down Mad River.

We kept away to the right, and finding ourselves on a great ascending ridge, also worked upward. Another half-hour of steady climbing; then as it was one o'clock, we concluded to rest a short time and eat our lunch. As I carried what little food I wanted in my pocket, I started off on a contour to the right, exploring. It appeared that we were on a great rounded ridge; and the farther to the right I went, the steeper it grew, for I was getting into one of those great gullies that descend to the base of the mountain. The woods were so much more open that, in looking up, the top of the mountain could be seen, the spruce-trees upon it seeming like bushes, they were so far away. Working my way back, I found the party about ready to start again.

From this point the grade was rapid, and nothing could be seen but trees and the great snowy slope rising steep above us. The trees were of large growth—great spruces, with a mixture of different kinds of hardwood—and they kept their size and were lofty to within a short distance of the summit. It took us one hour and a half from our resting-place to reach the top, and we did not stop once. First one, then another took the lead, breaking out the way; and the ladies were up with us all the time. The climbing was of the hardest kind: the snow soft and heavy, loading the shoe at every step. The rise was continuous, with no break of any kind for relief, no gully or cross ravine, no ledge until we reached the top. It was simply up, and at an angle that obliged one to lift the snow-shoes as high as possible, and make many steps with little progress. We spent no time looking at the distant prospect.

At about a quarter before three I sighted a rounded, snow-clad summit above us. We were soon on it; but it proved to be only one of many open ledges that jut out and fall away from the top. We passed about six of these, thinking each one the true summit; but finally rounding over one and crawling through the scrub, the top appeared at some distance to the east. At three o'clock—just five hours' time from the house—we stood upon it. Its area is quite small, covered with spruce growth, but not densely. The labor to clear it would be very little. The elevation is 4,189 feet. We, upon the surface of the snow, were about five feet higher. There is considerable short growth, from five to six feet in height, which kept the snow from being blown away; but the trees themselves were very loosely packed. Stepping on the top of one that projected above the snow, one of the party went down almost out of sight, and it took considerable floundering to get out again. We were quite warm from our exercise, and thought it imprudent to stop long, as a thin scud was floating over and the air was cool.

The lifting clouds gave us glimpses in all directions except the north. The long ridge of Tripyramid went off towards the south, and across a deep col the middle peak rose like an inverted wedge, not truncated in the least. The South Peak was very much more blunt and rounded. They looked faraway, but we would have liked nothing better than to have returned that way. Black Mountain, with all its spurs, peaks, and ravines, was near and impressive. The zigzag of the ridges which the path goes over shows plainly why it is the best although the longest, course up that mountain. Tecumseh and Osceola were dark and cloud-capped. One glimpse into the Swift River Valley made us wish for more.

We felt well repaid for our short-time view, and at a quarter-past three started down over the ledges and into the woods. We found it as hard to go down as it had been to go up. The soft snow would load the toe of the shoe, and we took several headers, but landed softly. About one third of the way down, looking through the thin growth of trees, a lovely picture was revealed to us in the west. Framed by the dark, sloping sides of Osceola on the left, and by Kancamagus on the right, with the gray clouds above, was an opening, through which the bright, clear sky and snowy mountain-peaks were revealed, bathed in the golden glow of sunlight.

We were soon down on the more gentle slope, where we made better time. We passed the log-jam, followed down on the right-hand side of the brook, avoiding the tributary and bluff, and turned into the ravine of Norway Brook. The background between Tecumseh and Osceola was a mass of very dark clouds, through the rifts and openings of which streamed the last rays of the setting sun. The deep, rich color in all its hues was something wonderful, and the snow on the river caught and reflected the rosy tints—a perfect winter picture. It lasted until we reached the woods; then darkness settled down. After crossing Cascade Brook, night was fairly upon us. We pushed forward at a lively pace up the long slope, then down through the clearing, and reached the house at a quarter-past six, just as the supper-bell was ringing.

"Flowers in the Waste Places"
by W. Whitman Bailey

From Among Rhode Island Wild Flowers *(1895)*

Born in West Point, New York, to a professor of chemistry, William Whitman Bailey (1843–1914) lost his parents and two of his three siblings at a young age under tragic circumstances. As a result, he developed health problems that would haunt him the remainder of his life. He attended Brown University but left without a degree. In 1862 he enlisted in a Rhode Island army regiment, but was discharged due to ill health. At last he found work as an industrial chemist, but became fascinated by botany as a student of Harvard's Asa Gray. After a brief stint with the U.S. Geological Survey, he taught classes at private schools, worked at the Columbia College herbarium, and offered summer classes at Harvard. In 1877 he initiated the first botany class at Brown and eventually became a professor.

Among Bailey's books are Botanical Collector's Handbook *(1881),* New England Wild Flowers and Their Seasons *(1895), and* Botanizing *(1899). Though a scientist, Bailey wrote in an evocative, poetic, and often conversational style that inspired a wide range of people. His descriptions of particular plants, localities, and seasons are delightful, but this excerpt from the introduction to* Among Rhode Island Wild Flowers *best illustrates his passion for exploring and finding wonders near at hand, even in waste places.*

"Flowers in the Waste Places"

The study of a limited area of country presents peculiar attractions. It is possible to compass it all. Thus, a collector may spend a delightful summer on Block Island, attempting by earnest and unremitting labor to discover and record every plant in this insular flora.

The same may be said of Conanicut, Prudence, Aquidneck, and other islands of Narragansett Bay. Even the islets abound in interest. Encamping upon one of them, the collector should lay out a scheme, and allow no plant to escape him.

Approached in the right spirit, even a single plant will afford matters for admiration or for lengthened study. In the sweet story of Picciola, we recall how a despairing prisoner was redeemed by a single plant. The small back-yard of a city, even, may prove a most delightful wilderness. It may require several or many seasons to discover and record its living inhabitants. A French writer described a "tour around his garden," and the book is immortal. One can always make journeyings in his own yard which have all the charm of adventure and discovery. There are the plants that are put in, and those that intrude. Who are we, to decide which are worthless? There is the all-pervasive purslane, easy to eradicate, though possessing immense vitality; there is shepherd's-purse,—cosmopolitan wanderer; and plantain, "the white-man's foot." Besides these, there are knot-weeds, big and little; hollyhocks, in whose silken pavilions the bee takes his siesta; pink and white funnels of bindweed, the all-embracing balsam-apple, catch-fly pinks, four-o'clocks, burdocks, and ground ivy. In the season, too, the golden-rods and asters light up their stars.

These plants are engaged in an unsparing struggle for existence. Woe to the weakling, for he will be crowded out. Look at the combat between that bramble, armed as it is with sharp prickles, and that bindweed that embraces it like some constricting serpent. The fight seems to be about equal, but the bindweed conquers. So, again, the mandrake will possess the land by means of its aggressive root-stocks, until its umbrellas are seen everywhere. Sunflowers, also, though annual, take care to scatter their seed—or invite the birds to aid them in so doing. For every seed these little fellows appropriate, they scatter forty. The result is that in the spring the yard becomes a nursery of baby sunflowers. Everywhere they spread their little hands. By and by they will rival Jack's beanstalk in height. Our neighbor's woodbine, a welcome interloper, tumbles over the fence, and with its prehensile tendrils lays hold of every point of vantage. It completely screens all unsightly fences,—for this was it ordained. Over the fence climbs that beautiful legume, the scarlet-runner, too poetic for a bean.

As intimated, it may require several seasons to explore, or at least to exhaust, even a small territory. Still, there is a definite end in view, and one which is attainable. This is not so when it is attempted to embrace the vegetation of a whole country or of the world. Even in the time of Linnaeus it was shown how stupendous was such an effort.

In Rhode Island, where modesty is the rule, everyone is convinced that any plant found within our limits, and therein native, is taller, more vigorous; if flowering, more beautiful; if fruit-producing, richer and rarer, than the same species in any neighboring State. The fact admits of no argument. Thus, State, county, or even village pride, may afford a certain stimulus to the observers' efforts. As for Rhode Island, it may be regarded as a chosen land, especially favored by nature. In old geographies it was well styled, "the Eden of America." Even the markets recognize the superiority of its productions.

There are no more interesting plants than those of waste places or shores, such as filled-in districts, like the Cove-basin and the tract around the Wilkesbarre Coal Yards in Providence. Here one naturally sees strangers, in foreign garb and with strange manners, tropical strays and waifs, of which we have many examples. These may maintain themselves for a while and then disappear, or they may come to stay.

It is always a delightful occupation to pry around such spots, with the chance of finding something new, and, if new, then most precious.

Many places about Providence, Newport, Bristol, and Pawtucket will bear further investigation for these Bohemians. Again, Westerly and Woonsocket, on the border of other States, are subject to incursions therefrom. These should be noted.

The amateur student of botany can materially aid the professional by keeping accurate notes of his finds, and better by retaining good pressed specimens to authenticate his statements.

Doctor Gray tells us, in his pleasant way, that plants have taken up modern customs—and travel by railway. Sometimes their advance is leisurely—by freight train; again, it is rapid—by the express. In other words, the operations of commerce tend to spread plants from one region to another. They come as fruits or seeds attached to bales of wool or cotton; as accidental accompaniments of hay and other fodder plants; in ballast earth transferred in process of railway building; and even adherent to the clothing of man. For this purpose many of them, like beggar-ticks, burdock, cockle-bur, etc., have prehensile spines or hooks, to act as grapnels.

Some plants are saunterers or loiterers by the way, preferring to abide in one locality for a long time, ere a new advance. They may first send out skirmishers to prospect and report. If things seem favorable the whole army may move on. Their approach must be noted, but the birds of the air, or the breeze itself, may thwart us, and drop a seed in the night. Again, certain persons—as they have an undoubted right to do—may confuse one's study of the native plants, by introducing foreign ones into the woods. Thus about Quinsnickett Hill one must not regard every plant seen as indigenous.

Against such practice there is no defence, but it is of less frequent occurrence than one might expect.

A ballast heap or railway filling is only excelled by the delightful ash-heaps of our cities. Blessings on the conservative wealthy who leave these odd corners to offend the public and educate the botanist!

Here we find the tall prince's feather cheek-by-jowl with aspiring sunflowers. Here golden-rods are tangled together with bindweeds and morning glories, hollyhocks pace like solemn sentinels, and portulacas and petunias; four o'clocks and evening primroses struggle with pigweeds and amaranths. Do you disbelieve in the struggle for existence? Study Darwinism one summer on an ash heap!

"Canoeing Down the Androscoggin" by George Elmer Browne

From Outing: An Illustrated Monthly Magazine of Sport, Travel and Recreation *(1898)*

An early twentieth-century American etcher and painter, George Elmer Browne (1871–1946) was born in Gloucester, Massachusetts, and exhibited artistic talent while attending public schools in Salem. He received his art education at the Museum of Fine Arts and Cowles School of Art in Boston and the Académie Julian, Paris. He specialized in landscape and marine images, and achieved membership in the National Academy and the Society of American Etchers. In 1930 he became president of the Allied Artists of America.

"Canoeing Down the Androscoggin" appeared in the July 1898 issue of Outing: An Illustrated Monthly Magazine of Sport, Travel and Recreation *accompanied by the author's illustrations. Here a landscape painter confronts the actual energy of the landscape through the river's hydraulic and aesthetic power. Browne's writing exhibits an artist's capacity to understand nature's details and beauty.*

"CANOEING DOWN THE ANDROSCOGGIN"

We camped near the little village of Derham the second night out from Lewiston, and the following day as we neared Lisbon were forced to break through a boom-chain before we could get down to the town. Then we were obliged to make another carry around the dam, and about four o'clock we started off in the direction of Brunswick.

It must have been near seven o'clock that evening when we came suddenly in sight of a large pulp mill that loomed up directly ahead of us on the left shore. I remember that the wind, which had increased to a gale since we pulled out from Lisbon, was rapidly driving us down toward this mill, and that it was fast becoming dark.

Suddenly we were hailed by some men, and the next moment we looked ahead, and there, not more than fifty feet away, the whole river seemed to plunge off into space.

"A fall!" shouted White from his place in the stern of the boat, and instantly I heard him shove an oar over the side and felt the boat swinging round against the current.

Quickly grasping an oar, I braced my feet, and as soon as the boat was headed for the shore in an angular direction away from the fall, I began pulling with all my might.

Much as we labored, I could see that we were making little headway against the wind and current, but it was our only chance of safety, and so we kept at the work. At least, with a joyous shout, we grated, and with a bound I cleared the side of the boat, and, striking the bank, with the painter grasped firmly in my hand, I pulled myself ashore and made fast the boat.

We reached Brunswick the next morning, after an uneventful cruise of about four miles. Here we made another carry around the dams and falls, and went into camp on a small sand-spit below the town.

The next day we pushed away from this, the last settlement of any kind on the great Androscoggin, and set out for Bath. The morning was a most delightful one. A refreshing breeze was rapidly clearing the valley of the mist as we headed downstream.

The nature of the country through which we now made our way was low and flat; and, strange to say, as we approached the mouth of the river the stream became very narrow, at one place not wider than thirty feet.

After possibly three hours' sail we came in sight of a long wooden bridge, which we presently reached; and as we passed between its supports and emerged on the other side, we knew, from the grand expanse of water that now confronted us, that our paddles had for the last time dipped in the waters of the good old Androscoggin, and we were drifting on Merrymeeting Bay.

Our course now took us among a long stretch of marsh and islands which, as we later learned, were visible only at low water. The bay now widened out on all sides, and the distant shore to the south was but barely visible. We pushed on, rounded a great cape, and came in full view of the mouth of the Kennebec.

We camped that night on the shore of a little island, where the fragrant smell of pine needles and the spreading boughs of the trees made the spot an ideal one.

Early the following morning, which was Sunday, after a sail of five miles we pulled ashore opposite the famous shipbuilding town of Bath, and went into camp.

"Purpose in Devices of Plants"
by Ellen Russell Emerson

From Nature and Human Nature *(1902)*

Born in New Sharon, Maine, Ellen Russell (1837–1907) met poet Henry Wadsworth Longfellow as a child, sparking a lifelong interest in both nature and Indian lore. After being sent to Boston's Mount Vernon Seminary at age 17, she began to write essays and poems, but her stay was cut short by brain fever. A few years later she married Edwin Emerson of Augusta, Maine, but continued her informal studies and writing, collecting Indian legends as an ethnologist. In Europe in the 1880s she researched library and museum records, eventually being the first woman elected to the Société *Américaine de France.*

Her books include Indian Myths *(1884),* Masks, Heads, and Faces *(1891), and* Nature and Human Nature *(1892), from which the following excerpt is taken. The book focuses on the different ways humans have interpreted the natural world through the arts. This excerpt from chapter 1 is an unusual mix of the scientific, literary, and anthropocentric, where everything is measured by comparison to humankind. It is emblematic of a transitional style of nature writing that has long since passed by.*

"PURPOSE IN DEVICES OF PLANTS"

Accommodation to circumstances is common in plant life, and it has been observed that a plant will turn and curve quite about in order to get into position to send its stem into the light, while as often the root of the stem will bend in the opposite direction, driving its tip beneath the soil, so avoiding the light, movements as direct and purposeful as any conscious act of the human being in providing against some adverse circumstance which threatens its welfare.

Arising with all the organs of vegetal life complete, root, stem, and leaves previously rolled up in the seed, the plant begins to develop the flower, that miracle of construction quite surpassing all antecedent parts, though prophesied by them. And the willpower which is disclosed in the maturing plant dominates the final stage when is achieved the birth of the seed, for reproduction is the end of the laborious cycle of activity,—that which may be termed centrifugal and centripetal forces raising the stem and extending the root with all that precision with which the planets are held in orbit. And the purpose of securing for itself perennial life demands avoidance of injury to both root and stem, and often by a twist on the part of one and the putting forth of thorns and prickles on the part of the other the plant will steadily impose itself to those destructive influences arising from environment or through foreign invasion, so showing that plant energy is as persistent as human energy. Has not a plant splintered a rock in order to get foot room, has it not turned aside from subterranean obstacles sensed without touch of rootlet? And what contortions are made, the gyrating stem turning upon itself at need of support when its course is straight as a driven stake, the point desired at last reached! A plant puts forth a stem in place of a leaf, and with this green fingertip awaits a propitious moment when, aided by the rising wind, it will approach a sturdy neighbor, and lo, the finger becomes a hook as strong as a parrot's beak, and thus moored the plant laughs in ruddy flowers and purple berries, garlanding living shores of green in grateful profusion.

It is pleasant to consider the maneuvers of plants in their effort to establish themselves happily in the land of their nativity, for it is in observation of these maneuvers is perceived that sensitiveness, fatuously limited to animal life, is developed in so-called inanimate life to a remarkable degree, and this too even in barren places, the desert abounding in so-called sensitive plants, there, as elsewhere, indeed, though in less degree, a concordant action being exercised to the end of overcoming unpropitious conditions.

On the desert is found the cactus, whose leaves are a reservoir of living water distilled from the atmosphere and whence is slaked the thirst of the hungry bud rising from amid a prickly guard, sentinels of this queen nymph, whose glory of color at last declares the chemics of the plant wisely combined those chemics maintained in equable proportion throughout the flowering period in the leaf's distillery, and whose abundance is maintained by the limitation of the circumference of each plant, that apparent arid space between neighbors a security to individual distillation.

Equal provision is exercised by the sand verbaena, its unctuous leaves a means of water-supply, this nectar appearing to impart such exhilaration to the flowers that they exhale fragrance in very delight and thanksgiving. And it is but necessary to watch the ineffectual invasion of an insect when a plant has eliminated from its water tank gummy juices to realize the astuteness of its devices, while if other examples are needed they appear to the observer of the ignorant foraging of a lamb whose maturing appetite sets it nibbling among those plants which have provided against such contingencies by a bristling guard of thorns set in tufts or in alternate rows. But another testimony should be added in order to give full weight to the foregoing evidences of the wisdom of plants, and that is the manufacture of poisons, concoctions of the more desperate of these children of the earth whose efficacy among varied measures adopted for self-preservation has given both the poison oak and ivy immunity from depredations at flowering period, so insuring berries for the late regalement of hardy birds. And these methods of self-preservation are anticipatory to renewed existence by way of the seed wherein the spark from the Essence of Life is preserved, and it is the care with which the plant protects itself in seedtime that declares most its wisdom. There is the lacquer covering leaf-buds filched by the purloining bee to seal up its offspring in safety in a happy imitation of the wise trees; and there is the albumen in the lyre-like seed-leaves of the maple, where is the *cella* of the young dryad of maple groves; there are also the plumes giving aerial flight to the too numerous progeny of the dandelion on whom crowding neighbors have the effect to ruffle up their mats and destroy the seclusion desired.

"The Proposed Eastern Forest Reserves" by Gifford Pinchot

From Appalachia: The Journal of the Appalachian
Mountain Club *(1908, first spoken in 1906)*

*Born at the summer home of his mother's family in Simsbury, Connecticut,
Gifford Pinchot (1865–1946) grew up in a world of wealth and privilege.
He attended private schools and graduated from Yale in 1889. After studying at the French National Forestry School and touring European forests, he
determined to bring the tradition of woodlands as public resources to the United
States. He was named first chief of the United States Forest Service when it
was created in 1905.*

*Pinchot advocated for a utilitarian, but sustainable, conservation: "to
make the forest produce the largest amount of whatever crop or service will be
most useful and keep producing it for generation after generation of men and
trees." This put him at odds with many conservationists who valued forests for
their beauty and non-economic values, most notably John Muir.*

*In this 1906 speech delivered to the Appalachian Mountain Club in Bos-
ton, Pinchot pitches plans for expanding national forests to a group concerned
with their value for physical challenge, beauty, and even spiritual renewal. His
arguments are classic utilitarian, but tempered with an interest in the long-
term health of forests. It's clear that Pinchot cared deeply about the woods, and
that was bound to appeal to his audience.*

"The Proposed Eastern Forest Reserves"

There is a good deal of mountain land through New England—medium mountain land, so to speak—which, while it is not absolutely forest land, is yet capable of producing more effectively under forest than it is under any other crop. Much of that land will be held by the lumbermen themselves under enlightened ideas which are coming to them so widely, and need not therefore be taken by the Government in order to be safe. Such timber as this produces rapidly, grows well, and is of value to the lumbermen. Many of these mountain forests in New Hampshire contain not only spruce, the most valuable tree, but also hard-wood trees.

In the attack on the New Hampshire forests that has been going on for many years, much of the best of the forests has already been destroyed, great areas have been cut, and even now the most important of the mountain forests that remain are threatened. It is a critical question whether those of the White Mountain region are to be treated as in these pictures, or whether they are to be taken under the protecting wing of the Government and handled as they ought to be.

I find it difficult to convey an impression to any audience, however intelligent, of the tremendous destruction that takes place through forest fires; and for that reason I have chosen for the pictures of the White Mountain region this evening mainly pictures showing destruction by fire. For, however serious the lumbering may be, the great question there is not the need of conservative lumbering instead of destructive lumbering, but first and for the most the protection against fire. The results are so bad, and the length of time during which they continue to inflict injury on the people who come after those who did the harm is so great, that no impression I can give you of the damage by fire is too strong.

The reasons why these forests should be preserved, different as the conditions are in different parts of the Appalachian chain, north and south, practically meet. We have got first the fact that it is wise policy to have these lands preserved, and for many different reasons. For example, we are now using, incredible as it may seem, ten times as much timber, valued in dollars, as we were in 1850, while the population of the United States has only increased three times. In other words, the census of 1850 gave us $60,000,000 as the value of the produce of the forests, while the census of 1900 gives $566,000,000, and during the same period the population has only increased from 23,000,000 to 76,000,000.

The timber question is far more than a business question, in the sense that it is utterly impossible for us to repair the damage of forest destruction in any reasonable time. You may start a mine which has been stopped, and there is little damage; you may let a farm lie fallow and take up the cultivation of it again, and the farm is better than it was; you may begin once more fisheries that have been abandoned, when the fish have returned; but the destruction of the forests means the destruction of the growth, the productive capacity of the land, through a long series of years.

The shortest possible time in which the damage of a timber famine can be repaired is fifty years. And all the signs point to the fact that unless the people of the United States, especially the Government of the United States, wake up to the present condition, we shall have a famine in that material, which, even more than steel, stands at the bottom of the productive industry of this country. For you can operate no mines, you can operate no railroads, you can have no farms, you can conduct no fisheries, you can conduct few manufactures, in the absence of timber. In this age of steel, timber is, nevertheless, one of the great essentials of civilization, and from a timber point of view we must preserve our forests. Therefore, since forest destruction is going on in the Southern Appalachians and in the Northern Appalachians, the White Mountains, it is a wise policy for us to stop that destruction, and to let the lands that are better capable of producing timber than anything else produce that timber crop.

—～—

It is perfectly clear that as an investment it would pay the Government to create these reserves. This has been the first year of the organization of the Forest Service, and the national forest reserves have this first year met nearly half of the total charge for Forest Service; and it is the confident expectation of those of us who are handling the matter that within from three to five years the Forest Service will be self-supporting, and a permanent source of revenue to the Government. And precisely the same method of handling will in the end give us the same sort of revenue from these forests. In other words, the purchase which is asked for is a purchase which in the very nature of things is bound to be a profitable one. Therefore, it is good statesmanship and it is good business to buy these forests. That is regarding it purely from a lumber point of view.

Now let us consider it for a moment from the point of view of water supply; and here is the nub of the question, North and South. It is estimated that there are 2,700,000 horse-power used for manufacturing in New England; and in the Southern States more than half a million horse-power (of which 180,000 are produced by water) are already in use, and not less than a million horse-power are capable of being developed.

It would be nothing less than suicide, from the commercial and manufacturing point of view, for you here, and for those in the South, to allow the destruction of the forests from which comes the water that turns your wheels. Not only is it necessary for you to protect yourselves against floods—one single flood at Holyoke some time ago cost $100,000,—but it is fair for you and for the South look forward to the maintenance and the increase of the means of wealth which you have at hand. It is a direct question of self-preservation in business for you, whether or not you are to allow the destruction of the sources from which so much of your wealth has sprung in the past, and from which, under proper conservation, still more will spring in the future.

Now if I am right in thinking that this is an inter-state question, and if the objection that other States will come and ask for the same thing is not valid, then why is not the thing done? why has not it been done already? The answer is a perfectly simple one: that the people who are interested in this matter have not made themselves heard. I have lived in Washington long enough to know that, whatever any other government on the earth may be, this Government of ours is a representative one, and that what the people ask for and mean to have they will get, be it right or wrong—for no man has lived in Washington long without seeing mistaken demands enforced on congressmen and senators, as well as demands that were right. It is simply a question of how much and how earnestly the people of the New England States desire the White Mountain reserve, and how much and how earnestly the people of the Southern States desire the Southern Appalachian reserve; and nothing else will secure them. President McKinley has spoken in favor of the movement; President Roosevelt has given it his hearty and his most effective support; your best men here in Massachusetts have pronounced in favor of it over and over again; we in Washington have put in our little word here and there where the occasion demanded it or where the occasion made it possible, we have spoken sometimes in season and sometimes out of season, all to no effect. The matter is purely one which rests with you.

"The Seeing Hand"
by Helen Keller

From The World I Live In *(1908)*

Born in rural Alabama, Helen Keller's (1880–1968) remarkable story of overcoming disability was already well known by the time she attended the Perkins Institute for the Blind in Boston, the Cambridge School for Young Women, and finally Radcliffe College, where she was the first deaf-blind person to earn a BA. She later moved to Easton, Connecticut, walking into her yard to smell the autumn air, holding onto a smooth wooden rail that helped her negotiate the rural landscape of her adopted New England home.

Many of Keller's books argue for disability rights and solutions to other social ills, but her most lasting have been her fascinating memoirs, which let millions of people into her unique world. The following extract is the first chapter from her book The World I Live In, *and describes the fascinating way in which a woman who both blind and deaf used her hands to interact with the natural world.*

"THE SEEING HAND"

I have just touched my dog. He was rolling on the grass, with pleasure in every muscle and limb. I wanted to catch a picture of him in my fingers, and I touched him as lightly as I would cobwebs; but lo, his fat body revolved, stiffened and solidified into an upright position, and his tongue gave my hand a lick! He pressed close to me, as if he were fain to crowd himself into my hand. He loved it with his tail, with his paw, with his tongue. If he could speak, I believe he would say with me that paradise is attained by touch; for in touch is all love and intelligence.

This small incident started me on a chat about hands, and if my chat is fortunate, I have to thank my dog-star. In any case, it is pleasant to have something to talk about that no one else has monopolized; it is like making a new path in the trackless woods, blazing the trail where no foot has pressed before. I am glad to take you by the hand and lead you along an untrodden way into a world where the hand is supreme. But at the very outset we encounter a difficulty. You are so accustomed to light, I fear you will stumble when I try to guide you through the land of darkness and silence. The blind are not supposed to be the best of guides. Still, though I cannot warrant not to lose you, I promise that you shall not be led into fire or water, or fall into a deep pit. If you will follow me patiently, you will find that "there's a sound so fine, nothing lives 'twixt it and silence," and that there is more meant in things than meets the eye.

My hand is to me what your hearing and sight together are to you. In large measure we travel the same highways, read the same books, speak the same language, yet our experiences are different. All my comings and goings turn on the hand as on a pivot. It is the hand that binds me to the world of men and women. The hand is my feeler with which I reach through isolation and darkness and seize every pleasure, every activity that my fingers encounter. With the dropping of a little word from another's hand into mine, a slight flutter of the fingers, began the intelligence, the joy, the fullness of my life. Like Job, I feel as if a hand had made me, fashioned me together round about and molded my very soul.

In all my experiences and thoughts I am conscious of a hand. Whatever moves me, whatever thrills me, is as a hand that touches me in the dark, and that touch is my reality. You might as well say that a sight which makes you glad, or a blow which brings the stinging tears to your eyes, is unreal as to say that those impressions are unreal which I have accumulated by means of touch. The delicate tremble of a butterfly's wings in my hand, the soft petals of violets curling in the cool folds of their leaves or lifting sweetly out of the meadow-grass, the clear, firm outline of face and limb, the smooth arch of a horse's neck and the velvety touch of his nose—all these, and a thousand resultant combinations, which take shape in my mind, constitute my world.

Ideas make the world we live in, and impressions furnish ideas. My world is built of touch-sensations, devoid of physical color and sound; but without color and sound it breathes and throbs with life. Every object is associated in my mind with tactual qualities which, combined in countless ways, give me a sense of power, of beauty, or of incongruity: for with my hands I can feel the comic as well as the beautiful in the outward appearance of things. Remember that you, dependent on your sight, do not realize how many things are tangible. All palpable things are mobile or rigid, solid or liquid, big or small, warm or cold, and these qualities are variously modified. The coolness of a water-lily rounding into bloom is different from the coolness of an evening wind in summer, and different again from the coolness of the rain that soaks into the hearts of growing things and gives them life and body. The velvet of the rose is not that of a ripe peach or of a baby's dimpled cheek. The hardness of the rock is to the hardness of wood what a man's deep bass is to a woman's voice when it is low. What I call beauty I find in certain combinations of all these qualities, and is largely derived from the flow of curved and straight lines which is over all things.

"What does the straight line mean to you?" I think you will ask.

It means several things. It symbolizes duty. It seems to have the quality of inexorableness that duty has. When I have something to do that must not be set aside, I feel as if I were going forward in a straight line, bound to arrive somewhere, or go on forever without swerving to the right or to the left.

That is what it means. To escape this moralizing you should ask, "How does the straight line feel?" It feels, as I suppose it looks, straight— a dull thought drawn out endlessly. Eloquence to the touch resides not in straight lines, but in unstraight lines, or in many curved and straight lines together. They appear and disappear, are now deep, now shallow, now broken off or lengthened or swelling. They rise and sink beneath my fingers, they are full of sudden starts and pauses, and their variety is inexhaustible and wonderful. So, you see I am not shut out from the region of the beautiful, though my hand cannot perceive the brilliant colors in the sunset or on the mountain, or reach into the blue depths of the sky.

Physics tells me that I am well off in a world which, I am told, knows neither color nor sound, but is made in terms of size, shape, and inherent qualities; for at least every object appears to my fingers standing solidly right side up, and is not an inverted image on the retina which, I understand, your brain is at infinite though unconscious labor to set back on its feet. A tangible object passes complete into my brain with the warmth of life upon it, and occupies the same place that it does in space; for, without egotism, the mind is as large as the universe.

When I think of hills, I think of the upward strength I tread upon. When water is the object of my thought, I feel the cool shock of the plunge and the quick yielding of the waves that crisp and curl and ripple about my body. The pleasing changes of rough and smooth, pliant and rigid, curved and straight in the bark and branches of a tree give the truth to my hand. The immovable rock, with its juts and warped surface, bends beneath my fingers into all manner of grooves and hollows. The bulge of a watermelon and the puffed-up rotundities of squashes that sprout, bud, and ripen in that strange garden planted somewhere behind my fingertips are the ludicrous in my tactual memory and imagination. My fingers are tickled to delight by the soft ripple of a baby's laugh, and find amusement in the lusty crow of the barnyard autocrat. Once I had a pet rooster that used to perch on my knee and stretch his neck and crow. A bird in my hand was then worth two in the barnyard.

My fingers cannot, of course, get the impression of a large whole at a glance; but I feel the parts, and my mind puts them together. I move around my house, touching object after object in order, before I can form an idea of the entire house. In other people's houses I can touch only what is shown me—the chief objects of interest, carvings on the wall, or a curious architectural feature, exhibited like the family album. Therefore, a house with which I am not familiar has for me, at first, no general effect or harmony of detail. It is not a complete conception, but a collection of object-impressions which, as they come to me, are disconnected and isolated. But my mind is full of associations, sensations, theories, and with them it constructs the house. The process reminds me of the building of Solomon's temple, where was neither saw, nor hammer, nor any tool heard while the stones were being laid one upon another. The silent worker is imagination which decrees reality out of chaos.

Without imagination what a poor thing my world would be! My garden would be a silent patch of earth strewn with sticks of a variety of shapes and smells. But when the eye of my mind is opened to its beauty, the bare ground brightens beneath my feet, and the hedge-row bursts into leaf, and the rose-tree shakes its fragrance everywhere. I know how budding trees look, and I enter into the amorous joy of the mating birds, and this is the miracle of imagination.

Twofold is the miracle when, through my fingers, my imagination reaches forth and meets the imagination of an artist which he has embodied in a sculptured form. Although, compared with the life-warm, mobile face of a friend, the marble is cold and pulseless and unresponsive, yet it is beautiful to my hand. Its flowing curves and bendings are a real pleasure; only breath is wanting; but under the spell of the imagination the marble thrills and becomes the divine reality of the ideal. Imagination puts a sentiment into every line and curve, and the statue in my touch is indeed the goddess herself who breathes and moves and enchants.

It is true, however, that some sculptures, even recognized masterpieces, do not please my hand. When I touch what there is of the Winged Victory, it reminds me at first of a headless, limbless dream that flies toward me in an unrestful sleep. The garments of the Victory thrust stiffly out behind, and do not resemble garments that I have felt flying, fluttering, folding, spreading in the wind. But imagination fulfils these imperfections, and straightway the Victory becomes a powerful and spirited figure with the sweep of sea-winds in her robes and the splendor of conquest in her wings.

I find in a beautiful statue perfection of bodily form, the qualities of balance and completeness. The Minerva, hung with a web of poetical allusion, gives me a sense of exhilaration that is almost physical; and like the luxuriant, wavy hair of Bacchus and Apollo, and the wreath of ivy, so suggestive of pagan holidays.

So imagination crowns the experience of my hands. And they learned their cunning from the wise hand of another, which, itself guided by imagination, led me safely in paths that I knew not, made darkness light before me, and made crooked ways straight.

"Starkfield" by Edith Wharton

From Ethan Frome *(1911)*

Edith Wharton (1862–1937) was born into a wealthy New York family and educated in private schools in the United States and Europe. In 1901 she designed and built her dream house, The Mount, in Lenox, Massachusetts, where she lived for a decade and wrote some of her most famous works. In all, she authored over forty books, including poetry and nonfiction volumes on architecture, interior design, travel, and gardens, but she is most renowned for her short stories and novels. Her books were popular, giving her great fame, a significant income, and the honor of being the first woman to win a Pulitzer Prize in fiction, for her novel The Age of Innocence (1920).*

Set in the fictitious town of Starkfield, Massachusetts, her novel Ethan Frome *is the story of a poor farmer living in bleak despair. He tastes a bit of short-lived hope when his wife's young cousin arrives to assist. Although Wharton was not known for nature writing, her knowledge of landscape serves her well. The character of Ethan Frome is so tightly bound to his place that the essence of one is indistinguishable from the other. The severe and melancholy landscape and Frome's personality are intimately fused, adding power to the story.*

"STARKFIELD"

The next morning, when I looked out, I saw the hollow-backed bay between the Varnum spruces, and Ethan Frome, throwing back his worn bear-skin, made room for me in the sleigh at his side. After that, for a week, he drove me over every morning to Corbury Flats, and on my return in the afternoon met me again and carried me back through the icy night to Starkfield. The distance each way was barely three miles, but the old bay's pace was slow, and even with firm snow under the runners we were nearly an hour on the way. Ethan Frome drove in silence, the reins loosely held in his left hand, his brown seamed profile, under the helmet-like peak of the cap, relieved against the banks of snow like the bronze image of a hero. He never turned his face to mine, or answered, except in monosyllables, the questions I put, or such slight pleasantries as I ventured. He seemed a part of the mute melancholy landscape, an incarnation of its frozen woe, with all that was warm and sentient in him fast bound below the surface; but there was nothing unfriendly in his silence. I simply felt that he lived in a depth of moral isolation too remote for casual access, and I had the sense that his loneliness was not merely the result of his personal plight, tragic as I guessed that to be, but had in it the profound accumulated cold of many Starkfield winters.

As we turned into the Corbury road the snow began to fall again, cutting off our last glimpse of the house; and Frome's silence fell with it, letting down between us the old veil of reticence. This time the wind did not cease with the return of the snow. Instead, it sprang up to a gale which now and then, from a tattered sky, flung pale sweeps of sunlight over a landscape chaotically tossed. But the bay was as good as Frome's word, and we pushed on to the Junction through the wild white scene.

In the afternoon the storm held off, and the clearness in the west seemed to my inexperienced eye the pledge of a fair evening. I finished my business as quickly as possible, and we set out for Starkfield with a good chance of getting there for supper. But at sunset the clouds gathered again, bringing an earlier night, and the snow began to fall straight and steadily from a sky without wind, in a soft universal diffusion more confusing than the gusts and eddies of the morning. It seemed to be a part of the thickening darkness, to be the winter night itself descending on us layer by layer.

The small ray of Frome's lantern was soon lost in this smothering medium, in which even his sense of direction, and the bay's homing instinct, finally ceased to serve us. Two or three times some ghostly landmark sprang up to warn us that we were astray, and then was sucked back into the mist; and when we finally regained our road the old horse began to show signs of exhaustion. I felt myself to blame for having accepted Frome's offer, and after a short discussion I persuaded him to let me get out of the sleigh and walk along through the snow at the bay's side. In this way we struggled on for another mile or two, and at last reached a point where Frome, peering into what seemed to me formless night, said: "That's my gate down yonder."

There was some hauling to be done at the lower end of the wood-lot, and Ethan was out early the next day.

The winter morning was as clear as crystal. The sunrise burned red in a pure sky, the shadows on the rim of the wood-lot were darkly blue, and beyond the white and scintillating fields patches of far-off forest hung like smoke.

It was in the early morning stillness, when his muscles were swinging to their familiar task and his lungs expanding with long draughts of mountain air, that Ethan did his clearest thinking. He and Zeena had not exchanged a word after the door of their room had closed on them. She had measured out some drops from a medicine-bottle on a chair by the bed and, after swallowing them, and wrapping her head in a piece of yellow flannel, had lain down with her face turned away. Ethan undressed hurriedly and blew out the light so that he should not see her when he took his place at her side. As he lay there he could hear Mattie moving about in her room, and her candle, sending its small ray across the landing, drew a scarcely perceptible line of light under his door. He kept his eyes fixed on the light till it vanished. Then the room grew perfectly black, and not a sound was audible but Zeena's asthmatic breathing. Ethan felt confusedly that there were many things he ought to think about, but through his tingling veins and tired brain only one sensation throbbed: the warmth of Mattie's shoulder against his. Why had he not kissed her when he held her there? A few hours earlier he would not have asked himself the question. Even a few minutes earlier, when they had stood alone outside the house, he would not have dared to think of kissing her. But since he had seen her lips in the lamplight he felt that they were his.

Now, in the bright morning air, her face was still before him. It was part of the sun's red and of the pure glitter on the snow. How the girl had changed since she had come to Starkfield! He remembered what a colourless slip of a thing she had looked the day he had met her at the station. And all the first winter, how she had shivered with cold when the northerly gales shook the thin clapboards and the snow beat like hail against the loose-hung windows!

As he lay there, the window-pane that faced him, growing gradually lighter, inlaid upon the darkness a square of moon-suffused sky. A crooked tree-branch crossed it, a branch of the apple-tree under which, on summer evenings, he had sometimes found Mattie sitting when he came up from the mill. Slowly the rim of the rainy vapours caught fire and burnt away, and a pure moon swung into the blue. Ethan, rising on his elbow, watched the landscape whiten and shape itself under the sculpture of the moon. This was the night on which he was to have taken Mattie coasting, and there hung the lamp to light them! He looked out at the slopes bathed in lustre, the silver-edged darkness of the woods, the spectral purple of the hills against the sky, and it seemed as though all the beauty of the night had been poured out to mock his wretchedness . . .

He fell asleep, and when he woke the chill of the winter dawn was in the room. He felt cold and stiff and hungry, and ashamed of being hungry. He rubbed his eyes and went to the window. A red sun stood over the grey rim of the fields, behind trees that looked black and brittle.

"Ipswich Shore"
by Charles Wendell Townsend

From Sand Dunes and Salt Marshes *(1913)*

A physician with a bent for natural history and exploring the outdoors, Charles Wendell Townsend (1859–1934) had a passion for birds. Born in Boston and an 1885 graduate of Harvard Medical School, he had a busy practice in obstetrics and pediatrics and was an expert in childhood nutrition.

Townsend was particularly taken with the natural beauty of the seacoast town of Ipswich, and in 1891 acquired a summer house there with a view of salt marshes, dunes, and the ocean. Among his many books on birds and nature is Sand Dunes and Salt Marshes *(1913), where he describes the shoreline of his beloved Ipswich, demonstrating his physician's penchant for scientific detail and a poet's talent for evocative description.*

"Ipswich Shore"

Sand dunes have a fascination all their own. In the multiplicity of their forms and colors, varying with the seasons and years, they are a constant source of pleasure, while in their wealth of plant and animal life their interest is never-ending. The beauty of the sand dunes is revealed at every turn, their secrets are legion. The course of their formation from the time they emerge out of the sea as reefs washed by every tide, until they have reached perfection in their wave-like crests fifty feet high is an absorbing study. Their surface records a continually changing story,—ripple-marks of the varying winds, magic circles made by the grass, and myriad tracks of living creatures.

The reefs along the beach are constantly changing. One of these I have watched and recorded since 1892. When first seen, it was already above high tide except at its northwest extremity, and connected with the beach off the Ipswich range-light. Like other reefs, its slope was gradual on the seaward, steep on the landward side, and so narrow that I used—in those barbaric days—to build my blind in the middle of the spit and shoot over decoys placed at the water's edge on both sides.

As the sea threw up more and more sand, and the wind seized it and blew it inland, the spit extended and broadened and cut off a lagoon of several acres in extent, so protected from the sea waves that a different marine life flourished there. It was a godsend to the old lighthouse-keeper, for he could dig at his door all the clams he needed without having to wend his way to the inland creeks. This was the only place on the outer side of the dunes where common clams were found, for on the unprotected beaches the massive sea-clam, an entirely different species, alone flourishes. The spit grew year by year, and in 1904 had become an elevated plain three hundred yards broad, which completely enclosed the shrunken lagoon, now brackish and stagnant. The clams had all died and another set of inhabitants flourished there, dominated by great masses of slimy algae. But the sands kept blowing, and in 1906 the pool was entirely effaced. Clumps of beach grass appeared in places, and the sand collected about them and formed the beginning of dunes.

Later, owing to some change in the currents along the shore, the waves demolished their own handiwork, and in 1908 veritable sub-fossils, the shells of the common clam, began to appear on the outside beach, standing in place with their empty valves pointing upward as in life.

While clumps of beach grass are often responsible for the birth of a dune as just described, any obstacle or irregularity, in whose lee the heavier grains of sand settle, may also start a dune on its progress. However started, their forms are many and various, yet, as they are all dependent on the winds, they are shaped by the strongest or dominant ones, and these are the winds which blow from the northwest, north and northeast, during the winter months. Certain secondary or transient modifications are due to other winds, particularly to the prevailing southwest breezes of summer, but a visit to the dunes in a snow-spitting northeaster of winter gives one an idea of aeolian power not often realized in the gentler summer season.

Smiling skies, gentle balmy breezes, flowers blooming and filling the air with their perfume, bird songs ringing from every clump of bushes and grove of trees, perfect gems of color in a setting of brilliant white sand—all of these are seductively enchanting. But the full glory of the dunes, to my mind, is to be found in the winter storms, when the biting wind sweeps with resistless force over them, driving snow and sand into the face of the toiling dune traveler, when the gulls scream noisily overhead, and flocks of ducks, restless in the foaming seas, scud by before the blasts, while over all the roar of the waves, pounding relentlessly on the beach, sounds a grand sea dirge. As one pauses for breath in the lee of a dune and watches the clouds rush by over the tumultuous ocean of sand, one feels to the full the primeval grandeur of the dunes and sees them in their true colors and stormy activities.

Ripple-marks form on the surface of the sand whenever it is dry and the wind blows. These are parallel ridges athwart the wind, with steep sides to leeward, gradually sloping ones to windward. Similar ripple-marks are left by the receding waves on the beach, or by the sweep of the tides in the estuaries, or by the rush of the brook to the sea. In the estuary the steep side of the ripple-mark is up-stream on the flood and down-stream on the ebb tide. In the bed of both water and wind stream the grains of sand are pushed along in parallel ridges up a gradual slope until they drop over and come to rest on the steep sheltered side.

In a gentle wind the ripple-marks advance so slowly that one is unconscious of any change, but in stronger blasts the changes are very manifest. On a blustering March day with a keen wind from the northwest I watched some ripple-marks that were four inches apart from crest to crest, and found that they were advancing at the rate of a foot in eight and a half minutes.

The most common form of dune at Ipswich is one whose longest axis runs from east to west across the prevailing winds, and these again may be divided into two classes. Both advance to the south like waves before the boreal blasts, but the commoner, unlike the water wave, presents its crest to the storm and retreats backward. The sharp, steep side of the dune is undercut and worn away by the wind, and streams out on the sweeping slope to leeward. Owing to the multitude of interlacing rootstocks and rootlets of the beach grass the crest sometimes overhangs like a breaking wave, and masses of roots and sand fall from time to time as the wind undercuts them. Indeed, this slope of the dune, the reverse of the normal one about to be described, is, I believe, due entirely to these beach grass roots—bricks made with straw.

These reversed waves of sand reach their fullest development at the southern end of the Ipswich dunes, where they form a series of parallel ridges, with their steep sides facing the north. They have advanced southward in the middle more than at either end, so that they describe the arcs of circles, and resemble a series of gigantic amphitheaters. One wave that I measured in 1903 could easily be traced for some 1,350 paces, or three-quarters of a mile, and it stretched from the estuary on the inside to the sea on the outside. Its breadth varied from forty to two hundred yards, and its height from twenty to fifty feet. The distance between the waves varies from a hundred yards to a quarter or half a mile.

The highest points or peaks of the dunes often show long ridges of sand extending in the wind's axis to leeward of them, and these longitudinal dunes are sometimes found by themselves, and constitute a distinct type, although not often developed to a great size at Ipswich. They are prone to form near the beach and appear to be indicative of unusually strong winds.

Every now and then in the amphitheater waves there are cross valleys with steep windswept walls. In the cuttings and on the sharp northward faces the stratifications in the sand are often marked, and the firmly packed layers stand out prominently, while the loosely formed ones are cut away. The strata often dip gently towards the south, for the sand is left by the wind on the southern or leeward slope, but they vary greatly and are irregularly superimposed. The angle of the northern slope of these dunes varies from thirty to ninety degrees, while that of the southern slope is about twelve degrees.

The other kind of transverse dune—the normal desert one—although rare at Ipswich, appears to form only where the wind is unhampered by the binding grass, and is one that resembles more closely a wave of the sea, for its steep crest is borne in front, while the long, sweeping side is left behind or to windward. In these respects it is but the magnification of the ripple-marks on the surface.

There are at the present time two very striking examples of this form of dune at Ipswich, one of which, like a devastating tidal wave, is overwhelming the southernmost of the pitch-pine woods, while the other, nearer the mouth of the Essex River, is burying in its progress a grove of white birches. Both of these are unprotected on the north for a considerable distance either by bushes or by grass, and Boreas rushes over them unimpeded. The northerly slope is hard and firmly packed, and extends gently upward at an average angle of nine degrees, whereas on the south the sand, freed from the mighty power, settles softly at an angle of rest generally as steep as thirty-two degrees. Here it is so loosely compacted that one may easily sink half-way to the knees.

Both of these dunes have crests higher than their victims, the trees. The pine grove has been so far imbedded that the remains of the buried trees are beginning to reappear on the northern side of the dune. The exposed wood is decayed and soft, but masses of hard pitch can be found here and there on the bark, so thoroughly infiltrated with sand that they look like sandstone or pieces of coral.

The rate at which the dunes advance varies greatly, but it depends chiefly on the season of the year. One of the fastest dunes is undoubtedly the large one just mentioned that is breaking over the birch grove, for here at the southern end of the dunes the sand is exposed to the full sweep of the north winds, and the region is widely destitute of grass or bushes. By means of marked trees I have been able to obtain exact measurements of the progress of the dune from time to time, for the edge of the sand as it advances into the grove is sharply defined.

"Landscape Painting"
by Henry Ward Ranger

From Art-Talks with Ranger *(1914)*

Henry Ward Ranger (1858–1916) grew up in Syracuse, New York, where he learned to draw and play piano. After studying art at Syracuse University, he worked as a photographer and painted watercolor landscapes. He moved to New York City and continued to study art in Paris and Holland, selling art to Paris galleries and Dutch collectors. Returning to America, Ranger became the founding member of the Old Lyme Art Colony, staying at Florence Griswold's Connecticut boardinghouse and inspiring others to join him in what became the largest art colony in the country. Though Ranger considered himself to be a "tonalist," the colony would also become one of the main centers of American Impressionism.

As is usually the case, after his death his paintings began selling for enormous prices, with his estate auctioned off for what was the highest average price paid for the works of a dead artist at the time. His bequest to the National Academy of Design was even larger, and allowed the National Collection, now the Smithsonian American Art Museum, to begin purchasing major works of American art. The following piece from Art-Talks *with* Ranger *extols the beauties of the New England landscapes he painted and loved.*

"LANDSCAPE PAINTING"

An artist often runs across the idea, pronounced or implied, that because he is a painter, he is necessarily narrow in his sympathies and consequently a poor judge of art; and that therefore his opinions must be taken with several grains of allowance. In a way, I am sorry to admit, it may be true. I know many laymen whose critical opinion I would take in preference to many of my own profession. But it must also be remembered that these are exceptional laymen: one in ten thousand, or perhaps one in a hundred thousand.

No one should dispute that the average artist is a better judge of art than the average layman. And I maintain that the exceptional artist is still superior in critical judgment to the exceptional layman. Ruskin says, and I think truly, that "the final judgment (of art) always has and always will come from the artist."

The popular mistake is to assume that because many men paint and are tagged as "artists," all are consequently on the same level of aim and attainment. The truth is quite to the contrary. If we look for a parallel in the arts of music and literature, it is obvious that we should not go to a writer of waltzes or of ragtime, no matter how eminent in his particular line, for a critical analysis of a new symphony. Neither would one go to a popular writer of "Shilling Shockers" for an opinion of a new poem. Like appeals to like—and the layman with symphonic sympathy and appreciation will probably be a better judge of what we call serious music than the professional musician whose sympathies and taste fall short of this standard. This simile seems as applicable to the art of painting as to the other arts, and should explain the injustice and the fallacy of the original contention: that an artist is necessarily an unsound judge of art.

Do not understand me as contemning the producer of popular music, literature, or pictures. The world would be drearier without them. They fill a popular want, and would not exist if they were not wanted. They give to many all the art their natures require, and give to some a stepping-stone to something higher. None of us should become so serious that an occasional funny print or popular song cannot be relished. We must sometimes let the bow relax.

Another popular fallacy is that the American is naturally devoid of art, and solely devoted to the pursuit of wealth and material things. My experience, which perhaps has been particularly happy, is that we have a large percentage of altruistic idealists. The numerous and increasing museum-foundations only serve as a small illustration of the case in point. I know that with many collectors it is not simply pride of possession; that their pictures, which they share with their friends and with the public by constant loans to exhibitions, have taught them—and this is the supreme test of understanding—to find their own pictures out-of-doors. And this is one of the great functions of an artist: not alone to produce a concrete work of art, but to teach the observer how to find the beauty around him.

No one realized the charms of sky and weather and heath or the beauties of lowland rivers until Constable interpreted them. No one realized fully the interest of the clipped poplars of France or the delicate, tree-veiled beauties of pond and stream until Corot translated them. And so, each artist has contributed his bit toward showing what a beautiful world we live in. And the American artist's mission should be to translate and emphasize the poetry of the land we were born in and love the most.

I feel that my little bit of New England, which I know and love so well, is reeking with poetic suggestion. I often say to my foreign friends in a spirit of paradox: It is the oldest pastoral landscape-country in the Western world. Our farms which were thoroughly tilled for a century or more have, for the past hundred years, been slipping back into picturesque neglect; while Europe has been forced to improve and utilize every agricultural resource, with the result that every lane almost has become a macadam road; the careless foliage that bordered road and stream has given way to scientific planting. The pond at Corot's Ville d'Avray has lost its charm. Holland has replaced the ground roads of the old Holland with brick pavements. And so it goes. But in New England, the country lanes are full of brush and grass and flowering weeds, with the little-used wagon track zigzagging between tumbled-down stone walls and rickety rail fences.

I never get into a farmer's back-fields with their ridges of rock, recurringly stripped of timber, without feeling what a race of unconscious heroes the pioneers must have been. I think of them as leaving their homes in small ships, and of their making a voyage, the dangers of which all who live on the coast can realize. I think of their innumerable hardships, of their fierce battles, and am amazed at their invincible courage. When I think that they had to fight the Indians for the privilege of landing, and realize their still more arduous conflict with soil and climate in their larger fight of conquering a living from the forest-grown and rock-ribbed hills, I am filled with reverence and wonder. Yet they did it.

Then, there are the little country graveyards—I should say, farm graveyards—for each family had its burial-place where the beloved dead could lie in sight of the house, and near the scenes of their labours. I say, when I pass these graveyards I always feel like saluting.

My little town has a church-record which shows that at one time in the early days all the men were carrying a rifle at the front, fighting; and the women had to discharge the deacons' duty, and pass the plate for collection.

I am sorry for anyone who knows this country, and yet does not feel its romantic charm. I would like to get into my pictures of this region a little of the love I feel for those who made it. As for me, a landscape to be paintable must be humanized. All landscapes that have been well painted are those in which the painter feels the influence of the hand of man and generations of labor. I think this is one reason why no man has made a success in painting outside his own country. For no matter how well he knows a foreign land superficially, he must still remain an alien. I realized, when living abroad, that a French farm, or even an English one, was not mine. While here, in my own country, I understand naturally why the wood-lot was kept, and why the lane over the hill to the barn must lead to a back pasture.

A farmer can't cut down a tree or build a fence or dig a ditch or throw a bridge across a rill without helping to humanize his land. And a sensitive person will unconsciously feel the spell woven by generations of husbandmen piling the stones from the fields into walls, often with their rifles lying close at hand; he will enter into their lives and share in imagination their troubles and rewards. A landscape is as human as an individual—so is a tree. Sometimes I feel that I, a poor descendant of these men, mark a decadence by merely painting amidst the scenes of their heroic labors instead of doing more virile work.

"Mount Hope"
by Clifton Johnson

From Highways and Byways of New England: Including the States of Massachusetts, New Hampshire, Rhode Island, Connecticut, Vermont, and Maine *(1915)*

Born in Hadley, Massachusetts, Clifton Johnson (1865–1940) grew up on a farm along the Connecticut River and peddled berries to locals. He attended Hopkins Academy, but dropped out to work at nearby bookstores. In 1893 he and his brother bought their own store in Springfield, Henry Johnson's Blank Books, an institution that lasted in the city for over a century. Johnson's work as a photographer was published around New England, and he illustrated the works of Henry David Thoreau.

The many books he wrote include New England Country *(1892),* The Country School in New England *(1894), and* What They Say in New England *(1897). The book from which this excerpt is taken,* Highways and Byways of New England *(1915), was part of a series that focused on history and rural life. The piece focuses on the layers of history on the small Mount Hope peninsula, and though it uses the offensive word "savages" to describe Native Americans, it is sympathetic to their plight. It is a sorrowful commentary on the many changes wrought by humans over the centuries, but also affirms the perennial power of nature.*

"Mount Hope"

No more fascinating character is to be found among the savages of our early New England history than King Philip, at whose hands the colonists suffered so much; and when I thought of visiting Rhode Island I decided that what I most wanted to see was Mount Hope, where, long years ago, this famous Indian chief had dwelt and where he met his tragic death. I expected as soon as I got into the vicinity of the mountain to see it rising against the sky in at least moderately imposing proportions; but one is obliged to have a quite favorable position to see it at all. In fact, it is nothing but a hill, and not much of a hill at that, and I wandered astray again and again on the local roadways as I searched for it one autumn morning.

The region between it and Bristol, the nearest town, two miles distant, is for the most part one of park-like fields that have fine trees along the borders, and sturdy stone-wall fences. This used to be farming country, but the better farms have been taken by city people who want a place for rural retirement in the summer, and the little farms have fallen into the hands of immigrants from Portugal. I sometimes saw men digging potatoes or cutting corn, but the cultivated fields were few, and agriculture as a means of livelihood is almost a thing of the past.

At length the pleasant, pastoral country was left behind and I came to bleak unfenced uplands whence I could look off on the sea overhung by a pearly haze and with a dazzling pathway across its surface sunward. Here I happened on two little boys watching some grazing cows. They were sitting among the bushes and ripened October grasses and weeds in a slight hollow, where the sun shone warm and they were somewhat sheltered from the brisk, cool wind that was blowing. The cows needed only occasional attention, and the hours of their vigil that chilly day must have dragged slowly. I tried to talk with them, but with slight success, for they were shy little Portuguese whose knowledge of English was very slender.

Mount Hope was now close at hand and I soon reached its bare, rounded summit. The land was thinly-grassed pasturage, and the turf was variegated with stunted goldenrod and white and purple asters, and there were multitudes of branching thistles, some of them still in blossom, but most gone to seed and dry-stalked. In spots grew clumps of huckleberry bushes and gay-leaved patches of little sumacs and poison ivy, while now and then occurred gray outcroppings of rock and neglected lines of stone-wall that the frosts had heaved into chaotic ruin.

The hill owes its name to the Indians who called it Monthaup, a title easily Anglicized to Mount Hope. It is the highest lift of land in all the rather level country around as far as the eye can reach, and it occupies a commanding position at the end of a peninsula hemmed about by irregular inlets from the sea. The steep southern side fronting toward one of the broader water-ways is broken by a rude crag of lichened quartz, and on the slope below the crag King Philip's home village had stood. The place was sheltered from the rough northwest winds, and there was a cool spring of water at the foot of the cliff. Moreover, close by the spring is a niche in the rock known as "King Philip's Seat." Possibly he used to sit there and meditate while he gazed off over the inlet to the wooded slopes of the shore beyond. Certainly, the niche is in form very well suited to its traditional use, and it would be much more perfect if visitors did not have the habit of chipping off pieces to carry away for mementoes. The spot is naturally very attractive, but unfortunately it is a picnic resort that has failed, and scattered roundabout are all sorts of ramshackle buildings— big and little, broken-windowed, leaky-roofed, and dubious in general.

For a long time the savage dwellers of the region were friendly with the whites, and Philip's father, Massasoit, not only ceded them land when they wanted it, but fed them when they were starving. Philip, as he grew older, perceived the increasing power of the English with alarm. They were overrunning the whole country, and the domain of the Indians was constantly contracting. So, at length he determined to act, and he journeyed from tribe to tribe inciting them to unite to drive the white men back whence they came. The struggle began in 1675, and many an exposed English village was wiped out, and hundreds of the settlers' lives were sacrificed.

But the savages suffered far more than their foes, and one by one the confederate tribes abandoned Philip to his fate. His brother and most trusted followers fell in battle, and when at length his wife and only son were taken prisoners, he exclaimed: "My heart breaks! Now I am ready to die."

"Spring Day"
by Amy Lowell

From Men, Women, and Ghosts *(1916)*

Born into a prominent Boston family, Amy Lowell (1874–1925) was a cousin of James Russell Lowell, went to private school, and traveled widely with her family in her youth. She was a voracious reader and self-educated as a poet. Her first book of verse, A Dome of Many-Coloured Glass, *was released in 1912. She would go on to be a leading exponent of Imagism, a poetic movement that favored simplicity and precise, concrete images.*

Lowell was a tireless advocate for modern poetry, writing books of criticism and a biography of English romantic poet John Keats. She was posthumously awarded the Pulitzer Prize for her 1925 poetry collection What's O'Clock? *Among her other poetry books are* Pictures of the Floating World *(1919),* East Wind *(1926), and* Ballads for Sale *(1927). The following "prose poem" comes from* Men, Women, and Ghosts *(1916) and beautifully describes a day's encounter with the natural world.*

"SPRING DAY"

Bath

The day is fresh-washed and fair, and there is a smell of tulips and narcissus in the air.

The sunshine pours in at the bath-room window and bores through the water in the bath-tub in lathes and planes of greenish-white. It cleaves the water into flaws like a jewel, and cracks it to bright light.

Little spots of sunshine lie on the surface of the water and dance, dance, and their reflections wobble deliciously over the ceiling; a stir of my finger sets them whirring, reeling. I move a foot, and the planes of light in the water jar. I lie back and laugh, and let the green-white water, the sun-flawed beryl water, flow over me. The day is almost too bright to bear, the green water covers me from the too bright day. I will lie here awhile and play with the water and the sun spots.

The sky is blue and high. A crow flaps by the window, and there is a whiff of tulips and narcissus in the air.

Breakfast Table

In the fresh-washed sunlight, the breakfast table is decked and white. It offers itself in flat surrender, tendering tastes, and smells, and colours, and metals, and grains, and the white cloth falls over its side, draped and wide. Wheels of white glitter in the silver coffee-pot, hot and spinning like catherine-wheels, they whirl, and twirl—and my eyes begin to smart, the little white, dazzling wheels prick them like darts. Placid and peaceful, the rolls of bread spread themselves in the sun to bask. A stack of butter-pats, pyramidal, shout orange through the white, scream, flutter, call: "Yellow! Yellow! Yellow!" Coffee steam rises in a stream, clouds the silver tea-service with mist, and twists up into the sunlight, revolved, involuted, suspiring higher and higher, fluting in a thin spiral up the high blue sky. A crow flies by and croaks at the coffee steam. The day is new and fair with good smells in the air.

Walk

Over the street the white clouds meet, and sheer away without touching.

On the sidewalks, boys are playing marbles. Glass marbles, with amber and blue hearts, roll together and part with a sweet clashing noise. The boys strike them with black and red striped agates. The glass marbles spit crimson when they are hit, and slip into the gutters under rushing brown water. I smell tulips and narcissus in the air, but there are no flowers anywhere, only white dust whipping up the street, and a girl with a gay Spring hat and blowing skirts. The dust and the wind flirt at her ankles and her neat, high-heeled patent leather shoes. Tap, tap, the little heels pat the pavement, and the wind rustles among the flowers on her hat.

A water-cart crawls slowly on the other side of the way. It is green and gay with new paint, and rumbles contentedly, sprinkling clear water over the white dust. Clear zigzagging water, which smells of tulips and narcissus.

The thickening branches make a pink *grisaille* against the blue sky.

Whoop! The clouds go dashing at each other and sheer away just in time. Whoop! And a man's hat careers down the street in front of the white dust, leaps into the branches of a tree, veers away and trundles ahead of the wind, jarring the sunlight into spokes of rose-colour and green.

A motor-car cuts a swathe through the bright air, sharp-beaked, irresistible, shouting to the wind to make way. A glare of dust and sunshine tosses together behind it, and settles down. The sky is quiet and high, and the morning is fair with fresh-washed air.

Midday and Afternoon

Swirl of crowded streets. Shock and recoil of traffic. The stock-still brick façade of an old church, against which the waves of people lurch and withdraw. Flare of sunshine down side-streets. Eddies of light in the windows of chemists' shops, with their blue, gold, purple jars, darting colours far into the crowd. Loud bangs and tremors, murmurings out of high windows, whirring of machine belts, blurring of horses and motors. A quick spin and shudder of brakes on an electric car, and the jar of a church-bell knocking against the metal blue of the sky. I am a piece of the town, a bit of blown dust, thrust along with the crowd. Proud to feel the pavement under me, reeling with feet. Feet tripping, skipping, lagging, dragging, plodding doggedly, or springing up and advancing on firm elastic insteps. A boy is selling papers, I smell them clean and new from the press. They are fresh like the air, and pungent as tulips and narcissus.

The blue sky pales to lemon, and great tongues of gold blind the shop-windows, putting out their contents in a flood of flame.

Night and Sleep

The day takes her ease in slippered yellow. Electric signs gleam out along the shop fronts, following each other. They grow, and grow, and blow into patterns of fire-flowers as the sky fades. Trades scream in spots of light at the unruffled night. Twinkle, jab, snap, that means a new play; and over the way: plop, drop, quiver, is the sidelong sliver of a watchmaker's sign with its length on another street. A gigantic mug of beer effervesces to the atmosphere over a tall building, but the sky is high and has her own stars, why should she heed ours?

I leave the city with speed. Wheels whirl to take me back to my trees and my quietness. The breeze which blows with me is fresh-washed and clean, it has come but recently from the high sky. There are no flowers in bloom yet, but the earth of my garden smells of tulips and narcissus.

My room is tranquil and friendly. Out of the window I can see the distant city, a band of twinkling gems, little flower-heads with no stems. I cannot see the beer-glass, nor the letters of the restaurants and shops I passed, now the signs blur and all together make the city, glowing on a night of fine weather, like a garden stirring and blowing for the Spring.

The night is fresh-washed and fair and there is a whiff of flowers in the air.

Wrap me close, sheets of lavender. Pour your blue and purple dreams into my ears. The breeze whispers at the shutters and mutters queer tales of old days, and cobbled streets, and youths leaping their horses down marble stairways. Pale blue lavender, you are the colour of the sky when it is fresh-washed and fair . . . I smell the stars . . . they are like tulips and narcissus . . . I smell them in the air.

"The White Mountains"
by Louise C. Hale

From We Discover New England *(1917)*

Born in Chicago, Louise Closser (1872–1933) studied at the Emerson College of Oratory in Boston before becoming an actress, debuting in 1894 and finding success nine years later in a Broadway production of Candida. *She also began to write novels, plays, and travel narratives, some of which were illustrated by her husband, actor and artist Walter Hale. She became a popular and acclaimed character actress on the stage and later in Hollywood, while her writing career continued.*

The following piece on the White Mountains was taken from her travel book, We Discover New England, *one of the earliest examples of the "motor tours" that soon became the primary way people experienced nature. We can see how using an automobile makes it easier to see more in one day, but also how it fragments the experience in a way that walking or even riding a horse did not.*

"THE WHITE MOUNTAINS"

We were immediately in the mountains when we turned toward the Profile House, mountains which we have endeavoured to garnish by fine roads and civilise by great hotels. But a mountain is uncompromising. One can wreathe it in garlands like a Roman Emperor and it will not lose its grimness. I am rather in awe of these great creatures, and I marvel that so many silly people can spend the summer among their heights and not grow uncomfortable.

It is said, however, that the rocky profile of the Old Man of the Mountain is scaling off a bit. Possibly its steady contemplation of the world is effecting a gentle softening toward mankind. He knows that all of us men and women, wriggling down below, are made of meaner clay, and he may appreciate that it is not so easy to be good and resolute when our hearts are not of flint.

The motorist could not very well miss seeing this great rock, but, for fear one should, an enterprising arrow marks the best view along the road by pointing heavenward. After this one might expect other arrows designating the moon, the sun, or the Dipper. A number of automobilists were looking at the Profile as solemnly as were we. There is little to be said about a great freak of nature, although one young woman who had brought her opera glasses bridged the chasm between almighty nature and nature simply human by remarking the resemblance of the Profile to "Grandpa."

Many of these automobiles continued south through Franconia Notch, and we would have spent more time in this district but that our itinerary forbade too much lingering. We retraced our path with the idea of the Bretton Woods for luncheon. For a distance we were not out of the woods, pine and birch wove their branches above us, and if one can find any fault with this wonderfully-laid track through the great forests, it is that the way is too enclosed for extended views.

The roads were magnificent, some of the turns made with "banked curves" for fast going, like a motor race track. Which is all very well for one who is driving rapidly, but causes the car of milder pace to fear that it may topple over. Much of this land is preserved forestry which Uncle Sam, like a good housewife, has husbanded (granting that Uncle Sam can be a housewife, and, if a housewife, can husband) for an indefinite future. Along the way boxes of tools are ready for the dreaded fires, and foresters in khaki with the best of motor-cycles were scouting along the road. The Illustrator's recollection of the Old Man of the Mountain was completely obliterated in his anxiety to remember whether he did or did not blow out "that match."

At Twin Mountain House we came into the open once more, meeting a railroad which was obsequiously shrinking across our path. Time was when, the railway crossed the road in an aggressive manner, other vehicles were interlopers, but in this paradise for automobiles it is distinctly second. We look upon a train in disapproval when it holds us up, and are inclined to show surprise if any other heads than pumpkins peer out from the windows. When motor trucks begin to carry freight, the fast express will pass away from shame.

"The Queen of the Swamp" by Walter Prichard Eaton

From In Berkshire Fields *(1920)*

Drama critic, author, and educator Walter Prichard Eaton (1878–1957) was born in Malden, Massachusetts, and graduated from Harvard. He worked for various periodicals as a drama critic, including the New York Sun *and* American Magazine. *Between 1933 and 1947 he was a professor of playwriting at Yale University. He wrote several books about the theater,* The Actor's Heritage: Scenes from the Theater of Yesterday and the Day Before *(1924) among them. However, he was probably best known for his essays about nature and the outdoors. Among his books on the subject are* Barn Doors and Byways *(1913),* Boy Scouts in the White Mountains: The Story of a Long Hike *(1914), and* Green Trails and Upland Pastures *(1917).*

This excerpt from In Berkshire Fields *(1920), about a trip to Bartholomew's Cobble in Ashley Falls, Massachusetts, demonstrates both the beauty and precision of Eaton's nature writing as well as his informal style and dry wit. The site is today a National Natural Landmark that hosts one of the greatest varieties of ferns in North America.*

"THE QUEEN OF THE SWAMP"

Not many people can remain indifferent to a showy lady's-slipper (*Cypripedium spectabile*). Any orchid commands respect from almost anybody, and orchids, as a species, have commanded extravagant devotion from a few. Of all our native New England orchids, of course, the showy lady's-slipper is the most beautiful; it is, indeed, the queen of our wild flowers, more beautiful, even, than the fringed gentian, and infinitely more rare. Its peculiar habitat makes it extremely difficult of cultivation except by experts with facilities to create the proper conditions of soil and moisture, and in a wild state it seems to be as averse to maintaining itself against the inroads of civilization—or as unable to do so—as the beaver or the varying hare. It is the secret queen of the deep swamps, and those of us who are its worshipers are yearly growing more and more loath to disclose its hiding place to alien eyes, not from any desire to maintain an exclusive aristocracy, but because we have learned from bitter experience that a showy lady's-slipper garden publicly discovered is a garden gone, to a greater degree, even, than in the case of the arbutus. We guard our secret to guard the very life of the plants.

The *Cypripedium spectabile* comes into flower with us about the middle of June, and very often while the swamps are still wet. (I am aware that the wild-flower manuals say the last of June, but if you search for it then in our swamps you will generally find but dried or faded flowers.) You search for it clad in hip rubber boots, and you find it, if at all, not without tears (as in rips) and sweat. Entering the swamp by a dim trail, the remains, perhaps, of an old logging-road, you pass borders of tall, fragrant brake and gracefully bending sprays of Solomon's seal, some of them six feet long. At first the woods are tolerably dry, and meadow-lilies (*Lilium canadensis*) grow gaily in the gloom. Then the dim trail gradually vanishes, by what seem like two or three forks, each leading to nowhere. You are in a tangle of thorny, ripping blackberry canes, through which you tear your way to plunge almost hip deep into black muck, or to find yourself full in the midst of a great bed of royal osmunda ferns. Now every vista of the woods looks like every other vista. Nowhere does the sense of direction fade so quickly as in a dense swamp. Trees are all around you, hornbeams, swamp maples, pines that cling to hassocks which lift them enough above water-level to enable them to survive, larches. To avoid the black ooze or the streams of dark water that never seem to flow, giving no aid to the sense of direction, you try to leap from hassock to jiggling hassock of the swamp grass, or the clumps of matted fern roots. Sometimes you do not succeed. Around your face buzz mosquitoes and tiny, annoying flies. You are extremely warm, for there is no breeze in here, and being rubber clad to the waist on a hot June day does not make for comfort. The vast uniformity of the swamp, and the slight distance in which your eye can cover the ground in any one direction, give to the searcher who does not know his country well, or is new to the game, a sense of hopelessness. Which is as it should be.

We did not know the swamp we entered one afternoon last June, and after beating it from end to end—a matter of a mile or more—and back again, in vain, I advocated giving up the search. My reason, however, was not discouragement. It was the exhaustion of my tobacco supply and the inexhaustibility of the mosquito supply. Only one woman in the party opposed my suggestion, but what are two men against one determined woman, especially when the other woman is neutral? We went back.

The sun was getting down into the west and I had gone twice into the muck over my boot-tops when I suddenly heard a soprano cry of triumph off on my left. Leaping as rapidly as I could from tussock to tussock (which is, by the way, the safest method by which to negotiate them), I came out into a small partial clearing, filled with a tall, rank grass, almost waist-high. In the center of this clearing, her yellow hair disheveled by the undergrowth she had fought, her face flushed, but her eyes, aglow with rapture, stood the determined member of our party. Even as I came into the clearing from one side the other searchers entered from the opposite shadow. Then, as the golden light of afternoon struck in over the tree-tops and made the tall grass golden, too, the four of us stood side by side and gazed upon the little gathering of woodland queens.

There were perhaps a dozen of them, rising on their tall, straight stems, from between the bright green, recurving leaves, till they bore their beautiful blossoms well above the golden grass-tops, fairy white slippers tinged with pink, each with its green-tinted, white lateral petals and up-pointing sepal worn like a three-pointed coronet. They were, indeed, the proud heads of queens, but cloistered queens, secluded, shy, and slimly beautiful. We touched them tenderly, and stooped to inhale their delicate perfume, which is less a perfume, perhaps, than a concentrated exhalation of the swamp verdure and richness. We picked just one, as proof to a skeptic world that we had found what we sought, and, after lingering till we had our exact bearings fixed for another season, we moved out of the swamp to a point where we could gain, unseen, a detour to another road. Our boots were hot and wet and excessively heavy. Our skirts (employing the domestic plural) were muddy and bedraggled and sagged with the weight of moisture. Skirts are most certainly not the costume for bog-trotting. Our hands were scratched, our faces swollen and itching, and I had no tobacco for my pipe. Wearily we clomped along the road. But in the lead clomped she of the golden hair and determined ways, and in her hand she bore like a banner of triumph—when she didn't hold it like a baby!—the long green stem with its big plaited leaves, and its blossom beyond compare. Four foolish folk we were, and happy as only they can be who have found the *Cypripedium spectabile* in the depths of its brooding swamp.

"Ascutney"
by Percy Goldthwait Stiles

From Wayfaring in New England *(1920)*

Hailing from the Boston area, Percy G. Stiles (1875–1936) graduated from the Massachusetts Institute of Technology in 1897 and earned a PhD from Johns Hopkins University in 1902. He became a widely published expert on nutrition, sleep, dreams, and physiology and was an assistant professor of physiology at Harvard Medical School. An inveterate walker since his college graduation, he would spend several days each year leisurely tramping the back roads and mountain trails of northern New England, even as motorized travel became increasingly popular. In 1920 he published Wayfaring in New England, *a memoir of his adventures.*

Stiles is a sage companion for whom walking was a high pleasure: "To say that the scenes have passed before me rather than I before them is to indicate correctly the delightful laziness of the pedestrian pastime." This excerpt about a trip to Vermont demonstrates his gift for description and observation.

"Ascutney"

Opposite, the dark green mass of the great mountain filled the eye. The small size of the trees near the top gave a delusive impression of distance and height. It seemed higher than Killington. It is not so high above the sea by nearly a thousand feet but it really rises higher above the surrounding farms. Mrs. Dudley was not at all pleased to see me and expressed annoyance that anyone should have sent me to her for a lodging. However, when I told her how far I had come she had compassion on me and said I might stay if I would put up with what they had. I consented with very good grace to put up with a supper of hot biscuits, maple syrup, milk, apple pie, and raspberry tarts.

Mr. Dudley, my host, proved to be a delightful character, so mild and benignant, deliberate and gentle, as to answer well to my notion of a Quaker. As we sat down to table his wife asked him if he had taken his medicine. He went meekly to get it, merely saying, "I wish you would forget that sometimes." By half past seven both my entertainers were so evidently having a struggle to keep awake that I asked to be shown to my room. It was hardly dark but I soon went to sleep.

On the morning of the sixth I was up at five o'clock. I went out to look at Ascutney while I waited impatiently for breakfast. The mercury stood at 50. Against the deep blue sky the ranks of diminishing spruces were clean cut to the mountain top. The air was crisp and bracing. At six we had our meal. I asked what I should pay and Mr. Dudley replied in what I thought a characteristic manner: "I don't know—would seventy-five cents be too much?"

The path from the Dudley farm was a plain one. Most of the way, in fact, it was a wood-road and a good part of it corduroy. It was very steep as it must be to rise 2500 feet or more in about two miles. So far as I remember there is not a clearing or a glimpse of distance all the way. The summit of Ascutney at the time of my ascent was considerably overgrown. It is cleft by shallow ravines into several knobs and these must be visited in succession to gain the various views. I passed about three hours in this way.

I thought the finest outlook was toward the west. In this direction the mountain-side falls very abruptly. From the brow of a white cliff I looked down over the serried array of the tree-tops which shrank with distance until it might have been moss rather than forest that clothed the lower slopes. From the edge of the woods extended the level farms of West Windsor, varied in coloring with different crops, and intersected by yellow roads which converged here and there upon church spires rising above the trees of village commons. Streams wound through this pleasant country, their banks touched with deeper green. One or two cemeteries were in sight, every stone gleaming.

All this was so close under my feet and so clear in detail and yet so reduced by three thousand feet of radiant depth that it seemed like the parks and lawns of moss that children like to lay out, with wooden blocks for houses and broken looking-glass for water. The map effect was remarkable. Farther away the land rolled up into hills becoming higher and more generally wooded until the central chain of the Green Mountains made the last terrace. The west wind blew fresh and cool. Three or four small clouds were coming steadily over from Killington trailing their shadows up and down the hills. They made the only motion in the outspread landscape.

The eastern view also has its charms. The eye ranges up and down the fertile Connecticut valley, its fields dotted with elms, and the broad river reflecting trees and bridges in its quiet surface. There is a corner of Lake Sunapee farther away and the large town of Claremont is visible but not obtrusive. Monadnock stands in lonely dignity in the southeast.

Ascutney has individuality. I think its outline from some quarters is displeasing, perhaps suggestive of deformity. But it rivals Monadnock in its isolated position. It stands detached from any range and lifts itself from the riverside meadows displaying its full height with no belittling feature. There is a great central dome with massive outstanding buttresses. When you are on top these outworks which keep the signs of encircling civilization at a due distance lend a sense of security and peace. The works of men are everywhere around—farms and villages with pygmy buildings, railroads with creeping trains plumed with steam, but you are removed to a sanctuary.

It was noon when I started down the mountain. I was not satiated with the view but so thirsty that the spring half a mile down the path had a superior attraction. There I ate the lunch Mrs. Dudley had given me. Then I came down to the road and followed it to Ascutneyville. This is a sleepy little place in the intervales by the Connecticut. A few large houses, the church, and the stores are ranged along the main street. There is a village green with a bandstand and a long, sagging toll-bridge stretches across to New Hampshire. I called on friends at the Acorn Inn and later departed for Cavendish. In the late twilight I completed the twelve miles and was in time for the eight o'clock train for Cuttingsville.

"The Beauty of the World"
by W. E. B. Du Bois

From Darkwater *(1920)*

Born in Great Barrington, Massachusetts, William Edward Burghardt Du Bois (1868–1963) grew up in a rural but integrated community. He became the first African American to earn a doctorate from Harvard, and became a history and economics professor at Atlanta University. His 1903 book, The Souls of Black Folk, *established him as one of the premier thinkers of the new century. In 1909 he helped found the National Association for the Advancement of Colored People, and he continued to fight for civil rights his entire life, helping to pass a federal law against lynching and supporting the Harlem Renaissance.*

Du Bois's works include biographies like John Brown *(1909), histories like* The Gift of Black Folk: The Negroes in the Making of America *(1924), and novels like* The Quest of the Silver Fleece *(1911). The following excerpt is from the first of three autobiographies he wrote,* Darkwater: Voices from Within the Veil *(1920). In it, he balances the horrors of racism and murder with the transcendent beauties of the natural world he found on Mount Desert Island.*

"THE BEAUTY OF THE WORLD"

Here, then, is beauty and ugliness, a wide vision of world-sacrifice, a fierce gleam of world-hate. Which is life and what is death and how shall we face so tantalizing a contradiction? Any explanation must necessarily be subtle and involved. No pert and easy word of encouragement, no merely dark despair, can lay hold of the roots of these things. And first and before all, we cannot forget that this world is beautiful. Grant all its ugliness and sin—the petty, horrible snarl of its putrid threads, which few have seen more near or more often than I—notwithstanding all this, the beauty of this world is not to be denied.

Casting my eyes about I dare not let them rest on the beauty of Love and Friend, for even if my tongue were cunning enough to sing this, the revelation of reality here is too sacred and the fancy too untrue. Of one world-beauty alone may we at once be brutally frank and that is the glory of physical nature; this, though the last of beauties, is divine!

And so, too, there are depths of human degradation which it is not fair for us to probe. With all their horrible prevalence, we cannot call them natural. But may we not compare the least of the world's beauty with the least of its ugliness—not murder, starvation, and rapine, with love and friendship and creation—but the glory of sea and sky and city, with the little hatefulnesses and thoughtfulnesses of race prejudice, that out of such juxtaposition we may, perhaps, deduce some rule of beauty and life—or death?

There mountains hurl themselves against the stars and at their feet lie black and leaden seas. Above float clouds—white, gray, and inken, while the clear, impalpable air springs and sparkles like new wine. Last night we floated on the calm bosom of the sea in the southernmost haven of Mount Desert. The water flamed and sparkled. The sun had gone, but above the crooked back of cumulus clouds, dark and pink with radiance, and on the other sky aloft to the eastward piled the gorgeous-curtained mists of evening. The radiance faded and a shadowy velvet veiled the mountains, a humid depth of gloom behind which lurked all the mysteries of life and death, while above, the clouds hung ashen and dull; lights twinkled and flashed along the shore, boats glided in the twilight, and the little puffing of motors droned away. Then was the hour to talk of life and the meaning of life, while above gleamed silently, suddenly, star on star.

Bar Harbor lies beneath a mighty mountain, a great, bare, black mountain that sleeps above the town; but as you leave, it rises suddenly, threateningly, until far away on Frenchman's Bay it looms above the town in withering vastness, as if to call all that little world petty save itself. Beneath the cool, wide stare of that great mountain, men cannot live as giddily as in some lesser summer's playground. Before the unveiled face of nature, as it lies naked on the Maine coast, rises a certain human awe.

God molded his world largely and mightily off this marvelous coast and meant that in the tired days of life men should come and worship here and renew their spirit. This I have done and turning I go to work again. As we go, ever the mountains of Mount Desert rise and greet us on our going—somber, rock-ribbed and silent, looking unmoved on the moving world, yet conscious of their everlasting strength.

About us beats the sea—the sail-flecked, restless sea, humming its tune about our flying keel, unmindful of the voices of men. The land sinks to meadows, black pine forests, with here and there a blue and wistful mountain. Then there are islands—bold rocks above the sea, curled meadows; through and about them roll ships, weather-beaten and patched of sail, strong-hulled and smoking, light gray and shining. All the colors of the sea lie about us—gray and yellowing greens and doubtful blues, blacks not quite black, tinted silvers and golds and dreaming whites. Long tongues of dark and golden land lick far out into the tossing waters, and the white gulls sail and scream above them. It is a mighty coast—ground out and pounded, scarred, crushed, and carven in massive, frightful lineaments. Everywhere stand the pines—the little dark and steadfast pines that smile not, neither weep, but wait and wait. Near us lie isles of flesh and blood, white cottages, tiled and meadowed. Afar lie shadow-lands, high mist-hidden hills, mountains boldly limned, yet shading to the sky, faint and unreal.

We skirt the pine-clad shores, chary of men, and know how bitterly winter kisses these lonely shores to fill yon row of beaked ice houses that creep up the hills. We are sailing due westward and the sun, yet two hours high, is blazoning a fiery glory on the sea that spreads and gleams like some broad, jeweled trail, to where the blue and distant shadow-land lifts its carven front aloft, leaving, as it gropes, shades of shadows beyond.

"Introduction, Review of Present Conditions and Recommendations for the Future" by Frederic C. Walcott

From Report on the Fish and Game
Situation in Connecticut *(1921)*

Born into a prominent upstate New York family, Frederic C. Walcott (1869–1949) graduated from Yale in 1891. He engaged in the family textile business and then became a banker in New York City. Walcott had a love of the outdoors and in 1909, with Yale classmate and fellow Boone & Crocket Club member Starling W. Childs, he began acquiring old charcoal land in Norfolk, Connecticut, to restore for forestry and wildlife conservation. From an original four hundred acres, the property would grow into several thousand and become known as Great Mountain Forest.

Walcott was president of the Connecticut State Board of Fisheries and Game and chairman of the Connecticut Water Commission in the 1920s. During that time, he was president pro tempore of the state senate. He served as a U.S. senator for Connecticut from 1929 to 1935. After losing his reelection bid, he served in a number of official capacities, including as a regent of the Smithsonian Institution.

While written from the perspective of a hunter and fisherman, this excerpt speaks to the larger values of nature. It recognizes the pressure put on natural resources by development and calls for solutions involving government. Its passionate championship of the outdoors anticipates the fervent advocacy that would become common in later environmental writing.

"Introduction, Review of Present Conditions and Recommendations for the Future"

Connecticut's population is concentrated in cities and small manufacturing towns to an extent not found in any other state in the Union with the possible exception of Massachusetts. Hence, the importance of teaching the people of Connecticut, young and old, the beauties and benefits of the country that they may find the recreations they need in park, field and forest and on the water. A love of nature insures both health and happiness. It teaches people simple living. It has a moral and ethical value in the life of a community, state or nation, that is incalculable.

In common with probably every one of the sportsmen in the United States, we should go a step beyond the protection and preservation of wild life. We believe that a man is a better man if he longs to go afield with rod and gun and dog, and the camera should be included; and that the realization of that longing brings him into close contact with the best, the most uplifting things in life. This is the best form of re-creation. The ultimate goal of nearly every true sportsman is to become almost unconsciously not only a lover of all nature, but an amateur field naturalist.

The real sportsmen of America are our best citizens—clean of mind and body, resourceful, strong and courageous. The sportsmen of the allied countries rid the world of imperialistic militarism, and the sportsmen of the civilized nations today stand as a solid bulwark against all forms of impractical and destructive radicalism. The love of nature—of clean, vigorous sport in the open—is the antidote to the softening, weakening influences of modern civilization. Our battle then is to recover the lost heritage which our ancestors wasted and failed to protect, and having regained it to protect it for our children and our children's children.

This is a many sided and a far-reaching question. It is nothing short of restoring the balance of nature interrupted by the growth of large towns and cities. Much progress has already been made toward this end, but the real progress has been made only in the last generation and a half, most of it in the last ten years and by a handful of devoted, self-sacrificing men to whom posterity will owe much. Reasonable success is now assured; the wild life can and will be saved. The best type of American citizen will persist and, with him, man's most wholesome companions, animate and inanimate—the dog, the gun and the rod. How can this be accomplished?

—

There is a loud call to duty. Strong men are needed, men of experience and vision to mold public opinion, to turn the agitated mind away from city strife and rebellion against life, toward the sunlight.

It is the workingman and his family who need most the call of the wild. When their eyes are opened to the mysterious, mystic powers of nature, their gratitude will be expressed in terms of better citizenship, our State, our Country better, its people far happier.

Bibliography

Agassiz, Elizabeth Cabot Cary. *A First Lesson in Natural History*. Boston:
Ginn D. C. Heath & Company, 1879.

Alcott, Louisa May. *Flower Fables*. Boston: George W. Briggs and Co.,
1855.

Bailey, W. Whitman. *Among Rhode Island Wild Flowers*. Providence, RI:
Preston and Rounds, 1895.

Barker, Fred C., and John S. Danforth. *Hunting and Trapping on the
Upper Magalloway River and Parmachenee Lake: First Winter in the
Wilderness*. Boston: D. Lothrop and Company, 1882.

Barnum, Phineas Taylor. *Humbugs of the World: An Account of Humbugs,
Delusions, Impositions, Quackeries, Deceits and Deceivers Generally, in
All Ages*. New York: Carleton, 1865.

Bolles, Frank. *Land of the Lingering Snow: Chronicles of a Stroller in New
England from January to June*. Cambridge, MA: Riverside Press,
1895.

Bradford, William. *History of Plimoth Plantation*. Boston: privately
printed, 1856.

Browne, George Elmer. "Canoeing Down the Androscoggin." *Outing:
An Illustrated Monthly Magazine of Sport, Travel and Recreation* 32
(July 1898).

Chase, Owen. *Narrative of the Most Extraordinary and Distressing Shipwreck of the Whale-Ship Essex, of Nantucket*. New York: W. B. Gilley,
1821.

Chubbuck, Isaac Y. "Up Tripyramid on Snow-Shoes." *Appalachia: The
Journal of the Appalachian Mountain Club*, vol. 7. Boston: Appalachian Mountain Club, 1895.

Creevey, Caroline Alathea Stickney. *Recreations in Botany.* New York: Harper & Brothers, 1893.

Drake, Samuel Adams. *Nooks and Corners of the New England Coast.* New York: Harper and Brothers, 1875.

Du Bois, William Edward Burghardt. *Darkwater: Voices from Within the Veil.* New York: Harcourt, Brace, and Howe, 1920.

Dwight, Timothy. *Travels in New England and New York.* London: W. Baynes and Son, and Ogle, Duncan & Co., 1823.

Eaton, Walter Prichard. *In Berkshire Fields.* New York: Harper and Brothers Company, 1920.

Eckstorm, Fannie Hardy. "Clearwater and Woods Hospitality." *Forest and Stream* 36, no. 9 (1891).

Edwards, Jonathan. "Some Early Writings of Jonathan Edwards A.D. 1714–1726." *Library of American Civilization.* Worcester, MA: American Antiquarian Society, 1896.

Emerson, Ellen Russell. *Nature and Human Nature.* Boston: Houghton, Mifflin and Co., 1902.

Emerson, Ralph Waldo. *The Boston Book: Being Specimens of Metropolitan Literature.* Boston: Ticknor, Reed, and Fields, 1850.

Flagg, Wilson. *Studies in the Field and Forest.* Boston: Little, Brown and Company, 1857.

Gibson, William Hamilton. *Strolls by Starlight and Sunshine.* New York: Harper and Brothers, 1891.

Hale, Louise C. *We Discover New England.* New York: Dodd, Mead, and Company, 1917.

Harris, Amanda B. *How We Went Birds'-Nesting: Field, Wood and Meadow Rambles.* Boston: D. Lothrop and Company, 1880.

Hawthorne, Nathaniel. *The Snow-Image and Other Twice-Told Tales.* Boston: Ticknor and Fields, 1865. Originally published in 1850.

Higginson, Thomas Wentworth. *Out-door Papers.* Boston: Ticknor and Fields, 1863.

Holmes, Oliver Wendell. *The Autocrat of the Breakfast-Table.* Boston: Houghton, Mifflin and Company, 1891.

Hubbard, Lucius. *Woods and Lakes of Maine: A Trip from Moosehead Lake to New Brunswick in a Birch-bark Canoe.* Boston: James R. Osgood and Company, 1884.

Jackson, Charles T. *Report on the Geological and Agricultural Survey of the State of Rhode-Island.* Providence, RI: B. Cranston & Co., 1840.

Jewett, Sarah Orne. *Strangers and Wayfarers.* Cambridge, MA: The Riverside Press, 1892. Originally published in *The Atlantic Monthly*, September 1889.

Johnson, Clifton. *Highways and Byways of New England: Including the States of Massachusetts, New Hampshire, Rhode Island, Connecticut, Vermont, and Maine.* New York: The Macmillan Company, 1915.

Josselyn, John. *New England Rarities, Discovered in Birds, Beasts, Fishes, Serpents, and Plants of that Country.* Boston: William Veazie, 1865.

Keller, Helen. *The World I Live In.* New York: The Century Company, 1908.

Lowell, Amy. *Men, Women, and Ghosts.* New York: The Macmillan Company, 1916.

Lowell, James Russell. *My Garden Acquaintance, and A Good Word for Winter.* Boston: Houghton, Mifflin and Company, 1871.

Mars, James. *Life of James Mars.* Hartford, CT: Case, Lockwood & Company, 1864.

Marsh, George Perkins. *Man and Nature.* New York: Charles Scribner & Co., 1864.

Olmsted, Frederick Law. *Notes on the Plan of Franklin Park and Other Matters.* Boston: City of Boston, Department of Parks, 1886.

O'Reilly, John Boyle. *Athletics and Manly Sport.* Boston: Pilot Publishing Company, 1890.

Percival, James Gates. *Life and Letters of James Gates Percival.* Boston: Ticknor and Fields, 1866.

Peters, Samuel. *A General History of Connecticut, from Its First Settlement Under George Fenwick to its Latest Period of Amity with Great Britain.* New York: D. Appleton and Company, 1877.

Pinchot, Gifford. "The Proposed Eastern Forest Reserves." *Appalachia: The Journal of the Appalachian Mountain Club*, vol. 11. Boston: Houghton Mifflin Company, 1908.

Prime, William Cowper. *Along New England Roads*. New York: Harper & Brothers, 1892.

Ranger, Henry Ward. *Art-Talks with Ranger*. Edited by Ralcy Hulsted Bell. New York: G. P. Putnam's, 1914.

Sigourney, Lydia. *Past Meridian*. New York: D. Appleton and Co., 1854.

Silliman, Benjamin. "Account of a Meteor." In *Memoirs of the Connecticut Academy of Arts and Sciences, 1810*. Vol. 1, part 1. New Haven, CT: Oliver Steele and Company, 1810.

Smith, John. *A Description of New England*. Rochester, NY: Genesee Press, 1898.

Steele, Thomas Sedgwick. *Paddle and Portage, from Moosehead Lake to the Aroostook River, Maine*. Boston: Estes and Lauriat, 1882.

Stiles, Percy Goldthwait. *Wayfaring in New England*. Privately printed, 1920.

Stowe, Harriet Beecher. *Poganuc People: Their Lives and Loves*. Boston: Houghton Mifflin Company, 1892.

Townsend, Charles Wendell. *Sand Dunes and Salt Marshes*. Boston: Dana Estes and Company, 1913.

Thaxter, Celia. *Among the Isles of Shoals*. Boston: Houghton Mifflin and Company, 1892.

Thompson, Zadock. *Natural History of Vermont*. Burlington, VT: published by the author, Stacey and Jameson, printers, 1853.

Thoreau, Henry D. *The Maine Woods*. Boston: Ticknor and Fields, 1864. Originally published in *The Union Magazine of Literature & Art*, October 1848.

Twain, Mark. *Mark Twain's Speeches*. New York: Harper and Brothers, 1910.

Walcott, Frederic C. *Report on the Fish and Game Situation in Connecticut*. Hartford, CT: State Board of Fisheries and Game, 1921.

Warner, Charles Dudley. *Being a Boy*. Boston: Houghton Mifflin and Company, 1877.

Webster, Noah. "Domestic Economy." *Connecticut Courant* 52, no. 2726 (1817).

Wharton, Edith. *Ethan Frome*. New York: Charles Scribner's Sons, 1911.

Winthrop, Theodore. *Life in the Open Air and Other Papers*. Boston: Ticknor and Fields, 1863.

Wright, Mabel Osgood. *The Friendship of Nature: A New England Chronicle of Birds and Flowers*. New York: Macmillan and Company, 1894.

About the Authors

David K. Leff is an award-winning essayist, former deputy commissioner of the Connecticut Department of Environmental Protection, and poet laureate, town meeting moderator, and historian of Canton, Connecticut. He is the author of six nonfiction books, three volumes of poetry, and two novels in verse, including *The Breach: Voices Haunting a New England Mill Town*. His 2016 travel adventure, *Canoeing Maine's Legendary Allagash: Thoreau, Romance and Survival of the Wild*, won a silver medal in the Nautilus Book Awards for memoir and a silver medal in the Independent Publisher Book Awards for regional nonfiction. Another Thoreau-oriented book, *Deep Travel: In Thoreau's Wake on the Concord and Merrimack*, was published in 2009 by the University of Iowa Press. In 2016–17 the National Park Service appointed David poet-in-residence for the New England National Scenic Trail (NET). His journals, correspondence, and other papers are archived at the University of Massachusetts Libraries in Amherst.

Eric D. Lehman is an associate professor at the University of Bridgeport and the author or editor of nineteen books, including seven from Globe Pequot Press: *Insiders' Guide to Connecticut, A Connecticut Christmas, Connecticut Waters, Connecticut Town Greens, Quotable New Englander, Yankee's New England Adventures*, and *New England at 400: From Plymouth Rock to Present Day*. His biography of Charles Stratton, *Becoming Tom Thumb*, won the Henry Russell Hitchcock Award from the Victorian Society of America and was chosen as one of the American Library Association's outstanding university press books of the year. His novella, *Shadows of Paris*, was the Novella of the Year in the Next Gen Indie Book Awards, won a Silver Medal for Romance in the Foreword Review Indie Book Awards, and was a finalist for the Connecticut Book Award.